How do white-collar offenders struggle to rebuild their selves and their future post-release? With his highly perceptive book on this topic Ben Hunter has contributed not just to the field of desistance studies, but to what might just as well be called existentialist criminology.

Ronnie Lippens, *Professor of Criminology, Keele University, UK*

This book makes a significant contribution to criminological debates concerning identity, existentialism, white-collar crime and desistance. Drawing on a range of published autobiographical accounts, Ben Hunter's existential approach critically examines how white-collar offenders' sense of self-identity is challenged and reconstructed by their experiences of both imprisonment and resettlement. This is a fascinating and unique study of deviant identities, and is a book I will certainly be recommending to students and colleagues.

James Hardie-Bick, *Lecturer in Sociology and Criminology, University of Sussex, UK*

# White-Collar Offenders and Desistance from Crime

The MPs' expenses scandal in England and Wales and the international banking crisis have both brought into focus a concern about 'elite' individuals and their treatment by criminal justice systems. This interest intersects with a well-established concern within criminology for the transgressions of such offenders. However, up until now there has been little sustained consideration of what happens to such offenders following conviction and little discussion of how they attempt to avoid reoffending in the wake of their punishment.

This study rectifies this omission by drawing upon white-collar offenders' own accounts of their punishment and their attempts to make new lives in the aftermath of it. Detailing the impact of imprisonment on white-collar offenders, their release from prison and efforts to be successful again, this book outlines the particular strategies white-collar offenders used to cope with the difficulties they encountered and also analyses the ways they tried to work out 'who they were' in the post-release worlds they found themselves in.

Representing the first sustained qualitative study of white-collar offenders and desistance from crime, this book will be of interest to academics and students engaged in the study of white-collar crime, desistance from crime and prison. The insights it offers into a particular group of offenders' experience of criminal justice would also make it useful for criminal justice practitioners and anyone who wishes to understand the challenges faced by a group of offenders who are assumed to have many advantages when it comes to desisting from crime.

**Ben Hunter** is Senior Lecturer in Criminology at University of Greenwich, UK. His research interests focus on desistance from crime, white-collar crime and the contributions of existential philosophy to understandings of offenders' lives.

# International Series on Desistance and Rehabilitation

The *International Series on Desistance and Rehabilitation* aims to provide a forum for critical debate and discussion surrounding the topics of why people stop offending and how they can be more effectively reintegrated into the communities and societies from which they came. The books published in the series will be international in outlook, but tightly focused on the unique, specific contexts and processes associated with desistance, rehabilitation and reform. Each book in the series will stand as an attempt to advance knowledge or theorising about the topics at hand, rather than being merely an extended report of a specific research project. As such, it is anticipated that some of the books included in the series will be primarily theoretical, whilst others will be more tightly focused on the sorts of initiatives which could be employed to encourage desistance. It is not our intention that books published in the series be limited to the contemporary period, as good studies of desistance, rehabilitation and reform undertaken by historians of crime are also welcome. In terms of authorship, we would welcome excellent PhD work, as well as contributions from more established academics and research teams. Most books are expected to be monographs, but edited collections are also encouraged.

*General Editor*
Stephen Farrall, University of Sheffield

*Editorial Board*
Ros Burnett, University of Oxford
Thomas LeBel, University of Wisconsin-Milwaukee, USA
Mark Halsey, Flinders University, Australia
Fergus McNeill, Glasgow University
Shadd Maruna, Queens University Belfast
Gwen Robinson, Sheffield University
Barry Godfrey, University of Liverpool

1 **The Dynamics of Desistance**
Charting pathways through change
*Deidre Healy*

2 **Criminal Behaviour in Context**
Space, place and desistance from crime
*Nick Flynn*

3 **Cultures of Desistance**
Rehabilitation, reintegration and ethnic minorities
*Adam Calverley*

4 **Offender Rehabilitation and Therapeutic Communities**
Enabling change the TC way
*Alisa Stevens*

5 **Desistance Transitions and the Impact of Probation**
*Sam King*

6 **Black Men, Invisibility and Desistance from Crime**
Towards a critical race theory of desistance
*Martin Glynn*

7 **White-Collar Offenders and Desistance from Crime**
Future selves and the constancy of change
*Ben Hunter*

8 **Offending and Desistance**
The importance of social relations
*Beth Weaver*

# White-Collar Offenders and Desistance from Crime
Future selves and the constancy of change

**Ben Hunter**

LONDON AND NEW YORK

First published 2015
by Routledge
2 Park Square, Milton Park, Abingdon, Oxon, OX14 4RN

and by Routledge
711 Third Avenue, New York, NY 10017

*Routledge is an imprint of the Taylor & Francis Group, an informa business*

© 2015 Ben Hunter

The right of Ben Hunter to be identified as author of this work has been asserted by him in accordance with sections 77 and 78 of the Copyright, Designs and Patents Act 1988.

All rights reserved. No part of this book may be reprinted or reproduced or utilised in any form or by any electronic, mechanical, or other means, now known or hereafter invented, including photocopying and recording, or in any information storage or retrieval system, without permission in writing from the publishers.

*British Library Cataloguing in Publication Data*
A catalogue record for this book is available from the British Library

*Library of Congress Cataloging in Publication Data*
Hunter, Benjamin William, 1978-
White-collar offenders and desistance from crime : future selves and the constancy of change / Ben Hunter. -- First Edition.
pages cm. -- (International series on desistance and rehabilitation ; 7)
1. White collar crimes. 2. Criminals--Rehabilitation. I. Title.
HV6768.H85 2015
365'.661--dc23
2014034881

ISBN: 978-1-138-79409-2 (hbk)
ISBN: 978-1-315-76057-5 (ebk)

Typeset in Times New Roman
by Fish Books Ltd.

To mum and dad. Thanks for everything.
And to Julie, for making existential angst far more fun
than it's supposed to be.

# Contents

| | |
|---|---|
| *List of illustrations* | xiii |
| *Acknowledgements* | xiv |
| *Foreword* | xv |
| | |
| Introduction: white-collar offenders and desistance from crime | 1 |

**1 The challenge of white-collar offenders' desistance**  10
*White-collar crime    10*
*Desistance from crime    14*
*White-collar offenders and desistance    24*
*Reconciling desistance research and white-collar crime    25*

**2 Searching for the self**  28
*The nature of existence    28*
*Existential sociology    32*
*Existential sociology and criminology    42*
*An existential framework for studying white-collar offenders    44*

**3 Autobiography and the search for 'truth'**  46
*The telling of the self    46*
*Autobiographies in sociology and criminology    49*
*Methodological issues in studying autobiographies    51*
*White-collar offenders' autobiographies    52*
*Analysing autobiographies    55*
*Comparing accounts    56*
*Are these unusual accounts?    58*

**4 Imprisonment and the assault on the self**  61
*Prisons and prisoners    61*
*White-collar offenders' prison accounts    66*
*First impressions    67*
*Prison time    70*
*Change and the self    74*
*A unique experience?    78*

xii *Contents*

**5    Who am I? Self and identity in the post-punishment world**                         83
*After a prison sentence    83*
*White-collar offenders' resettlement    85*
*Anticipating release    86*
*Leaving prison    94*
*Ex-prisoners in their post-release world    100*
*Discovering who one is    104*

**6    The journey to self: success, failure and change**                         107
*White-collar offenders and the post-punishment world    107*
*Returning to the familiar    108*
*Succeeding and failing    110*
*Responding to changes in the self    116*
*Agency and change    121*
*Life after punishment    127*

**7    Becoming who one was: professional-ex roles**                         129
*Ex roles and professional-exes    129*
*Professional-exes in the current study    132*
*Becoming a professional-ex    134*
*Deceitful pasts and the management of the professional-ex role    140*
*The professional-ex concept revisited    143*
*Past identities lived into the future    148*

**8    Becoming who one is: religious conversion narratives
and desistance**                         151
*Belief systems    151*
*Religious conversion    152*
*Religion and desistance from crime    154*
*Religious belief and white-collar offenders    156*
*Adopting new belief systems    156*
*Inner aspects to a belief system    166*
*Social aspects of belief    171*
*Conversion narratives and change    174*

**9    An existentially informed understanding of desistance**                         176

*Appendix: bibliography of white-collar offenders' autobiographies*                         188
*References*                         190
*Index*                         201

# Illustrations

## Figures

| | | |
|---|---|---|
| 5.1 | Prisoners who expressed anxiety over their future and guilt | 93 |
| 5.2 | Offenders who experienced blocked paths and stigma | 101 |
| 7.1 | Stages in becoming a white-collar professional-ex | 135 |

## Tables

| | | |
|---|---|---|
| 3.1 | Summary of sample, year of conviction and year of book publication | 53 |
| 3.2 | Offenders and subjects covered by their books | 54 |
| 4.1 | White-collar offenders' prison sentences and length of time served | 66 |
| 5.1 | White-collar offenders' time spent in prison | 87 |
| 5.2 | Anxious and confident prisoners | 87 |
| 6.1 | Offenders and information available | 108 |
| 6.2 | Profession prior to offence, at end of book and recently (offenders who could be traced) | 109 |
| 6.3 | White-collar offenders who cite failing and their goals | 111 |
| 6.4 | White-collar offenders who cite succeeding and their endeavours | 114 |
| 6.5 | Offenders who reported substantial and partial change | 117 |
| 6.6 | White-collar offenders who cite substantial change | 118 |
| 6.7 | Offenders who reported active and passive change | 121 |
| 6.8 | Offenders who experienced passive change and their reaction | 124 |
| 7.1 | White-collar offenders' professional-ex roles | 133 |
| 7.2 | Colson and Minkow's ex-role 'benefits' | 143 |
| 7.3 | Differences in the realisation of the professional-ex role | 147 |
| 8.1 | White-collar offenders' religious beliefs and first awareness of them | 156 |

# Acknowledgements

I am very grateful to Stephen Farrall for his helpful comments on the manuscript and for his support. Thanks also to the colleagues whose insights over the years have informed some of the ideas below, most especially Susanne Karstedt and Ronnie Lippens. Finally, thank you to Heidi Lee for her patience in getting me through the writing and submission process. May your individual existences be forever authentic.

# Foreword

The *International Series on Desistance and Rehabilitation* aims to provide a forum for critical debate and discussion surrounding the topics of why people stop offending and how they can be more effectively reintegrated into the communities and societies from which they came. The books published in the series will be international in outlook, but tightly focused on the unique, specific contexts and processes associated with desistance, rehabilitation and reform. Each book in the series will stand as an attempt to advance knowledge or theorising about the topics at hand, rather than being merely an extended report of a specific research project. As such, it is anticipated that some of the books included in the series will be primarily theoretical, whilst others will be more tightly focused on the sorts of initiatives which could be employed to encourage desistance. It is not our intention that books published in the series be limited to the contemporary period, as good studies of desistance, rehabilitation and reform undertaken by historians of crime are also welcome. In terms of authorship, we would welcome excellent PhD work, as well as contributions from more established academics and research teams. Most books are expected to be monographs, but edited collections are also encouraged.

It is a common refrain that studies of white-collar criminals are the exception rather than the rule in criminological endeavours. Despite the much, much larger economic, social and environmental costs which white-collar offenders can produce, their crimes and offending careers have not figured as much as they might have in criminological research. This is especially true when one thinks of studies of the trajectories of white-collar offenders, who, unlike street offenders, have not been subject to very much research which has sought to understand the nature of their engagement in crime throughout their lives. This – amongst other factors – is one of the reasons that I am so delighted that the Series can include Ben Hunter's study of 23 white-collar offenders and the more than 30 books which between them they had written. In this respect, as well as bringing new ideas derived from existential sociology to bear on an old topic, Hunter also continues the use of a methodology (namely the analyses of autobiographies) which a few notable scholars in criminology have employed. Through his use of some of the core tenets of existentialism, and in particular drawing upon some of the uses to which sociologists have sought to apply these ideas to real people's lives, Hunter is able to 'get inside' the white-collar offender through the use of this novel methodology. In so

xvi  *Foreword*

doing, and what I took from his investigation, is the similarities which can be drawn between those in his sample and the experiences of – for want of a better term – more 'mundane' former offenders. This book brings to the fore in key places the vulnerability of many of those he studied. As one of his authors wrote:

> A bar code! The ultimate stroke of dehumanisation! I was as significant as a box of corn flakes. Everything there was to know about me could be viewed on a computer screen by scanning my bar code.

Whilst another, on leaving prison reflected on what lay ahead of him:

> What possible good could I do that would ever make up for the evil I was responsible for causing?

Given that these represented some of the most advantageously positioned members of society, Hunter's work forces us not only to reflect on the pain of their own lives, but also consider in more detail how many 'ordinary' men and women who become embroiled in the criminal justice system must feel when faced with imprisonment and release. Hunter's contribution is not simply therefore a book about how and why white-collar offenders desist (although it is certainly that), but also a text which encourages us to reflect on what prison does to people. This book will appeal to those interested in criminal careers, white-collar offenders, desistance and existentialism, and I hope very much that those who read it will enjoy it has much as I have.

Stephen Farrall
Sheffield
December 2014

**The Editorial Board**

Ros Burnett (Oxford University, England)
Stephen Farrall (Sheffield University, England, General Editor)
Thomas LeBel (University of Wisconsin-Milwaukee, USA)
Mark Halsey (Flinders University, Australia)
Fergus McNeill (Glasgow University, Scotland)
Shadd Maruna (Queen's University, Belfast, Northern Ireland)
Gwen Robinson (Sheffield University, England)
Barry Godfrey (Liverpool University, England)

# Introduction

## White-collar offenders and desistance from crime

Martha Stewart was America's first self-made female billionaire (Fortune, 2005). Stewart's initial interests included the publication of books on cooking and entertaining, hosting her own lifestyle television show and also publishing a monthly magazine, *Martha Stewart Living*. Eventually, Stewart consolidated these various business interests under one company, Martha Stewart Living Omnimedia (MSLO). MSLO became a publicly traded company in 1999, with Stewart as Chairman and CEO. Revenues for 1999 increased 29 per cent compared to 1998 (MSLO, 1999, 1) attesting to the success of the Martha Stewart brand and as the company's value soared so did Stewart's personal wealth. However in 2004, aged 62, Stewart was sentenced to prison for conspiracy and obstruction of justice. The charges related to sales of shares that she owned in ImClone Systems Inc. in 2001 (CNN, 2004). By selling her shares a day before the stock price of ImClone fell, Stewart avoided a loss and her statements to investigators were held to have impeded the investigation of the case (CNN, 2004). She served five months in prison at Alderson Federal Prison Camp and was released in February 2005 to serve five months house arrest. She also agreed to settle insider trading charges with the Securities and Exchange Commission, agreeing to a five-year bar on her being a director of a public company and to paying disgorgement of $58,062 (Securities and Exchange Commission, 2006).

Less than a year after her release, Stewart had a new advice book, which made the *New York Times* bestseller list. *The Martha Rules* was a handbook containing advice for those who wished to set up their own business and be as 'successful' as Stewart (Stewart, 2005). Stewart also negotiated a daytime TV show, a satellite radio deal, a DVD deal, a music deal with Sony BMG and a partnership to build residential communities, all as part of the Martha Stewart brand (Fortune, 2005). MSLO had continued, run in her absence by a number of different personnel (Fortune, 2005). The negative publicity that Stewart's conviction attracted possibly hurt MSLO's profitability, but in 2008 MSLO announced a return to annual profitability for the first time since 2002 (MSLO, 2008). Stewart still held her shares in the company and, although at the time was barred from being a company director, was still heavily involved in the company she had founded.

Compare Stewart's story with that of Michael, whose life is outlined by Laub and Sampson (2003, 1–4). Michael was incarcerated at the age of ten for numerous

2  *Introduction*

petty offences and spent two years in reform school as a juvenile. As a young adult, Michael joined the United States army for seven years and following this he spent almost all of his working life in one form of employment or another. He lived with his wife of over 40 years. Official records and Michael's own account both indicate he did not offend again after leaving reform school.

Michael's account would be largely unsurprising to those who consider the behaviour of those who move from offending to a crime free life. His employment, his marriage and his age are all credible explanations for his desistance from crime (e.g. Laub and Sampson, 2001). Laub and Sampson (2003) explain Michael's move from offender to 'legitimate' citizen as the result of his active engagement with the opportunities provided him through work and his relationship with the woman who would become his wife. It was important that Michael valued his work and his relationship. His investment in these gradually precluded his involvement in crime, in part because such investment impacted upon the free time he had which could have been spent offending, but also because as a result of these he came to view himself differently, seeing himself as a non-offender (see also Sampson and Laub, 2005a).

Stewart's successful resettlement after her offence and imprisonment is difficult to reconcile with these explanations for Michael's desistance. Stewart had work at the time of her offence and was considerably older than Michael was when he began his offending. Explanations that appear to fit Michael's case seem inadequate for explaining Martha's successful resettlement following her punishment. She had all the 'advantages' traditionally associated with non-offending at the time of her offence.

This quandary, created by comparing Martha Stewart's case with Michael's is the starting point for this study. That Stewart has successfully 'moved on' following her release from prison does not seem contentious. The desistance literature has little to say, however, regarding how Martha's desistance and resettlement may have happened. This raises questions about how individuals convicted of white-collar offences such as Martha's come to desist from crime. Specifically, it encourages a number of questions. First, how do white-collar offenders desist from crime? Second, what experiences are relevant to them as they do so? Third, how might we frame an understanding of their desistance from crime? Fourth, in what ways do they (or do they not) differ from 'normal offenders'? Fifth, can an understanding of white-collar offenders' desistance contribute to desistance debates more generally and, if yes, what conclusions can we draw?

It would be trite to say that Martha Stewart could not help but lead a successful life following her release from prison given the financial resources she enjoyed as the majority shareholder of a billion dollar company and the personal resources she had such as her business acumen. Such 'explanations' fail to look beyond the fact of an ex-offender's desistance. More importantly, the fact that Stewart still offended despite the presence of these factors that are traditionally associated with non-offending suggests that these might have less impact for some offenders than others. White-collar offenders are one such group, their offending typically contrasted with those of other offenders by the use of non-physical means (Edelhertz,

*Introduction* 3

1970), the status of the offender (Sutherland, 1940) or both. This study investigates the important aspects of desistance for white-collar offenders, the first sustained qualitative investigation into their experiences of punishment, imprisonment and resettlement.

In investigating white-collar offenders' desistance from crime the study is well placed to take advantage of recent developments in the field of desistance that focus on the subjective aspects of offending. Some earlier research has considered similar processes (e.g. Shover, 1985; Cusson and Pinnsoneault, 1986). However, it is only recently that a sustained effort has been made to understand these aspects of desistance. Recent research has sought to understand how offenders who are attempting to desist are involved in creating and managing a new identity as an ex-offender (e.g. Maruna, 2001; Giordano *et al.*, 2002; Farrall, 2002, 2005; Maruna and Farrall, 2004; Farrall *et al.*, 2014). This work focuses on how individuals change and how they see themselves as capable of reconstructing who they are (Farrall, 2005). It also emphasises that desisting offenders take advantage of opportunities provided by their environment to fulfil goals in accordance with a future conception of themselves as non-offenders (Giordano *et al.*, 2002). Finally, such work has identified the importance of attempts to desist from crime being embedded within the context of the life as a whole. The 'stories' that ex-offenders construct about their deviant pasts are important in making such pasts meaningful for a future life in which they are a law-abiding citizen (Maruna and Roy, 2007). These aspects of desistance might be broadly termed as focusing on the subjective, 'internal' changes in offenders who desist from crime, without attending slavishly to an internal/external dichotomy of factors associated with desistance. Social actors shape and are shaped by their environments and changes in the external world will necessarily impact upon internal experiences.

White-collar crime and those who commit it remain absent from many studies of desistance from crime, including the recent work cited above. The importance of constructing an identity as someone who is a non-offender is as likely to be as important to someone in Martha Stewart's position as to any other offender. Questions regarding who one is and who one can be are not the sole preserve of 'street' offenders. This realisation, combined with the above research questions directs us to consider how white-collar offenders come to view their offending, how their view impacts upon the way they subsequently live their lives and how their view of who they 'are' changes as a result of their experiences in prison and beyond.

The study of desistance from crime is the study of change. Not merely change in behaviour, but how such changes are underpinned, preceded (and proceeded) by shifts in identity. These shifts relate to individuals' own efforts to construct a meaningful coherent life narrative, constructing the past to take account of the present and the future. Interwoven with this is the way they react to shifts in their world that impact upon them. These are the possible catalysts of 'internal' change, but also its consequences. Offenders – like all social actors – seek out situations that are in keeping with their prevailing sense of who they are (Kotarba and Bentley, 1998).

4    *Introduction*

Change is a fact of everyday life, recognisable in many forms. Religious conversion, retirement and marriage are examples of things that happen every day to many people, opportunities that are actively sought as much as they are mere occurrences that creep up on unsuspecting individuals. The change heralded by events such as these is a shift in self-conception and in the sense of who one is. More than this, such change and the events it is tied to put the past into a certain context. Events are recalled in a particular way for what they mean in the grand scheme of the life to that point. A particular present necessitates a particular past and while events that have occurred cannot be changed, the meaning attributed to them can be.

Existential thought, notably in the work of Kierkegaard (1844), Sartre (1958) and Heidegger (1926) emphasises the travails of living in the world, of feeling, of making choices as a result of feelings and building up meaning in line with these choices. It characterises existence as a future oriented endeavour and as the struggle to achieve authentic selfhood, with existence the fusion of thought, feeling and action (Macquarrie, 1972). Some of the concepts developed in existential philosophy have been applied to understanding individuals' everyday interactions with the world. Such 'existential sociology' (Douglas and Johnson, 1977; Kotarba and Fontana, 1984 and Kotarba and Johnson, 2002) privileges understanding the effort required by human existence within an ever-changing social world. This existence is characterised by the struggle to maintain a sense of who one is in the face of sometimes contradictory messages from the world more generally, messages that can also clash with one's own prevailing conception of self (Fontana, 1984). In studying humans in their interaction with the world, all aspects of existence are of interest to existential sociologists, although the way humans experience change is of particular interest. Some of the diverse topics studied by existential sociologists include the way in which nuns who wish to leave the convent come to terms with this wish (Ebaugh, 1984), the process of becoming a 'stalker' (Johnson, 2002) and how the stigmatised (in the United States) identity of 'blood donor' is managed (Espeland, 1984). Work that draws upon existential sociology provides a framework for understanding how significant changes in life are responded to for what they mean to the individual, how they interpret the reactions of others in terms of who they feel they are.

As the above suggests, the focus of existential sociology is upon individuals' interaction with their lived world, recognising that we are actively engaged in creating the world as we understand it (Fontana, 1984). This concerns the encounters that are relevant to us, the meaning we place upon the experiences that we have and our responses to change in our sense of who we are within the world (Douglas, 1984). Existential sociology in particular addresses the future oriented nature of existence, with our sense of self constantly unfolding in response to the experiences it has (Douglas, 1984). Important within such experiences are the emotions that are elicited by interaction with the world (Clark, 2002). How certain encounters and certain behaviours 'feel' provides us with important information for making sense of them and who we are.

Existential sociology therefore offers a framework to conceptualise the experiences of those convicted of a white-collar offence and who subsequently

*Introduction* 5

desist from crime. To become 'an offender', whether or not one accepts the label, represents a change in self based upon the new identity an offender label imparts. Resettlement will necessitate an attempt to manage this. Existential sociology provides a framework to analyse how desisters react to social encounters, managing, manipulating and reflecting upon them for the relevance they have. To think existentially about desistance means to recognise that the emotions elicited by the encounters inherent in the processes of desistance and resettlement are an important part of how individuals think about and attribute meaning to what is happening to them.

The method that this study employs reflects existential sociology's emphasis upon the meaning of events for individuals and their interaction with the world. The experiences of those who have desisted from white-collar crime are drawn from published autobiographical accounts written by 23 white-collar offenders about their offences, arrest and punishment. Some offenders are – or were – well known. Jonathan Aitken's, Charles Colson's and Alan Bond's cases attracted much publicity for example. Others are less 'celebrated' names who perhaps differ from other white-collar offenders only in their having published their experiences, sometimes financing publication themselves.

Autobiographical writing is well suited to a study that draws upon existentialist tenets. Autobiography is the writer's own account of the significant events of their life. Importantly, however, such writing contains the significant life events as identified by the author, the encounters that they feel shaped them and the experiences that they feel mattered most in the context of their life as a whole (Smith and Watson, 2002). This particular property of autobiographical writing highlights that to draw upon autobiography as a research tool means that notions of objective 'fact' should be relinquished in exchange for the 'truth' of events as the writer recalls them (McAdams, 1993). Autobiography privileges the writer's own account and while the 'fact' of some events can possibly be determined independently, how such events are interpreted by the writer e.g. how they made the writer feel, is a matter for them.

The strength of autobiography is that it presents the writer's own account of what has been important in their life. As a data source then, although autobiographies might initially be treated with caution for the lack of researcher involvement in their construction, the fact that they remain (mostly) free of outside influence in establishing what has been of relevance within the individual's life is actually an advantage (Maruna, 1997). Furthermore, autobiography frequently covers the whole life up to the point of writing and this therefore makes it possible for long periods of time to be recounted. Events that may have occurred decades ago can be placed within the context of the life, the meaning placed upon them differing by this historical lens that permits a more considered reflection of how past encounters shape who the writer is than is permitted in an interview (Cotterhill and Letherby, 1993).

Within criminology, autobiographical accounts represent something of an under-developed resource. Although a small number of studies have cited autobiographical accounts written by offenders (e.g. Shover and Hochstetler, 2006;

6  *Introduction*

Hunter, 2009), such studies have either been limited in scope or used autobiographical accounts as a supplement for other material. The extensive use that this study makes of such material will therefore serve to more fully demonstrate the contribution that autobiographical accounts can make to an understanding of the reality of offenders' lives.

The publication dates of the autobiographies drawn upon for this study vary widely, with the oldest published in 1972 and the most recent in 2009. It was important for this study to ascertain as far as possible what offenders were doing 'now', particularly if a significant amount of time had passed since their book was published. Therefore, the information drawn from the autobiographies of white-collar offenders was supplemented by media archive searches which provided details for some offenders regarding the direction their life had taken following the publication of their books. The information from such searches sometimes took the form of interviews offenders had given to various media, or perhaps reports on their whereabouts and activities. These helped to put their accounts into the context of their life course.

The rest of this book proceeds as follows. Chapter 1 outlines research on white-collar offenders and also considers what is known about how offenders more generally desist from crime. This juxtaposes more fully than above the inherent contradictions present if the research observations on desistance from crime are compared with those regarding white-collar offenders. The chapter considers the demographic characteristics of white-collar offenders alongside general observations of offenders' desistance from crime. It appears that white-collar offenders have many of the characteristics that are widely accepted to be associated with successful desistance and resettlement. More recent desistance research offers a means of exploring this apparent contradiction between the white-collar crime literature and desistance studies, emphasising the importance of changes in self-conception for offenders, their attempts to construct an environment consistent with who they feel they are and of acting in a way that demonstrates their reformed character. It also underlines the importance of envisioning a future free of offending and framing a criminal past so as to make it part of a coherent biography.

Chapter 2 introduces the conceptual framework of this study, drawing on existential sociology, itself derived from broader existentialist tenets. The chapter starts by summarising existentialist thought as present in prominent writings and in particular the emphasis on freedom, choice and responsibility as part of existence. The chapter then moves to outline existential sociology and the fundamental tenets that have inspired existential sociological thought. The focus here is on the importance of the self, values and emotions and how through the interaction of these individuals attribute meaning to their wider social world and identify their place within it. A particular emphasis is placed on shame as a powerful emotion of self-assessment and one that might be expected to be associated with the development of pro-social behaviour, specifically – in this instance – desistance. The chapter also draws links between existentialism, existential sociology and criminological thought to date, highlighting the oft-implicit links that criminology

*Introduction* 7

has drawn with existentialist foci. Such work cautions against forgetting that offenders are individual existents with their own concerns and are actively engaged in 'becoming'. Existential aspects of individuals' experience of crime, deviance and punishment have been noted in relation to gang membership (Scott, 2004), prison (Jose-Kampfer, 1990; Meisenhelder, 1985) and the transition from offender to non-offender (Farrall, 2005).

Chapter 3, recognising that the method employed is by no means common place, explores in detail the use of published autobiographical accounts for research on desistance. It considers what – in sociological terms – autobiographies are and, therefore, what they can contribute to an understanding of the writer's life. In doing this, the chapter considers the issue of 'truth' in regards to autobiographical accounts. Advantages of using autobiographical accounts are compared to other forms of qualitative research, while also discussing the potential problems of using such data. The chapter proceeds by outlining the limited number of other criminological studies that have drawn upon published autobiographical accounts, although as far as can be established, no study has done so on the scale to which they are employed here. The chapter concludes by providing a portrait of the sample of white-collar offenders whose autobiographies form the basis of the subsequent analysis.

The remaining five chapters comprise the analysis of white-collar offenders' accounts. Chapter 4 considers the experience of imprisonment for white-collar offenders, recognising that for some of these offenders experiences of resettlement and change were intimately tied to their incarceration. It investigates what aspects of imprisonment were of most importance to white-collar offenders and how their experience of imprisonment compared to that of other prisoners more generally. With this latter focus, the chapter acknowledges the debate surrounding white-collar offenders' 'special sensitivity' to prison (Mann *et al.*, 1980; Benson and Cullen, 1988) and the extent to which such a sensitivity was exhibited by the offenders whose accounts are the focus of this research. The analysis focuses on how white-collar offenders construed their prison time, particularly the way in which time spent in prison could be 'good' or 'bad' time. Explicit within this conception of the way prison time was spent and understood by prisoners was the implication for what this time meant in terms of individuals' sense of self. The threat to the sense of self was ever present while in prison. Consequently, a running theme throughout the experience of prison was how prisoners coped with what was happening to them and how the environment of the prison contrasted with the lives they had led prior to incarceration. Recognising this, the chapter investigates whether their former lives gave white-collar offenders a different perspective on prison compared to other prisoners (as indeed they have been held as doing, Shover and Hochstetler, 2006).

Chapters 5 and 6 focus upon the resettlement experiences of white-collar offenders following their release from prison. Chapter 5, recognising that resettlement starts in prison, considers how white-collar offenders came to view their impending release from prison, what they anticipated might be waiting for them in the 'outside' world, and what they subsequently found when they re-entered it. It

8  *Introduction*

identifies the feelings of anxiety that were present for many prisoners as they considered release from prison and explores the root of this anxiety. In focusing upon the initial aftermath of release the chapter identifies the most immediate concerns for newly released prisoners. It outlines how they coped with challenges in the aftermath of release as their expectations of what was waiting for them were reconciled with the reality of resettlement and how they negotiated a sense of self in the world. Further, the chapter explores how white-collar offenders made decisions over plans for the direction of their lives. This chapter identifies how their understanding of their present was tied to their future and the selves they could become.

Chapter 6 identifies the more long-term experiences associated with resettlement for white-collar offenders and identifies how they attempt to move on with their lives following release from prison. Prison had been a serious disruption to the lives of offenders and, in asking 'how would they move on from this?' the chapter identifies how white-collar offenders responded to success and failure in the endeavours they wished to pursue. Reactions to success and failure are considered in terms of anxiety and perspectives on the future and how changes in identity were perceived. The chapter further investigates whether or not white-collar offenders actively embraced and engaged with prospects for change or felt that their change was something that 'happened to' them. This leads to an explanation of the role of acknowledged guilt in accounting for the way offenders experience change.

Chapters 7 and 8 consider in detail specific routes to change as engaged with by white-collar offenders. Chapter 7 explores the concept of the professional ex – a previously deviant identity being used as a specific occupational strategy (Brown, 1991) – and revisits this within the context of white-collar offenders' resettlement experiences. This chapter focuses in detail upon two particular white-collar offenders to identify their experiences as they adopted professional-ex roles. It details how professional-ex identities were formed as white-collar offenders drew upon past deviant identities as a means of proceeding with their life. The analysis follows the process by which professional-ex roles became attractive as options and how they were subsequently pursued. Finally, the chapter compares these white-collar offenders' professional-ex roles with the way in which professional-ex statuses have been conceptualised more generally.

Chapter 8 analyses change in self within the context of conversion to a religious belief system. The chapter begins by outlining the literature on conversion to religion that has detailed the processes involved and the various factors that are relevant in the lives of potential converts. It proceeds to an exploration of the contribution that conversion to religion has made to the study of desistance. The chapter then outlines the process through which white-collar offenders took on religious beliefs. However, conversion was not a straightforward process and doubts as to the efficacy of religious belief assailed the potential converts. What is particularly important is how religious conversion influenced the meaning offenders placed upon their pasts, particularly with regard to casting past offending in a different light. Besides these 'internal' aspects of belief, the chapter explores the social dimensions of religious conversion. New, religiously focused, peer groups helped offenders' make sense of their experiences and also certified offenders' change.

The concluding chapter situates the findings with regard to wider research and explores several questions. Do white-collar offenders' previous 'high lives' make the prison experience harsher for them compared to other offenders? Do their previously successful pasts equip them better for resettlement following prison? Is it more difficult to demonstrate change in who one is (i.e. a change to non-offender) if the life prior to the offence is replete with indications of normalcy? In answering these questions, policy implications will be drawn for the resettlement of offenders more generally.

# 1 The challenge of white-collar offenders' desistance

The study of white-collar crime has, like desistance-focused research, received much attention from academics. However, observations regarding the demographic characteristics of white-collar offenders have rarely been considered with respect to knowledge on desistance. This chapter rectifies this. The first section considers some of the conceptual issues inherent in any attempt to study white-collar crime, along with the observed realities of who the 'average' white-collar offender is. The chapter then moves to outline the substantial literature on criminal careers and desistance, noting the developments in this field over the last two decades and the recent emphasis on understanding how those who are attempting to desist experience the process. The final section of the chapter brings together the first two, demonstrating that a consideration of traditional explanations for desistance appears unsuitable for considering desistance from white-collar crime. It is argued that attending to the subjective experience of desisting from crime will help to situate the experiences of those convicted of a white-collar crime within current desistance debates.

## White-collar crime

It has become traditional (obligatory?) to begin any discussion on white-collar crime by highlighting the definitional issues that trouble its study. Arising out of a perceived class bias in the way in which crime and criminals were perceived, Sutherland (1940, 1945, 1983) sought to bring the concept of a rather different sort of offender to the attention of social scientists. Definitions of white-collar crime have tended to either focus upon the offender or the offence, with the former following Sutherland (1940, 1983) in prioritising an individual's social status or respectability as of key importance. The latter are concerned with the offence itself, the manner in which it is carried out and the means of doing so (e.g. Wheeler *et al.*, 1982; Shapiro, 1990). Offender based definitions highlight that individuals of high status may be as crime prone as any other, but bring under their purview the problem that concepts such as respectability are resistant to being measured (Croall, 2001). Simultaneously, the opportunities to commit the types of crime Sutherland (1940) was originally attempting to highlight with his definition are now distributed far more evenly than when the concept of white-collar crime was first raised

(Weisburd *et al.*, 2001). Offence-based definitions are troubled by the observation that an extremely wide variety of crime may be included in such definitions. Both crimes by employees of small businesses and war crimes can be identified as 'white-collar' under certain definitions Croall (2001).

In any event, and as Weisburd *et al.* (2001) note, the purpose of the concept of white-collar crime is to highlight a type of crime and a type of offender rather different from those reflected in the literature more generally:

> High social status is not a trait that is normally associated with crime, nor indeed is white-collar occupational status. Street criminals often use guns or knives to steal from their victims, they do not rely on paper instruments or computers as methods for committing their offenses. In some basic sense, the different definitions of white-collar crime intersect with one another.
>
> (Weisburd *et al.*, 2001, 9)

This study utilises the definition suggested by Edelhertz (1970, 3) under which white-collar crime is:

> An illegal act or series of illegal acts committed by non-physical means and by concealment or guile, to obtain money or property, to avoid the loss of money or property, or to obtain business or personal advantage.

Although still broad, this offence-based definition does not place an occupation as being of importance. Simultaneously it recognises that offending may take place to gain or avoid losing non-physical assets i.e. that both potential gain and potential loss may be motivations for white-collar crime (Wheeler, 1992, although see Piquero, 2012 for an empirical test of this 'fear of falling'). For the purposes of this study, a white-collar offender is anyone convicted of a white-collar offence under the above definition.

### *Researching white-collar crime*

It may once have been fair to say that white-collar crime was a hidden problem largely ignored by criminologists, a fact that Sutherland bemoaned and was behind his original intent when he brought the field's attention to the concept. However, that is hardly true today. Over two decades ago Gottfredson and Hirschi (1990, 180) suggested that no concept within criminology was more secure. This is not least because white-collar crime and offenders were regularly used as the stick with which to beat supposedly general theories of crime, demonstrating their short-comings in describing the behaviour of this most complex group of offenders and crimes. Such security is seemingly inviolable now, with Shover and Hochstetler (2006, 4) similarly convinced of white-collar crime as having captured scholarly and lay public attention and being firmly rooted in everyday parlance. Numerous core texts introduce students to the concept (Croall, 2001; Friedrichs, 2009) and edited collections explore its intricacies (Simpson and Weisburd, 2009) or bring

## 12   *White-collar offenders' desistance*

together key readings (Shover and Wright, 2001). Journals publish special editions that consider white-collar offending (Karstedt *et al.*, 2006; Benson, 2013), 'state of the field' reviews (Simpson, 2013) or articles that organise and rank by frequency of citations the scholars engaged in white-collar crime research (Wright *et al.*, 2001).

Despite this however, it seems that, generally speaking, white-collar crime is a difficult subject for researchers to engage with, notwithstanding Weisburd *et al.* (2001), who present statistical portraits of white-collar offenders. Shover and Hochstetler lament the lack of statistical data on white-collar offenders' activities, noting that what is known about white-collar offenders is 'pale in quality and comprehensiveness beside the bountiful and readily available data on street crime' (2006, 13). When it comes to studying corporate violations of the law, researchers have emphasised case studies as a means of understanding misconduct by large organisations (e.g. Geis, 1968; Vaughan, 2001). Studies of the lives of individual white-collar offenders are, as Shover and Hochstetler allude to, not particularly extensive. Relatively few and far between are those studies that do provide an informative look at specific situations and 'varieties' of white-collar offender (Cressey, 1971; Levi, 1981; Benson, 1985; Jesilow *et al.*, 1993). Perhaps due to the fact that such a diverse range of behaviours can fall under the umbrella of white-collar crime definitions, these provide snapshots of rather specific environments, situating motivation within those confines or having a particular theoretical focus (neutralization theory for example: Copes *et al.*, 2013).

One potential reason for this scarcity is the difficulty of conducting research with those who have either committed or are committing white-collar offences. Levi observes that the ethnographer who chooses white-collar crime as their topic of study may face problems simply being able to afford to share space with those they wish to learn about (1981, 327). Shover and Hunter (2010) note that ongoing legal action and the oft-convoluted nature of their cases, combined with a desire to put the experience of criminal justice behind them once they have been punished means that there is practically no good time to try to elicit interviews with white-collar offenders.[1] These difficulties in collecting research data on white-collar offenders pose significant challenges for researchers and have seen the adoption by some of what may be considered unconventional means. Shover and Hochstetler (2006) for example, draw upon published autobiographical accounts by white-collar offenders for their data.

Maybe because of these difficulties in accessing the white-collar crime experience, explanations for white-collar crime have, generally speaking, been rather lacking within criminological theory (Croall, 2001, 80), particularly where corporate crime is the focus of enquiry (Slapper and Tombs, 1999, 110). The relationship of white-collar crime to more general observations regarding criminal behaviour is patchy at best, with general theories of crime increasingly seen as limited in use for understanding white-collar offending (see Croall, 2001, 79–101 and Nelken, 2012 for an exploration of the relationship between white-collar crime and criminological theories more generally). Nelken argues that what hampers this search for an explanation for white-collar crime may be that causes of crime may

White-collar offenders' desistance 13

vary by offence type and, relatedly, that particular formulations of white-collar crime (e.g. is breach of trust important? can it take place outside of an occupation?) will locate explanations differently (2012). Nevertheless, white-collar crime continues to be considered occasionally with respect to other established frameworks. Of most relevance here is Weisburd *et al.*'s application of the criminal career approach to white-collar crime, which will be more fully explored below.

### *Identifying white-collar offenders*

Popular stereotype holds the white-collar offender as the antithesis of the street offender. While crime is associated with male youths who experience a large degree of disadvantage (Weisburd *et al.*, 1991), white-collar crime 'has been linked to advantaged older men from stable homes living in well-kept communities' (Weisburd *et al.*, 1991, 47).

The reality is somewhat different, notwithstanding the fact that types of white-collar crime differ widely (Croall, 2001). Weisburd *et al.* (2001), following Weisburd *et al.* (1991) identify four groupings of white-collar offenders along a spectrum of social and demographic characteristics. Those at the 'high' end were more likely to be company owners, have greater resources and were more likely to be graduates. Of those at the 'low' end less than half were in full time employment. Additionally, for certain types of offences (e.g. bank embezzlement), offenders were almost as likely to be female as male (Weisburd *et al.*, 2001; see also Levi, 1994). Further to this, white-collar offenders are far closer in terms of demographic characteristics to non-deviant individuals, frequently being married and of 'average' socio-economic status (Levi, 1988). Benson and Kerley (2001) make similar observations. In short, white-collar offenders are typically 'ordinary people leading middle class lives' (Benson and Kerley, 2001, 129).

Following Weisburd *et al.* (2001, 26) however, it is worth noting that such observations still fit with the overall goal of white-collar crime research and Sutherland's (1940) original intention when introducing the concept i.e. to highlight a rather different type of offender than had been conceived of previously. The average white-collar offender presented in the above studies is not the elite corporate executive of popular stereotype. However he or she is still more likely to be married, be of greater average age and have higher socio-economic status than the majority of street offenders (Weisburd *et al.*, 1991).[2] This observation is curious when considered alongside criminal career research, and desistance from crime in particular. It is this body of work we consider next.

### *The criminal career paradigm*

One means of studying the offending behaviour of individuals has been through an understanding of the concept of the criminal career (Greenberg 1996a; 1996b), identified as 'the longitudinal sequence of offences committed by an individual offender' (Farrington, 1992, 521). Expressed formally, criminal careers have an onset, when the first offence is committed and duration, measured as the length of

## 14 *White-collar offenders' desistance*

time between onset and the career's end, when the individual desists from offending (Farrington, 1992). Rather than being a theory of crime the criminal career approach presents a framework within which offending can be studied (Blumstein *et al.*, 1988a). It does not treat 'crime' as a unitary construct, permitting differentiation between offence types and allowing different aspects of offending behaviour to be considered in isolation (Blumstein *et al.*, 1988). This allows different aspects of the criminal career to have different factors associated with them (Farrington, 1997). For example, the factors related to onset may be very different from those related to desistance from crime instead of simply being the same processes in reverse (see Farrington and Hawkins, 1991).

Much criminal career research reflects this differentiation between the elements of the criminal career. Methodologically, the criminal career approach utilises self-report and conviction data and longitudinal designs to track patterns of offending over the life course (e.g. Laub and Sampson, 2003, 14–15). Such designs focus on what prompts individuals to start offending, which factors differentiate seriousness and duration of offending for different offenders and what is associated with the cessation of offending (Blumstein *et al.*, 1988a).

Important within the criminal career paradigm is the manner in which age relates to offending. The observation that whether or not one participates in crime is almost inextricably linked to age (Farrington, 1992) drove attempts to uncover the importance of life events and the way in which these might impact upon individuals' offending behaviour (Greenberg, 1996a). Wolfgang *et al.* (1972) highlight the importance of a longitudinal methodology for identifying patterns of offending, specifically with relation to age and crime.

In the 1980s the criminal career paradigm was challenged, most vociferously by Gottfredson and Hirschi (1986, 1987, 1988) who denied the theoretical and methodological use of the approach. Criminology seems to have moved on from such debates, not least thanks to the valuable contributions that longitudinal studies have made towards understanding the different aspects of the criminal career (see below for desistance-focused examples). Those interested could return to Gottfredson and Hirschi's original critique and Blumstein *et al.*'s rebuttal (1988a, 1988b). There is no desire to repeat them here. Instead this chapter will now focus on a particular aspect of the criminal career: desistance from crime.

### Desistance from crime

There has been a steady rise in desistance research over the last two decades. Numerous studies have led to special editions of journals (Farrall and Maruna, 2004), review articles (Laub and Sampson, 2001) and edited collections (Farrall, 2000). Even a cursory glance at this work reveals that the study of desistance has many conceptual, definitional and measurement related issues inherent in it. Overviews of the field are available elsewhere (Laub and Sampson, 2001; Farrall *et al.*, 2014). The following review is concerned with the aspects of desistance that are of most relevance to the study of white-collar crime.

### Defining and conceptualising desistance

Attempts to identify desistance must deal with the realities of observed offender behaviour. Most individuals who might be termed offenders spend large proportions of their time not offending (e.g. Clarke and Cornish, 1985) and 'lulls' in an offending 'career' can potentially be quite substantial (Barnett *et al.*, 1989). Related to this is the problem of the length of time an individual must be 'crime free' before they can be characterised as a desister, based upon the realisation that truly knowing someone has desisted from crime is not possible until their death (Farrington, 1992).

Specific definitions of desistance cannot and should not be developed in isolation from a particular research question (Laub and Sampson, 2001). Nevertheless, desistance (however so defined) has in recent years increasingly come to be viewed as a 'process', distinct from the termination of offending, itself identified as an 'event' (Maruna, 2001; Bushway *et al.*, 2001; Laub and Sampson, 2003). In clarifying the distinction between termination and desistance, Maruna (2001, 26) suggests that while a study of termination of offending asks the question 'why' – e.g. why did that person not offend again – the study of desistance directs us to ask 'how'. For example, how do individuals live in a manner consistent with decisions to live a crime free life? How do they cope with challenges to the maintenance of an identity as an ex-offender?

Maruna and Farrall (2004), in identifying desistance as a process term it 'secondary desistance', distinct from the 'primary desistance' which is characterised by any 'gap' in offending behaviour. Secondary desistance represents:

> the movement from the behaviour of non-offending to the assumption of a role or identity of a non-offender or 'changed person'.
>
> (Maruna and Farrall, 2004, 174)

Secondary desistance is therefore concerned with change within the offender of who they feel 'they' are and a shift in priorities away from those which are congruent with offending. To emphasise desistance as a process is to emphasise that the move from 'offender' to 'non-offender' is a gradual one, through which the individual comes to take on the latter self-identity (Maruna and Farrall, 2004). The focus of this conceptualisation of desistance is upon the opportunities offenders engage with to achieve a 'state' of non-offending (Maruna, 2001; Giordano *et al.*, 2002; Farrall *et al.*, 2014). For example, an offer of employment may be accepted because it offers the opportunity to gain money which would otherwise be obtained through crime.

More recent work on desistance reflects this concern with understanding how individuals come to desist from crime and the interplay between subjective experiences and active attempts to move away from crime. Such work will be considered in a later section. First, some of the generally accepted correlates of desistance are noted.

## 16 White-collar offenders' desistance

### Why do people desist from crime?

Desistance research has identified several correlates of desistance, placing the most emphasis on the process of aging (e.g. Shover, 1983, 1985), gaining of employment (Uggen and Kruttschnitt, 1998) and forming romantic relationships (Horney *et al.*, 1995). Such work has almost exclusively focused upon white, male offenders (although see Elliot, 1994; Calverley, 2013; and Giordano *et al.*, 2002 for respective exceptions) involved in 'street crime'.

Long championed as one of the most robust findings in social science research, the observation that the older offenders get the more likely they are to desist is well documented (e.g. Gottfredson and Hirschi, 1990; Shover and Thompson, 1992, although see Laub and Sampson, 2003, 16–17 for a more nuanced summary of the age effect). Some explanations for this focus upon the direct impact of aging on the physical prowess needed to commit many types of crime (e.g. Farrington, 1986). Others, however, cite the indirect effects of aging. Shover (1983, 1985) outlines this latter explanation for the 'age effect' following interviews with 36 male property offenders and data from autobiographies of comparable individuals. The aging process for Shover's (1983) participants brought with it a recasting of the offending behaviour that had characterised their younger years as foolish and wrong. Looking to the future, they felt that time was something that they had increasingly little of and that if their lives were to be worthwhile they would have to take advantage of the few opportunities available to them. Finally, there was a shift in their desires and a recasting of what was important to them as a result of this greater sense of perspective. Material wealth was no longer as important to them as 'contentment' and 'peace' (Shover, 1983, 211).

Similar results were reported by Cusson and Pinsonneault (1986) following interviews with 17 offenders convicted of armed robbery. Several of their sample experienced a gradual building of a lack of willingness to offend that followed successive periods of punishment (1986, 76). With age came the realisation that involvement in crime was increasingly hazardous. Apprehension became more likely, with longer sentences for repeat conviction, and prison life was increasingly difficult for the strain it placed upon them. Beyond this, time spent in prison was increasingly seen as wasted, detracting from the possibility of having a 'real life'. Finally feelings of excitement that offending engendered were replaced by fears of detection of offending and of violence from police that permeated every aspect of offenders' lives. These realisations led to a re-evaluation of how the future was viewed, such that it was perceived as a dead end if offenders were to continue their lives in their current form. The future became something that took on a concrete – and undesirable – form and aspirations e.g. to accumulate wealth, were recast in light of this (Cusson and Pinsonneault, 1986).

The link between gaining employment and desistance is also well documented (Meisenhelder, 1977; Shover, 1983; Sampson and Laub, 1993; Uggen and Kruttschnitt, 1998; Pezzin, 1995; Laub and Sampson, 2003). Explanations for this relationship have traditionally focused upon changes in routine activities and the assertion that commitment to a job increases social control (Laub and Sampson, 2003). In addition to these benefits, work provides a sense of identity and meaning to the employee that is incompatible with continued offending, as it did for many of Farrall's (2002) offenders. Farrall (2002) notes that the effect of employment upon offending was partly explained by the reduced time it afforded his sample to 'hang around', which might lead to offending, but also had an impact upon how individuals saw themselves and also in how they were seen by others. This shift was important for helping would-be desisters to understand that their attempts to lead a 'normal' life could be successful.

The forming of romantic partnerships is also linked to desistance (Shover, 1983; Cusson and Pinsonneault, 1986; Warr, 1988; Horney *et al.*, 1995). Such relationships are held to provide a means of informal social control and the forming of social bonds that steer the individual away from offending. Additionally, Shover (1983, 1985) asserts that relationships contribute to the reinforcement of an identity that is not centred upon offending, prompting a change in routine activities. However, in exploring the links between marriage and desistance further, Laub *et al.* (1998) emphasise the importance of the quality of the marital relationship. A good marriage i.e. one where the potential desister is committed to the relationship, was associated with desistance from crime, more so than one where such commitment was lacking. In addition, the impact of marriage on offending is asserted to hold regardless of the spouse's own deviance (Sampson and Laub, 1993).

The role of marriage and employment in prompting desistance from crime have also been held to be age graded i.e. they only impact offenders' behaviour if they occur at a certain age (Uggen, 2000). Amongst Uggen's (2000) sample, employment was only related to desistance for those aged 27 and older. Laub *et al.* (1998) suggest that a 'good' marriage that takes place early in the life can grow to have a preventative effect upon criminal behaviour, the timing being important because the social bonds which marriage introduces to the life need time to develop.

The observations regarding the above factors associated with desistance from crime are more or less widely accepted (Laub and Sampson, 2001). In recent years, research has attempted to further consider the subjective processes that are concomitant with transitions in the life course such as gaining employment or marriage and therefore concomitant with desistance from crime. The work of Maruna (2001), Sampson and Laub (1993; Laub and Sampson, 2003), Giordano *et al.* (2002) and Farrall (2002, 2005; Maruna and Farrall, 2004; Farrall and Calverley, 2006; Farrall *et al.*, 2014) is most prominent in this movement, while the work of Bottoms *et al.* (2004) makes more theoretical contributions. The particular emphasis of this work is on how desistance is constructed by the desister.

## *Maruna*

Maruna's (2001) study of 50 young offenders and ex-offenders sought to identify how desistance from crime and their previous deviant life is reflected upon by offenders. For Maruna's sample a significant part of desisting from crime was being able to reframe the past as something that was detached from who they 'really' were. This was a key part of what Maruna terms a 'redemption script':

## 18 *White-collar offenders' desistance*

The redemption script begins by establishing the goodness and conventionality of the narrator – a victim of society who gets involved with crime and drugs to achieve some sort of power over otherwise bleak circumstances...Yet, with the help of some outside force, someone who 'believed in' the ex-offender, the narrator is able to accomplish what he or she was 'always meant to do'.

(Maruna, 2001, 87)

For offenders, 'reading' from a redemption script meant to cast themselves as a victim of circumstances, virtually driven to offend, but who ultimately made good. Important for desistance was the recasting of the life so as to make sense of it within the context of who the offender was now and also who they wanted to be. Deviant pasts can therefore be acknowledged and even accepted so long as such acceptance is accompanied by the caveat that it was the 'past person' who was deviant (see also Maruna and Roy, 2007; Vaughan, 2007). Maruna's participants did not reject their past deviance, but rather changed the meaning it had for who they were now. Important as well was that offenders had a sense that their future was within their control, that their desires were achievable and that they were masters of their own destiny. Without this there was no impetus to attempt to desist from crime.

### *Sampson and Laub*

Sampson and Laub (1993, 2005a, 2005b; Laub and Sampson, 2003) argue for the importance of understanding the entire life course and its relationship to offending. Sampson and Laub (1993) reviewed the life histories of 500 delinquent and 500 non-delinquent men, originally collected by Glueck and Glueck (1950 in Laub and Sampson, 2003, 5) and subsequently interviewed 52 of the sample ten years later (Laub and Sampson, 2003). Their analysis argues for the importance of informal social control in helping to foster desistance from crime.

The central argument put forward by Sampson and Laub (1993 and reiterated by Laub and Sampson, 2003) is that offenders desist as a result of turning points in the life course that are influenced by structural factors. A turning point is that which leads to a change in the life course by altering a trajectory e.g. marriage can be a turning point for some offenders in that it is retrospectively identified as encouraging them to desist from crime, thus changing a criminal trajectory (Sampson and Laub, 1993). These turning points lead to sustained behaviour change. Engaging with turning points is not a conscious decision for many. Rather, engagement comes about as a result of habit through continued routine in a particular role. As a result, a turning point is not usually a discrete event but more a lasting change that occurs over time (Laub and Sampson, 1993). Laub and Sampson (2003) hold that the influence of turning points exists regardless of factors rooted in childhood such as onset of offending. From this, they argue that it is not useful to group offenders according to different 'typologies' grounded in early childhood risk factors (e.g. Moffitt, 1993), as these have little predictive power in identifying distinct criminal trajectories (Laub and Sampson, 2003, 110).

Furthermore, they assert that while there are different ways in which offenders may come to desist (e.g. marriage, employment) these all have common elements to them:

> What appears to be important about these institutional or structural turning points is that they all involve, to varying degrees: 1) *New situations that 'knife off' the past from the present.*[3] 2) *New situations that provide opportunity for supervision and monitoring in addition to opportunities for social support and growth.* 3) *New situations that change and structure routine activities.* 4) *New situations that provide the opportunity for identity transformation.*
> (Sampson and Laub, 2005b, 171–172, emphasis in original)

For example, military service was noted as an important turning point for some of Laub and Sampson's (2003) interviewees. Military service: 1) removed offenders from neighbourhoods and peers conducive to crime 2) provided a code of conduct for individuals if they wished to remain in military service, but also offered training in skills that could be used after service had ended 3) gave a clear structure to offenders' lives and 4) introduced offenders to new ways of thinking about themselves, seeing that they had skills they could employ in pursuit of legitimate goals and encouraging them to think about their antisocial behaviour and what it meant for their life.

In an update to their 1993 study, Laub and Sampson (2003) interviewed 52 of the men involved in the Glueck's original study. Laub and Sampson (2003) sought to explicate the role of agency and the interaction between human agency and turning points. For example, regarding marriage, the mere fact of a marriage was not enough to suddenly prompt desistance; instead, what was important was that the individual wanted the marriage to be a success. Consequently, it is necessary to understand the interplay between human agency and the structure offered by opportunities in the environment. Desistance involves recognising potential turning points as such and wishing to engage with them. Thus, Laub and Sampson (2003) conclude that opportunities are mediated by perceptions and human decision making. Neither agency nor structure can solely explain life course transitions in criminal behaviour (see also Farrall and Bowling, 1999).

### *Giordano* et al.

Further explication of the way in which engagement with opportunities to desist from crime may take place has been suggested by Giordano *et al.* (2002; also Farrall and Bowling, 1999). They also highlight the importance of the changes in perception of the self that underlie individuals' desistance. Their theory of cognitive transformation was developed from 197 interviews with male and female offenders.

Giordano *et al.* (2002) emphasise the choices that actors make, particularly with regards to creating an environment for themselves that is conducive to desistance. They therefore emphasise the role of human agency in desistance instead of

## 20    *White-collar offenders' desistance*

suggesting that offenders are merely beings who are subject to environmental influence. While the environment provides the structure to make changes possible, the offender must still recognise this possibility and take advantage of it. Taking advantage of the possibility of change provided by the environment is termed 'appropriating hooks for change' (Giordano *et al.*, 2002, 992). Giordano *et al.* avoid terms such as 'turning points' to emphasise the importance of offenders engaging with opportunities for sustained behaviour change.

As part of the process of cognitive transformation, Giordano *et al.* (2002, 1000–1002) highlight four stages that the offender goes through. First, there must be a shift in a basic openness to change, with the offender feeling that offending is not 'for them' any more. The second is the shift in openness to a specific hook for change. Examples of such a hook could be factors traditionally associated with desistance, such as employment or marriage. However, the mere presence of a hook is not sufficient. Instead, the individual's attitude towards a hook is relevant and this highlights the importance of attending to the shift that takes place within the individual to make a specific hook more attractive or salient. The offender must regard the hook and the future it promises as positive and also incompatible with continued deviance.

Third, having identified a specific hook for change, the offender must be able to envision a future self to replace the one they currently have. This 'replacement self' gives them a goal to work towards and can help with decision making in novel situations by providing a cognitive blueprint for making decisions i.e. choices can be made in line with what 'that sort of person' would do. Examples of a replacement self include the desire to be a good father or an honest person and the nature of the replacement self may be suggested by the particular hook for change appropriated by the individual. Giordano *et al.* assert that it is this replacement self that is more crucial to lasting behaviour change than any particular 'hook' because it will allow the individual to navigate novel situations after the hook associated with it is no longer present. For example, where marriage is the hook for change a replacement self centred upon being a good husband could still be of use in the absence of one's wife (Giordano *et al.*, 2002). Fourth, there is a change in the way deviant behaviour is viewed, such that it no longer holds the meaning that it once did for the individual. Consequently there is no desire to offend.

Hooks for change are deemed to be most effective at helping in the cognitive transformation process when they: 1) provide a detailed cognitive blueprint for behaviour 2) contain a projective element i.e. are based upon future concerns rather than past issues 3) are connected to positively valued themes e.g. wanting to desist so as to be a good father instead of wanting to desist so as to no longer have to spend time in prison and 4) act as a gateway to conforming others.

### *Farrall* et al.

Farrall and others (Farrall, 2002, 2005; Maruna and Farrall, 2004; Farrall and Calverley, 2006; Farrall *et al.*, 2014) have sought to elucidate more fully the perspective of would-be desisters in coming to terms with their circumstances.

*White-collar offenders' desistance* 21

They also emphasise the relationship between the individual and their environment and how this impacts upon the experience of desistance. Farrall's (2002) study of 199 men and women who were on probation explored the processes that are relevant to desistance from crime and the role of probation in facilitating or inhibiting desistance. Farrall identified three 'groups' of offenders. The 'confident' were those who in their opinion and that of their probation officer had a good chance of desisting. 'Optimists' gave themselves a good chance of desisting but this opinion was not shared by their probation officers. The 'pessimists' were those offenders who did not give themselves much chance of desisting and whose probation officers agreed with that assessment. Farrall (2002, 113) draws the link between agency, structure and desistance by noting that offenders' motivation to desist influenced the way they approached obstacles to desistance such as their use of drugs or the influence of their friends and family. Fewer of the 'confident' group experienced such obstacles (Farrall, 2002, 108). For the optimists and pessimists their ability to solve obstacles was related to their ability to desist, with those who could not solve obstacles far more likely to reoffend than those who could. These trends suggest a means of considering how motivation to desist impacts upon one's chances. Feeling able to desist impacted upon how opportunities to move away from offending were viewed but, importantly, those who were most successful were able to buttress their motivation with a supporting environment. For example, the desire to desist that one of Farrall's interviewees expressed, was supported by his partner (Farrall, 2002, 114).

Follow ups to Farrall's (2002) study have been completed with the original cohort by Farrall and Calverley (2006) and Farrall *et al.* (2014). These have focused – amongst other things – upon what desistance is like for the desister. They explore how it 'felt' to desist, the pleasure to be taken from a newly crime free life and the importance of living as an ex-offender. In doing this Farrall *et al.* make explicit the connections between events potential desisters encounter, how these are perceived and reacted to and the dynamic interplay between the two. The principal contribution of this work is to identify what is happening 'within' the desister. For many of Farrall *et al.*'s participants, desistance from crime was an emotional experience (Farrall and Calveley, 2006, Chapter 5; Farrall *et al.*, 2014, Chapter 7). Efforts to desist gradually brought about a restructuring of the way certain facets of the life were viewed. Pleasurable feelings such as an increase in self-worth and being trusted again that desisters took from spending time with family supplanted the 'positive' emotions individuals took from engaging in crime. At the same time, this past involvement in offending came to be viewed differently, with offenders noting the destructive elements of their past behaviour. Concomitant with this was the realisation that they were not recognised as an offender any more, with a consequent reduction in the stigma they felt and an increase in feelings of self-worth.

In a similar vein to Giordano *et al.*'s (2002) conceptualisation of desistance, Farrall and Bowling (1999) and later Maruna and Farrall (2004) also sought to take account of the way in which offenders construct an environment that is conducive to their own desistance. In doing this Maruna and Farrall (2004) make

## 22 *White-collar offenders' desistance*

more explicit that desistance is not explicable solely in terms of either structure or agency. Drawing upon and expanding Giddens' (1984) concept of structuration and applying notions of pro-social labelling, Maruna and Farrall (2004) assert the importance of societal reactions framed within a context of the ex-offender feeling they have made their own effort to desist.

### *Bottoms* et al.

Bottoms *et al.* (2004) direct us to focus on the absence of criminal behaviour and, consequently, are interested in any 'significant lull or crime free gap in the course of a criminal career' (2004, 371). They argue that the two 'camps' of desistance researchers, those asserting the importance of cognitive transformation (Giordano *et al.*, 2002; Maruna, 2001) and those positing desistance as a result of informal social control and key turning points (Sampson and Laub, 1993; Laub and Sampson, 2003) are essentially recreating the structure-agency debate. Although recognising a narrowing of this divide in recent times, Bottoms *et al.* (2004) nevertheless advocate working towards a more interactive framework, identifying five concepts that will aid an understanding of desistance: programmed potential, structures, culture and habitus, situational contexts and agency (Bottoms *et al.*, 2004, 372–374).

Programmed potential means applying what is known about the likelihood of individuals offending again based upon their demographic and social character-istics (notwithstanding some caveats about using aggregate data to predict behaviour). Using this information we can make some assessment of the likelihood of an individual offender's chance of offending again within a short period.

'Structures' are defined as 'social arrangements external to the individual which enable or limit action by that individual' (Bottoms *et al.*, 2004, 372). For example, employment may enable opportunities for successfully desisting. Obtaining work is likely to be more difficult with a criminal conviction than without however. This, for Bottoms *et al.* (2004), is one of the structural constraints inherent in the 'world' of employment.

Culture and habitus refer 1) to the social world where members share certain beliefs and patterns of behaviour (culture) and 2) to the predisposition of people to act in a particular manner based upon the structure imposed by a shared social experience, even when removed from the context of that social experience (habitus). Situational contexts are the locales that individuals find themselves with-in, which may or may not be conducive to offending. Limiting one's presence in situations conducive to offending may be deliberate (e.g. through decisions not to frequent particular locations) or accidental (e.g. time is spent elsewhere, perhaps as a result of new and meaningful pursuits).

Situational context, culture/habitus and structures can be described as the social context within which offending or conformity will take place. Behaviour is likely to be shaped by and interact with this context. Finally, agency, in relation to desist-ance is understood as active participation in the process. Bottoms *et al.* (2004) argue that taking agency seriously means to attend to the actor's own understanding of their actions while simultaneously recognising that they may not be aware of all

## White-collar offenders' desistance   23

that is relevant within their life. Offenders' lack of self-awareness and contextual awareness are likely to hamper attempts that just focus on their subjective accounts of desistance.

### *Summary*

The work noted above is suggested as contributing towards an understanding of the phenomenology of desistance. Maruna's work shows the importance of desisters being able to make sense of a deviant past within the context of a present and future where they no longer offend, casting the past in positive (or at least, non-negative) terms. With the appropriate narrative for one's life, a criminal past can be construed as perhaps even necessary for the real, non-deviant, person to emerge. In contrast to Maruna, who focused upon short-term processes of desistance and ex-offenders' feelings shortly after they had started to desist, the longitudinal data Sampson and Laub utilised allowed them to track individuals' lives across a substantial period of time. Desisters' personal conceptions of themselves changed as they developed from adolescence to adulthood. That is, they came to see themselves in different ways or to realise that their lives could change. This was often done with a view to a future self and therefore had a prospective element e.g. they came to see themselves as 'capable' of being a 'family man' instead of an offender. As much as desistance is a process, Maruna's desisters were, in the main, quite close to the start of that process, some still 'finding their feet'. For them, their closeness to their offending lives was something they were very much aware of. Sampson and Laub's participants in contrast, were in some cases looking back over decades' worth of crime free life.

Farrall *et al.*'s work (in particular Farrall, *et al.*, 2014) similarly benefits from its longitudinal nature, providing a rich portrait of the lives of offenders and their efforts and experiences of the desistance process. As well as further highlighting the importance of process noted by Giordano and Sampson and Laub, Farrall *et al.* draw our attention to the importance of emotional aspects of desistance and the importance of the presentation of self as a non-offender.

Giordano *et al.* demonstrate the importance of the choices that individuals make in coming to desist and the relevance of their being receptive to opportunities presented by the environment. In doing this and drawing attention to the notion of cognitive blueprints for a future self, they make explicit the importance for desisters of visualising a future in which they do not offend so that choices may be made in accordance with that future. Although theoretical, Bottom *et al.*'s (2004) framework explicates and further underlines the importance of the interaction between individual cognitions and the external environment. Potential desisters not only have a role in shaping their environment but must also react to and make sense of external events and structures.

The contribution such work makes is to bring out what the experience of desistance is like for the desister and make relevant an understanding of how the mere presence of elements conducive to desistance is not a guarantee that such desistance will take place. Although the above studies focused on 'street' offenders, the manner in which offenders who successfully desist from crime are able to

## 24 *White-collar offenders' desistance*

identify possibilities for change within their environment, 'manage' their personal narratives and do so through reconciling an immutable past with a desired future self can provide important insights for other offender populations. This concern is the focus of the current research, which seeks to understand the desistance of offenders convicted of a white-collar crime.

## White-collar offenders and desistance

The criminal careers literature has, with one or two exceptions, left the issue of white-collar crime and, of most relevance here, white-collar offenders' desistance, unstudied. Some of the best cited authors in white-collar crime research (e.g. Geis, Levi, Croall) have not directed their efforts towards understanding what experiences are significant to those convicted of a white-collar offence. Although the life course perspective has been employed to a limited extent to understand white-collar offenders (e.g. Benson and Kerley, 2001; Piquero and Benson, 2004), such work has considered desistance from crime briefly, if at all. Weisburd *et al.* (2001) provide a rare exception with a statistical portrait of the criminal careers of 968 convicted white-collar offenders (selected using an offence-based definition) drawn from information gained from pre-sentence investigation reports and supplemented by records of their offence history for up to ten years after the criterion offence. Weisburd *et al.* draw tentative conclusions about the desistance of their sample, highlighting that, for white-collar offenders, desistance occurs later in life than for other offenders. For white-collar offenders, the gradual aging out of crime was explained as a result of gradual shifts in the way criminal activity is viewed (Weisburd *et al.*, 2001), with aspirations for this group changing similarly to such processes in other offenders (e.g. Shover, 1983). However, the nature of Weisburd *et al.*'s data make this assertion impossible to confirm:

> Goals and aspirations change for these offenders as for other people as they get older. We suspect that such changes influence the willingness of offenders to be involved in criminality, irrespective of opportunity structures and other prerequisites for offending.
>
> (Weisburd *et al.*, 2001, 41)

Weisburd *et al.*'s (2001) observations, while admittedly somewhat limited in their scope, provide an opportunity for a rethink on common wisdom regarding desistance from crime. Desistance studies highlight the importance of age, marriage, employment and contact with the criminal justice system for an understanding of why individuals desist from crime. As has been indicated, however, white-collar offenders are, on average, older, more likely to be married and employed at the time of their offences than other offenders (Benson and Kerley, 2001).

Some age related explanations for desistance place an emphasis on the deterioration of the physical skills needed to commit many types of street crime (Farrington, 1986). Weisburd *et al.* (2001), however, suggest this is not a reasonable explanation for white-collar offenders' desistance as the physical fitness necessary to commit street crime is not necessary to perpetrate white-collar offences. Indeed, if there were to be any expected relationship between age and white-collar crime, Weisburd *et al.* (1991) suggest that it would be in the opposite direction to that observed with crime more generally. As individuals get older, they are presented with greater opportunity and ability to commit white-collar offences e.g. through a greater understanding of institutional working practices. Weisburd *et al.*'s data (2001; see also Benson and Kerley, 2001) indicate that white-collar offenders do gradually 'age out' of crime, but the observation remains that they start and end their criminal careers far later on average than other offenders. The quantitative nature of Weisburd *et al.*'s data make it difficult to consider the extent to which processes of maturation more generally (e.g. Shover, 1983; Cusson and Pinnsoneault, 1986) are associated with desistance from white-collar crime. However, such explanations are frequently held to underlie the observation that crime declines almost inexorably with age (e.g. Shover, 1983). Therefore a consideration of Weisburd *et al.*'s data would suggest that if such maturation did take place it did so substantially later in the life than existing research would suggest.

Of those in Weisburd *et al.*'s sample who had only one or two arrests (*low rate* offenders in Weisburd *et al.*'s terminology), two thirds were married at the time of their arrest (Weisburd *et al.*, 2001, 55). The greater average age (compared to 'street' offenders) of the offenders in their study makes it seem unlikely that the marriage bonds had insufficient time to strengthen, which is deemed important by some conceptualisations of the relationship between marriage and offending (Laub *et al.*, 1998). However, regarding recidivism, being married did increase the time until they offended again (Weisburd *et al.*, 2001, 104). Ninety-one per cent of Weisburd *et al.*'s 968 offenders were in employment at the time of the offence that led to their inclusion in the study, suggesting that the mere presence of employment may not be enough to prevent offending.

## Reconciling desistance research and white-collar crime

The above represents what is understood about how white-collar offenders come to stop offending. A focus on external factors such as the presence or absence of employment or marriage (for example) seems inadequate for accounting for white-collar offenders' desistance. Even in citing the 'traditional' factors that aid desistance, the supposed age-graded notion of them (Laub *et al.*, 1998; Uggen, 2000) is problematic when the greater average age of white-collar offenders is considered (Weisburd *et al.*, 2001; Benson and Moore, 1992). Shover and Hochstetler (2006) note that the odds of recidivism are low for white-collar offenders, and associate this with general observations within the desistance literature i.e. that white-collar offenders have all the 'advantages' associated with desistance from crime.

If white-collar offenders get married, find jobs and have other 'positive' life events when age-graded accounts of desistance predict they will do the most good however, then there has, given their greater average age, been plenty of time for their influence to take hold. The question then becomes: if these influences do not encourage conventional behaviour, what is responsible for white-collar offenders'

## 26   *White-collar offenders' desistance*

desistance? Even if such events are not age graded then the question still remains: what is responsible for desistance amongst this group of offenders who apparently have all the 'advantages' associated with leading a law abiding life? As Weisburd *et al.* observe:

> it does not seem reasonable to argue that growing stability in adulthood is a major factor in inhibiting criminality in our sample, as is suggested for those offenders who begin their criminal careers as teenagers.
>
> (Weisburd *et al.*, 2001, 41)

This concern is echoed by Benson and Kerley (2001) who suggest that white-collar crime and – potentially – white-collar desistance appears to be more a function of adult life experiences rather than underlying and undetectable personality traits or social background. Additionally, Piquero and Benson (2004) note that given the later start and end of white-collar offender criminal careers, citing early family background and biological characteristics will be insufficient to account for white-collar offenders' patterns of offending. White-collar offenders therefore offer 'a unique challenge to life course explanations of criminal behaviour'. (Piquero and Benson, 2004, 158).

Although an appreciation of the importance of understanding white-collar offenders' behaviour is demonstrated by the above authors, the issue of white-collar desistance is still largely absent from their considerations. What the above comments on white-collar offenders' desistance make explicit is that the mere presence or absence of particular factors is not sufficient for desistance from crime to take place. Looking beyond the presence of such factors is in keeping with the recent work on desistance cited above and the focus of such work on the necessity of offenders actively engaging with opportunities for desistance. To consider white-collar offenders' desistance from crime it therefore seems appropriate to follow the route taken by the desistance literature more generally and focus upon the internal processes that underlie desistance from crime e.g. shifts in values and beliefs and the lived experience of desistance. Pursuing these through a qualitative methodology would contribute both to the wider body of literature on white-collar crime and criminal careers research.

As desistance studies have emphasised, part of the desistance process involves making choices in line with who one wishes to be and also accounting for a deviant past. There is no understanding of how these processes operate for white-collar offenders. This is the emphasis of the current study: to consider the experiences of a group of white-collar offenders who have subsequently desisted from crime. What this study outlines are the processes that accompanied desistance and how white-collar offenders made sense of their experiences. In doing this the study aims to situate white-collar offenders with regards to the observations that have emerged from the desistance literature noted above.

The research questions for this study are: 1) What were the significant experiences of white-collar offenders who desisted from crime? 2) How did these experiences relate to their desistance from crime? 3) Is their desistance a result of shifts in values and beliefs regarding themselves and their behaviour? 4) How do they come to make sense of what has happened to them and 5) how do the experiences of white-collar offenders who desist compare to those of other desisters?

These questions reflect the importance of a focus on the subjective experience of desistance, which the above review emphasises. Answering them will be done by drawing upon a body of work that seems particularly well suited to explaining issues of motivation and change and for understanding the importance of one's place within the world. The following chapter outlines a conceptual framework underpinned by existential sociology and this work's place in helping to illuminate the issue of white-collar offenders' desistance from crime.

## Notes

1   Shover and Hunter draw upon an offender-based definition, but their comments still hold when we consider white-collar offenders as those who commit a certain type of crime. The demographic characteristics of offenders focused upon by researchers are in keeping with the general tenor of offender-based definitions (see for example Benson and Kerley, 2001; Weisburd *et al.*, 2001).
2   Reviews regarding concerns over the conceptual issues inherent in white-collar crime research can be found elsewhere (Croall, 2001; Nelken, 2012).
3   However, see Maruna and Roy (2007) for a more detailed consideration of the concept of 'knifing off'.

# 2  Searching for the self

The previous chapter established the importance of attending to the subjective aspects of desistance and resettlement to account for change amongst white-collar offenders. This chapter outlines a means of investigating this lived reality of attempts to desist from crime and resettle in the wake of conviction and punishment by presenting work drawn from existential philosophy and the accompanying sociology that this has inspired. The chapter starts with a summary of the literature that has considered existentialism as a school of thought. This is followed by a focus on existential sociology, which draws upon existentialist tenets to provide a means of considering human behaviour, making salient a focus upon emotions and the search for a meaningful self. A number of studies that have identified processes that have some concordance with existential sociology's tenets will be used to illustrate the efficacy of this approach for studying offenders' behaviour. Of particular relevance for a consideration of behaviour and behaviour change is the role of shame and so the chapter concludes by suggesting how shame may be related to desistance from crime.

## The nature of existence

Existentialism is perhaps best conceived of as a 'style of philosophising' rather than a distinct philosophy (Macquarrie, 1972, 14). The principal subject of existentialism is the individual being, who attempts to gain authentic selfhood and a sense of meaning through the exercise of freedom, choice and responsibility.

To exist is to be in encounter with the world and Macquarrie (1972, 69–76) identifies three 'characteristics' of existence. First, existence is dynamic and future oriented. The self strives constantly to achieve meaning. In any given moment, man, as a being who exists, is trying to move beyond what he currently is. From this, it is not possible to describe an individual in terms of a definite set of characteristics because this denies all the future possibilities that one might become. Because the self is constantly 'becoming', however, there is always a tension in the self; one's future self is always, to a greater or lesser extent, separate from the self as it stands in any particular moment (see for example Sartre, 1958, 113). Second, to exist is to be unique. This uniqueness is a vital characteristic of existence. No other has the experiences that I have, and it is this that lies at the centre of existence;

it is 'my' existence and no other's. I have a perspective on the world that belongs to me and only to me (Macquarrie, 1972). Third, to exist is to be possessed of self-relatedness. That is, to be able to both determine oneself and to be determined by external factors (Macquarrie, 1972). In sum then, to exist is to assert uniqueness through one's own existence, to have feelings, experiences and encounters that are relevant to oneself only.

Uniqueness of self is achieved through thinking, as a result of this thinking exercising choice and realising that choice through action (Sartre, 1958, 440). Freedom of choice and the exercise of that freedom is the means of deciding upon a future and making a commitment to pursuing one particular self over all others (Sartre, 1958, 465). Such a choice can never be completely free i.e. that literally any option is available to the individual; first, because one's past choices will have a bearing on the range of possible options open to the individual (Sartre, 1958, 517; Heidegger, 1926, 313) and second, because of the need to attain authentic existence, achieved when one can cite a unity of existence such that choices one makes are consistent with one another and the conception of self, and also when freedom and choice can be exercised without reference to external factors. As Macquarrie describes,

> Existence is authentic to the extent that the existent has taken possession of himself and, shall we say, has moulded himself in his own image. Inauthentic existence on the other hand, is moulded by external influences, whether these be circumstances, moral codes, political or ecclesiastical authorities, or whatever.
>
> (1972, 206)

Inauthentic existence is that characterised by Sartre's 'bad faith' (1958, 90) and alluded to by Nietzsche with his concept of 'slave morality' (1886, sec 259). The inauthentic existent hides behind slavish devotion to a role or makes excuses to deny their freedom to choose. Meaningful existence is achieved through attaining authentic selfhood.

### Emotions and the world

To exist is to directly participate in the world, as opposed to merely observing it, and it is through feelings that we interact with our world. Through feelings and emotions individuals engage with the situations they encounter and make sense of them and because of this emotions are important in understanding how the individual interacts with (i.e. exists within) their world (Grossman, 1984). Some emotions have been considered in more detail than others because they represent states that are considered fundamental to the individual as he or she exists. For example, as noted above, freedom and choice are of critical importance in understanding individuals' existence, but such freedom is also the root of anxiety. Anxiety arises out of our awareness of the full range of possible choices available to us and the sense that we might choose to do almost anything, even acts that might previously have been inconceivable. For example we are free to act in ways contradictory to

30  *Existential sociology*

our efforts to construct a unitary self-identity (Kierkegaard, 1844). Anxiety is therefore how one comes to recognise the freedom of choice one has. To feel anxious about an act is to know that one could perform it; one would not feel anxious about an act that could never happen (Grossman, 1984). To know that one is capable of such an act then is to have highlighted the extent of one's freedom of action.

To anxiety we might add guilt. Guilt is a product of the constant discrepancy between the self as it currently stands and a future ideal self (Macquarrie, 1972, 202). To feel guilt is to know that one has failed in attempting to achieve that self. However, guilt may ultimately be a positive experience because it can provide the individual with the will to change, and to strive to realise their future potential self (Macquarrie, 1972). A positive, future oriented emphasis on the experience of guilt ties it to another emotion that has been considered by a number of authors: hope.[1] To hope is to desire a particular outcome (Lazarus, 1999), an outcome that has to be perceived as being, at the very least, possible (Simpson, 2004). This attributes a future oriented aspect to hope, focused on the 'betterment' of the individual's situation. It is because of this that hope may act as a motivating force, as the individual acts to bring about that which they hope for (Bovens, 1999), although it is possible to be hopeful for outcomes that may be perceived as being beyond the individual's control (Lazarus, 1999). However, our hopes, once formed, are not pursued unchangingly, for as our knowledge of the situation shifts so too may our specific hopes regarding it (Simpson, 2004).

Just as information from the environment may impact upon what is hoped for, however, specific hopes acts as an information filter, such that new experiences will be interpreted and understood in relation to what is hoped for (Simpson, 2004; Smith and Sparkes, 2005). This thus increases the chance that we will act in a manner perceived as beneficial for bringing about the desired outcome (Bovens, 1999).

Perhaps the greatest contribution of hope to a consideration of human existence may be noted when it is considered in terms of its antithesis, despair. With hope, we may act to affect a change in our circumstances, staving off the inaction which we might otherwise fall into when faced with a negative situation (Lazarus, 1999). Even if a negative situation is one which we may feel we have no control over, to have hope is to recognise that it will not last indefinitely, providing a reason to 'carry on' (Bovens, 1999). To be able to hope is crucial because 'without it, there would be little to sustain us' (Lazarus, 1999, 654). In order for the self to grow and project itself forward, it is necessary to have hope, because without it we would become immobilised by the despair of some situations we encounter, unable to see a way beyond them.

Hoping is linked to existence because through hoping individuals express their values and desires. It is not possible to hope for something that one does not value and therefore to hope for something is to provide a reflection of oneself (Simpson, 2004). Furthermore, by reflecting upon hopes and the way in which these may change, individuals come to situate themselves within the world (Bovens, 1999). However, just as an emotion we might term negative, e.g. guilt, may bring with it

*Existential sociology* 31

positive implications because it may provide the impetus to change (Macquarrie, 1972, 203), so hope also has, in part, negative connotations. To hope is to risk the disappointment that a desired outcome will not come about (Simpson, 2004). Simpson conceives of hoping for a particular outcome as making an 'investment' (2004, 442) towards it. Doing this commits the individual to wanting a particular outcome, while a failure to realise it is then likely to be accompanied by a sense of loss or pain (Bovens, 1999). In addition to this, if others are made aware of our hopes they may reject them, by association rejecting a part of us (Simpson, 2004).

## *Action*

While thinking and feeling are both important elements contributing to one's own existence, it is through action that our existence becomes realised (Sartre, 1958, 498). Action is not merely the observable act, but is rather the fusion of thinking and feeling and the meaning this fusion has for the self. From this then it may be seen that action represents the total person. As one acts, they are in the process of projecting themselves forward, of making themselves, of existing (Morrison, 1995, Chapter 15).

It follows from this that action, as existentialists use the term, is intentional. That is, an act is intended to bring about a certain consequence (Sartre, 1958, 455). What is also present in existentialist writings however is a sense of tragedy (Grossman, 1984) and the sense that the very act of existence as characterised by exercising choice and realising that choice through action is one that has an inherent sadness to it (Macquarrie, 1972). It has already been noted that one never has a total freedom of possibilities when making a choice because of the way in which past choices constrain future opportunities (Sartre, 1958, 517). Beyond this, another dimension to the anxiety inherent in realising one's freedom of choice is to realise what is lost by choosing (Sartre, 1958, 520). In choosing we select a particular future and therefore a particular future self, but consequently reject all other future selves. Exercising choice is therefore as much about what is rejected as what is embraced (Macquarrie, 1972, 182). Inherent in every choice is the concern that through deciding to pursue one possibility others must be rejected, with the consequence that a reduction of future choices becomes inevitable. Related to this concern is that the consequences of a choice may not be fully realised until some point in the future. In this way then, there is a sense of trepidation over any such choice because one's future self can only be guessed at (Macquarrie, 1972, 183) and a future self can never being committed to in the sure knowledge that such a self is achievable.

## *Past, present and future*

An individual's past and future are intimately connected for the meaning placed upon the events of our personal history. The meaning placed upon the past may in fact be constructed and reconstructed as needed to serve the present. In this way, the past is always open to new meaning and to new interpretation, existing only as

## 32 _Existential sociology_

it is recalled in a given situation and with regard for the meaning placed upon that situation (Kenyon, 2000, 14). In turn, the way the present is interpreted is constituted by the future and the specific goals that are of concern to the individual. Part of existence involves managing the tension between our past, present and future self. Who we are now and who we may yet become are grounded in who we were. This is what Heidegger (1926, 373) means when he stresses 'I am as having been' and also as Sartre describes,

> the freedom which escapes toward the future can not give itself any past it likes according its fancy... It has to be its own past, and this past is irremediable... If the past does not determine our actions, at least it is such that we can not take a new decision except _in terms of it._
>
> (1958, 517, emphasis in original)

We therefore must become our past and in this way we already are our future. However, although we may not be able to change our past, we can change the meaning of it (Sartre, 1958, 519–520) and it is in this way that we actively construct a future for ourselves. The meaning I place upon the past is a function of my present aspirations, which in turn, as we have seen, are directed towards who I wish to be. For example, the offender who wishes to desist from crime may cite negative experiences as prompting them to do so such as being caught while burgling a house, suffering physical injury or fearing for one's life for example. The future project constituted by wishing to be an ex-offender cites these experiences as evidence that crime is not worth it. If the same offender later reoffends then these same experiences may be cast somewhat differently. With a different future project, the same experiences may be interpreted for the excitement they bring, the 'rush' that offending engenders a key part of the life that is now missing and a reason to offend again (equally, offenders may reject an authentic existence by asserting they were 'driven' to offend).

This necessarily brief overview of existentialism has concentrated on the key aspects of existence that will inform the forthcoming analysis. This chapter now considers the application of existentialist thought within sociology.

## Existential sociology

Sociology has sought to utilise the ideas suggested in existentialist thought for a consideration of human behaviour (e.g. Douglas and Johnson, 1977; Kotarba and Fontana, 1984 and Kotarba and Johnson, 2002). The goal of this existential sociology is to study people within their everyday world (Fontana, 1984, 4).

Existential sociology draws upon many of the important concepts inherent within existentialist thought more generally but rejects the often rather bleak view of existence that is frequently characterised as being present in such writings (e.g. Nietzsche, 1887; Sartre, 1958; Heidegger, 1926) and characterised by such themes as dread, fear and loneliness (Kotarba, 1984; Douglas, 1984).[2] Despite this less 'grim' aspect to existential sociology, however, the influence of the existential

*Existential sociology* 33

literature may be seen in the core concerns of existential sociological thought; specifically: individuals' search for a meaningful self-identity; the role of feelings and emotions; and finally, the importance of individuals' values and beliefs. These concerns provide a means of understanding that individuals' behaviour may change.

### A meaningful self-identity

Douglas argues that all individuals hold a sense of self that cannot necessarily be rationalised (1984). Our sense of self develops to aid us in negotiating the various situations we will encounter over the course of our life. Above all, individuals strive to achieve a secure and meaningful self to ward off the isolation and meaninglessness that threaten to pervade all human existence (Manning, 1973). It is through the sense of self that the individual relates to the world and comes to understand their place within it (Johnson and Kotarba, 2002), it constituting a set of guidelines for positioning ourselves in the world, for acting and for situating our actions with regard to our past, present and future (1984, 97). These temporal aspects of the self are important for an understanding of how our lives form a whole, giving a sense of coherence for acting. As Douglas notes:

> Where do I come from? Where am I? Where am I going? must be answered,
> at least in some implicit way to *give physical direction to our life processes*.
> (Douglas, 1984, 82, emphasis in original)

The future oriented, constant drive to realise an ideal self, prompts us to seek out new experiences to imbue existence with meaning rather than simply partaking of the same experience constantly, which would lead to a lack of growth (Frankl, 1978). Only through this expansion and growth of the self can life become meaningful and the sense of self is made real through the social roles we engage with, roles that must often be manipulated so as to help meet our needs and desires (Kotarba, 1984, 226). In noting this then, we can see that the self is not passively 'decided' by the social situations we are part of. Such situations are approached by us and shaped in accordance with our prevailing conception of who we are. Concrete situations are therefore the way actors inform their understanding of who they are.

Fundamental to the conceptualisation of the self is an understanding of how it reacts to the possibility of its own change. Events within the world can suggest the possibility of change because they impact upon some aspect of our existence (Kotarba, 1984, 229). If change can be accommodated within the current conception of the self then the individual is unlikely to feel ontological insecurity: a threatening of the entire self (Yalom, 1980; Fontana, 2002). Instead, such change might promote, at most, a period of heightened self-reflection if the change in the sense of self is one that puts it in sharp contrast to the currently held perception (Douglas, 1984, 77). Conversely, if the individual feels they lack the resources to cope with change then it may be perceived as threatening and accompanied by the

## 34 *Existential sociology*

dread that is concomitant with their inner self – their very being – being at risk (Douglas, 1984; Hunter, 2011 demonstrates the impact of this on white-collar offenders).

The self evolves through social encounters and who one 'is' is constructed through interaction with others and will necessarily be reconstructed as one moves between social encounters and social institutions (Goffman, 1963, 1969; Douglas, 1977, Ebaugh, 1984). Such movement may lead to insecurity, but it is a situational insecurity and will no longer be present once the situation has been left behind (Douglas, 1984, 94). Only when the self feels *basically* insecure will the barriers that inhibit its growth be present across a variety of situations (Douglas, 1984, 94). An important related issue to the notion that others define who we are is that answering questions about our self can be done through an understanding of others' beliefs about us.

In addition to providing the drive to seek out new experiences, the self is also reflective, considering the way in which situations relate to the values we hold and the emotions we experience. These reflections are used for determining the best course of action in a given situation, prompting action in such a way so as to protect the self from the possible shame/guilt that may arise from failing to act in accordance with the beliefs and values that the individual has (Scheff, 2000).

### *Values and beliefs*

The values that we hold are likely to be derived from cultural values and those expressed by our own social groups (Douglas, 1984, 83). Living in accordance with our values is likely to produce feelings of pride while, conversely, acting in a manner contradictory to them may bring about shame as the individual is forced to confront (via their actions) the possibility that they are less capable or have less integrity than the self is comfortable with (Scheff, 2000). In this way then, our values help us to orient ourselves in relation to the world. The values that individuals hold themselves to become self-reinforcing, protecting the self from shame by prompting behaviour more in accordance with the prevailing conception of self. To live according to our values is not restrictive however, because they are a part of who we are (Douglas, 1984, 83). Douglas describes the problems that would be faced by a self without values:

> Socially we would be continuously *lost*. An individual who violates his own basic rules or those of the groups in which he is emotionally grounded feels that he has betrayed his self, and he experiences the pain of severe guilt or shame; this pain in turn reinforces the rules, making it more likely that he will not betray his self next time.
>
> (Douglas, 1984, 83, emphasis in original)

It is also the case however that individuals may manage to circumvent the barriers to guilt-free behaviour imposed by certain standards and develop new values if they frequently experience guilt and shame prompted by the conflict between self and actions. This may be done by associating the new value with positive emotions (Douglas, 1984). Our values then, are important for providing us with guidance on how to act in a given situation. However, it is emotions that provide us with the drive to act.

### Feelings and emotions

Existential sociologists also prioritise emotions, particularly as they relate to providing the impetus for human action. From this perspective, emotions sit alongside rational action as explanations for behaviour (Clark, 2002). As emotions emerge from our interaction with our world, they are therefore social products that hold importance because they confirm or alter the relationships we have with others (Clark, 2002).

Existential sociology's focus is upon the free will of the individual and therefore argues against a deterministic view of social encounters that sees them as constraining individual choice. Instead, all contexts are socially constructed by actors, whose sense of agency and free will contributes to the formation of the 'rules' of a given situation (Johnson and Kotarba, 2002). Particularly strong emotions may overcome even these rules however, because essentially humans are not rational actors, but animals who are inclined to act upon their feelings (Douglas, 1977). Reason, although still employed by individuals is 'weak' and prone to high levels of variability depending upon the situation the individual is in and their interpretation of it.

Although the rules that society has and the values that individuals hold themselves to can constrain the impulse of feelings, equally they may be prey to them. When this happens, feelings and emotions may be used to reframe values so as to cast them in a manner that is more acceptable for the individual and therefore become 'the reasons behind our reasoned accounts' (Douglas, 1977, 51). In this position, feelings are all pervading, underlying and driving forward all aspects of the human experience. A focus on emotions leads us to consider what, for some writers, is one of the most powerful emotions that relates specifically to social interaction and behaviour change, shame.

### Shame

Shame is an emotion comprised of moral and social elements. It is a moral emotion, because to feel shame is to recognise that one has transgressed one's own rules of how a person should conduct his or her self (Taylor, 1985). The individual who feels shame recognises that their behaviour is incompatible with the values they believe themselves to hold and that this reflects negatively upon them. This ties shame to notions of responsibility, at least where shame is as a result of behaviour that calls one's character into question (Manion, 2002). Shame then, represents a perceived lack of fit between one's values/ideal self and one's actions (Ford, 1996) and as values are themselves derived from those we interact with (Douglas, 1984), this attributes a social element to shame (Taylor, 1985). It is social because it

36  *Existential sociology*

represents an unfavourable judgement by one's honour group: the group the individual belongs to that shares common values and ideals, holding each other to these (Taylor, 1985, 54–57). To fail to live to the standards of the group is to lose esteem in the eyes of the group and to be shamed.

In noting the importance of the 'honour group', Taylor (1985) makes explicit the necessity of an audience to prompt an individual to feel shame. The individual who finds his or her behaviour under scrutiny will be forced to recognise the audience's perspective on their activity. This perspective will not necessarily be a critical one and, even if it is, will not necessarily cause shame (the individual may not care for the audience's opinion for example). However, sometimes it may, and this conception of an audience is a unique characteristic of shame, that it involves an other-to-self message, a message with unfavourable connotations that discredits the self or rejects it in some way (Retzinger, 1991).

An audience can be symbolic as well; one need not necessarily be observed to feel shame over one's actions. What is important is that the individual's way of viewing their self shifts in such a manner that they can view their behaviour in a way that is free of bias. In this way then, the different views an audience may have regarding our behaviour (e.g. critical, indifferent, admiring) become a metaphor for our own self judgements (Taylor, 1985). Shame therefore represents an unfavourable judgement of the self, where that judgement is taken from a point of view that the individual has until, that time, not recognised. The notion of an audience and what it means in terms of judging one's own behaviour is significant for understanding the power of shame to have a profound effect upon an individual (Taylor, 1985). In adopting, even briefly, the role of impartial observer, the individual is unable to hide from him or her self the aspects of their personality that they might otherwise deny and, for Schneider, this is another of shame's unique qualities. It forces the self to be its own judge:

> Normally, the self refuses to see itself; it looks away; it hides from itself. To know oneself is *painful*. There is much that, left to ourselves, we would just as soon overlook. As long as we are left to our own devices, we are willing to participate in much self-deception to avoid the pain of shameful self-revelation.
> (1992, 26, emphasis in original)

Shame is also an emotion of self-assessment, with the individual comparing their behaviour to the ideals and values that they hold (Taylor, 1985). However, in contrast to guilt, which also entails a judgement over one's behaviour, shame speaks to a far more fundamental problem. Lynd (1958) makes the distinction between guilt as directed to certain specific acts (i.e. what one did) while shame is more fundamental, representing a problem with the self as a whole or certain aspects of it (i.e. what one is). This accounts for the very fundamental nature of shame, as a basic emotion that threatens either the core personality of the individual or specific aspects of it (Manion, 2002). Shame conveys to the individual that as a person they are 'wrong' (Scheff, 2000) and that in some way they have 'failed' as a human being (Manion, 2002). As a result of its all-encompassing nature, shame

*Existential sociology* 37

can be temporarily crippling to the individual, leaving them, for a time, unsure of how to proceed (Manion, 2002). Instead of building gradually, shame 'surprises' the individual, appearing quickly and suddenly calling one's behaviour into question (Schneider, 1992).

Despite this negative aspect to shame, however, there are positive elements to the experience. Shame serves as an emotion of self-protection by making our values explicit through comparison with our behaviour and therefore experiencing shame provides the individual with the opportunity to reappraise those values and (assuming the individual still wishes to live by them) make a fresh commitment to them through behaviour that is consistent with them (Manion, 2002). Shame's function as a social emotion is relevant here as well. Having an awareness of shame and knowing what may prompt/prevent it aids social interaction by providing a means of monitoring the self in our interactions with others (Goffman, 1963). Indeed, for Scheff (2000), having a sense of shame is a necessity if we are to negotiate relationships with others successfully, because it represents a threat to the individual's bond with society. As such, a threat may occur at any time and it must be constantly guarded against. Manion (2002) also makes reference to this aspect of shame, asserting that it alerts us to a threat that we will lose the esteem of others.

Ford (1996) suggests that the power of shame lies in its ability to be a catalyst for behaviour change, representing as it does the ultimate lack of fit between one's ideal self and one's actions. Shame then, is future directed, with the goal of 'bettering' the individual (Schneider, 1992) and this links experiencing shame to the search for an ideal self. A final positive aspect to the experience of shame is that it may be taken as an indication that the individual who feels it may still maintain a degree of self-respect. One can only feel shame in the presence of self-respect because to have self-respect is to attempt to protect the self from shame by adhering to the values it has internalised (Taylor, 1985). Ultimately then, shame can only represent a positive evaluation because we can only feel shame in the presence of other positive feelings about ourselves. To possess a sense of shame is therefore to possess a desirable moral characteristic (Schneider, 1992). Where an individual lacks shame, they lack the ability to care about and value the self (Schneider, 1992).

### *Shame and desistance*

What the foregoing sections make clear is that existential sociology is fundamentally concerned with change. As part of our existence in the world, the self is grounded in particular situations and settings and the ever-shifting nature of these presents us with challenges as we attempt to maintain a unitary sense of self. Emotions are an important part of this because through understanding emotions we can locate how we understand ourselves. Manion (2002) notes that we might reasonably expect shame, in some instances, to be linked to the development of morally positive traits, with an accompanying change in behaviour. The above conceptualisation of shame emphasises its ability to provide the impetus for behaviour change. Shame then, may be a prompt for the individual to behave 'better' in the future (Manion, 2002).

38  *Existential sociology*

If the experience of shame is stultifying, then it prevents the growth of the self while the shame is being experienced, because all focus is directed upon it (Manion, 2002). However, such a period can only ever be transitory because to exist in a sustained period of shame would be to deny the self one of its fundamental properties, that of growing, seeking to achieve its ever-unreachable ideal (Douglas, 1984). Such a conceptualisation of shame makes it not immediately apparent how it may impact upon behavioural change in the long term, given shame's transitory nature. Although, as noted above, some authors have considered shame as a catalyst for behaviour change (Ford, 1996; Schneider, 1992), such a conceptualisation may not fully encapsulate the role of shame in this regard. Therefore, this section will tentatively suggest a means by which we might consider the relationship between shame and the type of behaviour change of interest here, desistance from crime. The notion that feelings of shame may be related to desistance is hardly new (e.g. Braithwaite, 1989; Liebrich, 1996). However the intention here is to consider in more detail the relationship that shame has to concepts of the self and the relevance of this for desistance.

With its relation to the interplay between values and behaviour change, an understanding of shame provides one means of considering how 'internal' processes may prompt individuals to desist from crime. For some individuals, offending behaviour may be far enough removed from the values they associate with their self that they may experience shame. This may be directly, because the offence itself is inconsistent with their values e.g. 'I'm not the sort of person who steals'. Alternatively, any shame experienced by an individual who offends might be directed not at the offence but at the impact it has had on their life e.g. where a conviction impacts upon the ability to perform socially valued roles such as caring for one's family. Coping with shame experienced either directly or indirectly as a result of an offence might be done through desisting in an attempt to affirm that the person is not 'an offender', reflecting upon their shame to consider the meaning it has for them (Douglas, 1984).

Shame as conceptualised above represents something of an overwhelming emotion. If an offence does not prompt feelings of shame then this might suggest that, for the individual, their behaviour is not incompatible with the values they consider to be of importance (Ford, 1996). If, however, the individual does experience shame as a result of their offending then the feelings must be confronted and 'managed' in some way. Such management could (for example) be in the form of rationalisations that cast the individual's behaviour in a positive light (see Benson, 1985, for an example of this when applied to white-collar crime) or a 'victimisation narrative' (Schrock, 2002), which prevents feelings of shame through the construction of a perception that the individual is being unjustly treated. Within this narrative, feelings of shame may be viewed as being intended by one's persecutors, with the accompanying anger this entails lessening the chance for any feelings of shame (Schrock, 2002). Such strategies help by allowing the individual to maintain a favourable conception of their self and help to nullify the 'paralysis' that accompanies the shame, allowing the self to continue to grow. Retzinger (1991) and Scheff (2000; Scheff and Retzinger, 1991) also identify the way in which shame, if unacknowledged can lead to anger.

*Existential sociology*  39

Such strategies may not always be possible, however. For example, the incident may be too far removed from the individual's conception of their self to allow for justifications to mitigate the shame. Alternatively, an offender may be prevented from conceptualising their actions in a positive light by others who know of the offence and react in a manner that makes a positive conceptualisation untenable. It is suggested that, in such an instance, making a commitment to change or acting so as to reaffirm their basic self may be possible strategies for managing shame, as others have suggested (Lewis, 1971; Manion, 2002). With regards to making a commitment to change, the individual may feel they no longer wish to 'be' the 'sort of person' who does 'that' and resolves to remedy this by identifying a 'new' self they hope to become (in keeping with the perspective that shame may act as catalyst for change, Ford, 1996; Manion, 2002). Shame acts then, to prompt the search for a new conception of the self. This strategy may work to mitigate the shame felt because it allows the individual to place some distance between their 'old' self and the self they will be. If the incident that caused the shame is viewed as an aberration when set against the rest of the self, however, then the shame may be managed to some extent by a reaffirmation of the self by acting in ways more in keeping with the self concept, e.g. an apology illustrates that the individual knows they have behaved unacceptably (Schrock, 2002). In either case, the memory of feeling shame is a reminder of why cessation of the behaviour which caused the shame is important.

A suggestion that individuals might make use of management strategies for coping with shame should not be taken to reflect a conception that that such strategies are chosen consciously by individuals or that such strategies are as distinct or mutually exclusive as the above may suggest. For example, a victimisation narrative may be used as a means of justifying an act, or a commitment to change may only extend to some areas of the individual's life while in other areas the individual acts to reaffirm their self through behaviour salient to 'them'. It is the case, however, that an individual may feel shame for their actions retrospectively. Shame does not necessarily happen immediately and it is possible that reflecting back on past actions may cause feelings of shame which were perhaps absent at the time. This may be because the consequences of the act have only just become realised or are now viewed differently. Therefore, an alternative relationship between shame and change is that shame at past actions, rather than being a cause of a shift in values and beliefs, may be a consequence of such a shift casting the past in different terms. Actions that once were unproblematic from the point of view of the self may now be seen as fundamentally wrong.

For some who desist from crime, however, the role of shame may be more subtle, acting more on the possibility of it occurring. Where, for example, an individual has experienced a gradual restructuring of their values (e.g. as a result of changes in friendship networks, Giordano *et al.*, 2002) then shame may aid efforts to desist through the threat it represents to the individual. In this instance, rather than desistance being prompted by a sudden experience of shame, it might be 'encouraged' out of a desire to avoid feeling shame by acting in a manner inconsistent with one's (new) values. Previous offending would not cause shame

## 40 *Existential sociology*

despite being incompatible with new values because it is not the behaviour that the 'sort of person' the individual now is would engage in (Maruna, 2001). In this instance, shame's relation to desistance might be as a threat of the negative feelings that would be experienced should the individual transgress once more (Manion, 2002). This gradual manner of desistance is in keeping with research observations that change does not happen 'overnight' (Laub and Sampson, 2003; Farrall *et al.*, 2014). It also highlights the interplay between 'external' changes such as shifts in friendship networks and 'internal' processes such as alterations in values. Acting to avoid feelings of shame may elicit more 'positive' emotions that serve to highlight the efficacy of change in the individual's life (for an example of how positive emotions are associated with desistance see Farrall and Calverley, 2006, Chapter 5). This last observation also cautions against the temptation to view shame as the only emotion of relevance for a consideration of desistance. Instead, it should perhaps be viewed as just one emotion that may be considered of importance when considering change over time (Giordano *et al.*, 2007), albeit a significant one.

### *Phenomenological sociology and existential sociology*

Existential sociology has been identified as one of a range of sociologies that seek to understand self (see Lester, 1984). Comparisons can be drawn most closely between existential sociology and phenomenology as a sociological enterprise. This latter is distinct from phenomenological thinking more generally and perhaps best exemplified in the work of Schutz (1967). The phenomenological sociology of Schutz concentrated on the particular actions that individuals undertake as rational courses of action and that are a consequence of other events and also undertaken in order to cause particular outcomes. For Schutz, actions have objective meaning and it is through understanding this meaning that we can understand the subjective experience of the person who acts.

Phenomenological sociology and existential sociology both seek to understand the meaning individuals place on their circumstances and the relationship this has with action. Both approaches advocate methods that capture participants in their natural environment, and identify how they understand that environment (Lester, 1984, 57). Where existential sociology differs however is in identifying individuals as feeling subjects who express their own uniqueness in situations that are specific to them (Lester, 1984, 57).

Existential sociology holds that situations are not necessarily 'acted out' through conformity to rules, but through the emotions that are elicited through such conformity (Lester, 1984). For example failing to live up to others' expectations of us in a particular situation might produce feelings of shame, while doing so might engender pride. This contrasts with phenomenological sociology's emphasis on the typicality of social interactions and the way in which actors draw upon a stock of knowledge to determine how it is appropriate to act in a given situation, based on a shared understanding of the ways a 'typical' person engaged in a particular role would act (e.g. Schutz, 1967, 17).

Existential sociology 41

Phenomenological sociology aims to understand the basis of the knowledge we have. That is, how we come to understand our world. The basis of 'truth' can be identified by understanding how the individual relates to his world. But for existential sociologists, the world is also the setting for thoughts and feelings (Fontana and Van de Water, 1977). As the foregoing made clear, emotions are a vital part of existence and cannot be ignored. It is this emphasis on emotion that is at the core of the difference between existential sociology and other sociological perspectives on subjectivity e.g. symbolic interaction.

A further difference between the sociology of existentialism and that of phenomenology is that the former holds that there is such a thing as a 'true self' that exists (Lester, 1984). Existence is concerned with understanding and expressing that self and there are 'good' and 'bad' ways of doing so, emphasised by the distinction between authentic and inauthentic existence (Lester, 1984).

Existential sociology also differs from phenomenological approaches to sociology in emphasising that we cannot understand human meaning through an identification of abstract categories of behaviour grounded in rationally motivated action (Altheide, 1977). Difference, not routine, characterises existence. Altheide further criticises phenomenological sociology for conceptualising the cognitive processes which underlie specific acts as rather invariant:

A meaningful social science must be able to make sense out of what is important to actual people, and not merely reduce them to actors who 'do' social life… Knowledge of the invariant procedures cannot tell us why one man kills and another loves. But this is precisely the kind of thing we desire to know in our daily lives.

(Altheide, 1977, 148)

Difference is not solely a characteristic used to distinguish between two individuals, but also within the same individual across time. Implicit within this then is that for *difference* we might also read *change*. Human life is change and an adequate sociology of human action and interaction should be able to account for this. Particular ways of thinking and particular activities that are attractive at one time cease to be so at another and become supplanted by others that sometimes contrast sharply. Perhaps nowhere is this more apparent than when those who engage in offending 'change their ways', desist from crime and take up very different lives from those which they had previously. Existential sociology is best placed to understand and conceptualise such shifts. It emphasises that there are no hard and fast 'ways' to desist and that every offender's situation is different. Finally, as will be indicated below, desistance focused research has begun to emphasise the role of emotion in desistance. Existential sociology is sympathetic to the role of emotion in the life more generally and, in fact, celebrates it, making it a particularly useful framework within which to consider desistance from crime.

## 42  *Existential sociology*

## Existential sociology and criminology

Some of the concerns that have occupied existential sociologists in relation to how individuals move within society and experience change can be identified within criminological literature. It is worth noting, however, that of these studies, only Farrall (2005; also Farrall and Calverley, 2006; Farrall *et al.*, 2014) and Hunter (2009; 2011) explicitly draw upon existential sociology. The remainder may be better thought of as emphasising some existential aspects of offending. The most obvious link is the focus of criminology on the emotional aspects of offending. Involvement in crime has been explained as fulfilling an emotional need (Adler, 1985; Scott, 2004). Katz has argued for the importance of understanding the emotional pleasure associated with offending, the powerful enjoyment that being an offender brings and the consequent attraction of crime (1988). Morrison (1995) follows Katz in attempting to highlight the importance of understanding how it feels to offend. Morrison argues that a failure to comprehend this emotional component to offending is to deny the lived reality of crime for the offender and that social science risks losing *individuals* (a cardinal sin for existentialists) by attempting to generalise and therefore is 'in danger of forgetting that the offender is an existential phenomenon' (1995, 360).

The relevance of the emotional component of offending has begun to take even more prominence in recent years. As Loader and deHaan (2004, 244) remark, a greater understanding of the emotional aspects of offending 'might enrich criminological research and reflection; helping us construct explanations of criminal behaviour and social censures'. Scott (2004) shows that the 'sensuality' of offending and being part of a gang not only gave members a sense of belonging, but also relieved the boredom that was otherwise prevalent in their lives. In addition, gang members' almost compulsive acquisition and exhibition of material items (e.g. clothes, shoes) as a means of preserving their status was interpreted as being the way in which they can 'defend their place in the world' (Scott, 2004, 124), helping to make meaning in their lives. In desisting from crime, several of the gang members recognised that to be successful would require a complete reworking of their lives, including their outlook on the world, as a means of reinventing their self (Scott, 2004). Other studies have hinted at the internal conflict that some offenders may experience as a consequence of the lack of fit between the person they perceive themselves being and the actions they undertake as they are involved with crime and deviance (Adler, 1992; Ford, 1996).

Jose-Kampfer outlines how being imprisoned represented an 'existential death' for the women in her study (1990, 110). The reports given by long-term female prisoners suggested they were in mourning for the life they had lost upon their incarceration, but were in an environment not conducive to adequately resolving this. A link to the timelessness of their prison experience was made by women citing that they were held 'out of their existence', suggesting a limbo period in which they were removed from the outside world. This was emphasised by the loss of previous world roles and the 'unreality' of the prison existence. They were unable to exist as they conceived of their selves.

*Existential sociology* 43

Meisenhelder's (1985) study of the way in which time in prison was experienced by prisoners draws upon the concept of time as understood within existentialism (e.g. Sartre, 1958). A sense of crushing futility was experienced as the structure of prison life left prisoners without any sense of future. Very little that is done in prison, Meisenhelder (1985) argues, is done with regard to what happens after prison time has been served and consequently time passes very slowly because nothing is being worked towards i.e. there is no discernable future. Prison time, for prisoners, was essentially 'futureless'. Prison constituted individual identity in terms of who one was 'now' (a prisoner) and who one had been (an offender) but denied an opportunity to have any meaningful future project (see also Hunter, 2011).

In rebellion against this imposition of time were attempts by prisoners to manage time, making it pass more quickly through the initiation of events that would serve to act as a distraction from the present e.g. by creating disruptions to the prison routine. Time was created rather than merely being served (Meisenhelder, 1985). Meisenhelder notes, however, that – ironically – such strategies merely served to orient prisoners to the past, as they were relived by prisoners to detract from their present.

More recent work has drawn explicit links between existentialism, existential sociology and the lives of offenders. This work indicates how the interplay between internal and external factors is important for long-term identity change. Positive responses from colleagues, for example, helped Farrall's (2005) interviewee to confirm to herself that the 'normal' persona she was attempting to achieve was legitimate. Farrall illustrates how gaining legitimate employment can aid a process of desistance by demonstrating to the individual that there is potential for them to be 'someone else', giving hope that their efforts to desist can be successful. Such a future oriented realisation helps in the identification of a meaningful future self. Some of Farrall and Calverley's (2006, Chapter 5) desisters expressed similar realisations. They were focused upon their families, who they felt they had previously neglected, but had been given the chance to 'make amends' by taking on roles which they had not fully engaged with previously. Farrall and Calverley also highlight the way in which emotions underlie the desistance process. Emotions such as shame and guilt prompted individuals to try to affect a change in their lives, while feeling good about changes that had taken place served to reinforce the idea that these changes were worthwhile (these themes are developed by Farrall *et al.*, 2014). Hunter's (2011) interviews with imprisoned white-collar offenders further emphasise the role of emotions and the importance of a future self as an existential concern for prisoners. White-collar offenders recognised that their place in the world had changed as a result of their convictions, their pasts constituted by the particular futures each identified as awaiting them upon release.

In the previous chapter, the theory of cognitive transformation (Giordano *et al.*, 2002) was outlined. In highlighting the importance of individuals' attitudes towards specific hooks for change, the theory of cognitive transformation suggests the importance of attending to the meaning individuals place upon their own circumstances. Observations that offenders are concerned about their 'future self' (Farrall, 2005; Hunter, 2009, 2011) have some concordance with existential sociology's

## 44 *Existential sociology*

concept of the self as a future oriented, dynamic entity. They also find common ground with the concept of the ideal self that individuals strive to achieve (Douglas, 1984; Fontana, 1984). Additionally, the efforts that individuals made to try and achieve a future replacement self, accompanied by the angst that they experienced while attempting to do so have resonance with the search for meaning in the face of the futility of existence that has characterised existentialist writing (e.g. Sartre, 1958). In this work, then, are suggested some ways that the concerns of existential sociology might be applied to consider desistance from crime. It also offers a conception of how changes in values may take place, based upon associations with new peer groups.

A further example of how existentialist thought may be implicitly present in desistance focused research is given by Maruna (2001). The narratives of reform told by Maruna's interviewees emphasised their own agency in constructing a legitimate life for themselves. Desisting from crime required a means of constructing past deviance in a particular way so as to portray them as victims of circumstance who could not help but offend (see also Maruna and Roy, 2005; Vaughan, 2007). The past could not be changed, but the meaning they placed upon it could (Sartre, 1958).

Mention should also be made of Braithwaite's (1989) theory of shaming and the way in which this relates to desistance from crime. Braithwaite's use of the term shame is more sociological than is used in the discussion above, with shaming something that is 'done to' offenders by peer groups and by society, rather than being an emotion that they feel. Nevertheless, within a framework that draws upon existential sociology Braithwaite's (1989) work highlights the importance of offenders' interaction with the world in which they live and the relationship between the identity society provides them with and their own sense of who they are.

## An existential framework for studying white-collar offenders

The above discussion of existentialism and existential sociology focuses on the aspects of this work that will be used to frame an understanding of the desistance and resettlement experiences of white-collar offenders. Of particular interest given work on desistance more generally is how white-collar offenders experience change in their 'outer world' and the impact this has upon their sense of self. An existentially inspired framework directs us to consider how offenders understand themselves as a precursor to identifying how they understand their own lives. Inherent in this is knowing the relationship that white-collar offenders have with their own particular 'worlds', the way they shape and are shaped by them. Finally, underlying all of this is the emotional aspect to white-collar offenders' desistance. How do feelings surrounding the processes involved in punishment and subsequent resettlement impact upon white-collar offenders' own understandings of who they are and who they wish to be?

These considerations are in keeping with the presence of the concerns of existentialism within criminological thought more generally, and the efficacy of using such concerns for an understanding of offenders' experiences. The focus that existential sociology places upon how individuals attempt to make meaning in their lives through their interaction with the world and how emotions drive action and may prompt change provides a means of accessing the processes that underlie the desistance of white-collar offenders. Through a focus on self and responses to transitions of that self, an understanding of the significant experiences of white-collar offenders who are attempting to live a legitimate life may be understood.

## Notes

1   In identifying hope as an emotion, Lazarus (1999) observes that an emotion is that which arises from the presumed fate of a specific endeavour. In accordance with this, for Lazarus, 'hope is a response to goal outcomes, and, as such, it should be treated as an emotion' (Lazarus, 1999, 663).
2   It is probably rather unfair to portray existentialism as an unremittingly bleak enterprise. Being alone in the world and free to choose for example is potentially empowering and should be a cause for celebration. Nevertheless, existential sociology has characterised existential thought more generally in such a manner.

# 3 Autobiography and the search for 'truth'

The telling of lives has a rich tradition in sociology. The written and oral accounts of individuals represent a valuable means of gaining access to subjective experience and how they understand themselves. In this study, the experiences of white-collar offenders who have desisted from crime are drawn from published autobiographical accounts written by such offenders i.e. accounts which are commercially available and written to be sold. This chapter provides a rationale for the use of autobiographical accounts as a means of understanding human experience. The chapter starts by outlining what autobiography is and the particular insights autobiographical accounts give, focusing on the issue of truth and subjectivity. Some of the potential problems inherent to a study of autobiography are noted, but it is also observed that these issues are only problematic if certain, rather inflexible notions of 'truth' are privileged by researchers. Such notions ignore the unique contributions of autobiography for understanding the way in which particular human experiences are recounted by those who have lived them. Investigation of individuals through their autobiographical accounts is by no means unprecedented and so the chapter moves to consider similar methodological approaches that have been employed within criminology. Following this the sample of offenders is outlined, noting the particular characteristics of the members of the sample and the potentially unusual nature of this group of offenders.

## The telling of the self

It is through the telling of stories that individuals attain meaning and self-identity, reaffirming their sense of unity and purpose (McAdams, 1993). This gives individuals' accounts a unique place in contributing to an understanding of their experiences, with the relevance of historical facts relegated to a secondary role behind establishing the 'truth' of events for the individual. Autobiography is one such way of telling the life story. For Lejeune, autobiography is:

> A retrospective prose narrative produced by a real person concerning his own existence, focusing on his individual life, in particular on the development of his personality.
>
> (Lejeune, 1982, 193)

An autobiography is focused upon the past or, perhaps more appropriately, a particular the past recalled by the author, who tells the story of their life. Autobiography therefore represents one of the forms of 'human documents' (Plummer, 2001, 18) through which individuals express themselves. Autobiographies recall and revisit past events, which are interpreted and recounted for the meaning they hold to the writer and in this sense construction of an autobiography is the search for a sense of who one is (Plummer, 2001). Recounting the life is an active process however, with the meaning of events constructed and reconstructed as the past is recalled (Smith and Watson, 2002). Smith and Watson (2002) refer to autobiographies as one example of a life narrative. As a text, a life narrative is:

> a historically situated practice of self-representation. In such texts, narrators selectively engage their lived experience through personal storytelling, Located in specific times and places, they are at the same time in dialogue with the personal processes and archives of memory.
>
> (Smith and Watson, 2002, 14)

Only through a life narrative such as that represented by autobiographical text may we encounter the writer's self (Smith and Watson, 2002). The individual is the only one who may comment on their own subjectively viewed experiences. This subjectivity means autobiographies include what has been relevant for the writer, the life experiences that were of importance and the encounters that shaped them (Smith and Watson, 2002). They are therefore a means of understanding how the self experiences itself and how the past is understood by the writer (Plummer, 2001; Smith and Watson, 2002) and this suggests that accessing data on individual thoughts and feelings is best achieved through using autobiographical data (Cotterhill and Letherby, 1993). These permit a telling of the 'entire picture' of the life, rather than a recounting of specific incidents free of historic and relational context. This, Cotterhill and Letherby (1993) note, affords autobiographical accounts a privileged place in any consideration of an individual's past.

Attending to narratives in such a manner means to relinquish notions of 'fact' and recognise that, just as an individual experiences events subjectively, they will also come to recall and recount these events in a similarly personal manner. Smith and Watson argue that 'truth' in autobiography represents an interaction between author and reader with the goal of arriving at a shared understanding of the life (2002, 13). Any use of autobiography as a research tool must reflect this. Plummer, who views life history as analogous to autobiography, being the full-length account of a person's life in his or her own words, makes this point explicit:

> It is however clear what [life documents e.g. autobiography] are not, they refuse to be social scientists' second-order accounts that claim to be external and objective truth... They all attempt to enter the subjective world of informants, taking them seriously on their own terms and thereby providing first hand, intimately involved accounts of life... What matters, therefore, in life

48 *Autobiography*

> history research is the facilitation of as full a subjective view as possible, not the naïve delusion that one has trapped the bedrock of truth.
>
> (Plummer, 1983, 14)

In representing the writer's truth, a reading of an autobiography should privilege an understanding of the writer's experience and interpretation of the events of their life. However, external 'fact' still has a place in autobiography as many accounts will deal with events that are in some manner verifiable. What is of relevance is the way such events were experienced by the writer.

Written autobiography differs from other methods of understanding the life – oral history for example – because there is no interviewer involvement in their construction.[1] They are 'fixed' as presented to an audience, and although we can investigate the data, we cannot investigate the person who constructed such data. Far from being a disadvantage for those wishing to understand human existence, assessment of autobiographical accounts may represent a truer reading of individual experience because such accounts add to that which can be obtained through external observation of the life (Gusdorf, 1980). The autobiographer reflects on their life, their significant experiences and what these mean in terms of the life as a whole. This is what makes autobiographical accounts unique as a form of data. Their focus is on the person and this makes them superior to biographical accounts' emphasis on events (Evans, 1993).

With an emphasis on the writer's self and the subjective aspects of experience, certain characteristics of autobiographical texts are likely to be prominent. Sometimes narrators work to make the self-representation of their life conform to particular identity frames so as to affirm who they are to others but also to themselves (Smith and Watson, 2002). Sheridan (1993) argues that the construction of an autobiography is a means of confirming one's existence to oneself. Further, construction of an autobiography helps one to understand who 'they' are, as the generation of a coherent life story allows the teller to gain a sense of meaning. It gives the author the opportunity to situate their life and their sense of self with regard to broader historical and social contexts (McAdams, 1993).

Constructing a narrative is an important part of understanding who one is, but narrators write with an audience in mind. Through this we may see the possibility of the autobiography acting in the writer's best interests. As Gusdorf notes 'One is never better served than by oneself' (1980, 36) and also 'Memoirs are always … a revenge on history' (1980, 36). The autobiography then, should be viewed as the production of the life (de Man, 1979, 70), representing the life as it is recalled by the teller at the moment of writing (Plummer, 2001). Further, autobiographies are a means of creating 'posthumous propaganda' (Gusdorf, 1980, 36) for the teller of their own life story and a means of self-justification for a life. To the characteristics of autobiography, we might add a further dimension for autobiographical texts that are written for publication. The desire to make money must be viewed as a drive to publish one's life story, although this should not necessarily impact upon the writer's subjective experience.

Through these properties of such texts, it is clear that autobiography may be best thought of as a performance, the intended audience having an impact upon the 'type' of self that is constructed through the telling of one's own life story (Smith and Watson, 2002). In turn, this will impact upon the 'truth' that the account aims to present and furthermore to how the reader should respond (Smith and Watson, 2002). In sacrificing 'the' truth for 'a' truth, autobiography permits the understanding of far more about the individual than might be inferred from a reading of the 'facts' of their life. The way in which accounts are constructed provide important indications as to the writer's sense of who they are (e.g. Oleson, 2003). When we search for autobiographical truth then, we search for the writer's own conception of self and their interpretation of events.

The self that is constructed through an autobiographical account may be identified first through what is said about events within the life and how they were experienced and second by the way in which the account is constructed. This latter construction of the self may be identified in the 'tone' of the writing. Is the autobiographical 'I' bitter, conciliatory or regretful for example? In addition, identifying the intended audience for the autobiography may provide useful insights into the way the self is constructed by the author. Other questions that may be asked regard the 'aim' of the writing. For example, does the text aim to provide the 'true' account of a particular event or series of events (Smith and Watson, 2002)? Such issues will likely have a bearing on how the self is presented.

## Autobiographies in sociology and criminology

The use of autobiographical material in sociological research is well established. Working out of the Chicago School of Sociology, Thomas and Znaneicki's early work *The Polish Peasant in Europe and America* (Bulmer 1984, 45–64) made an important contribution to sociology for the emphasis it placed on understanding the sociological subject's subjective experience of their world. The methodology used to investigate the lives of Polish immigrants to America included the analysis of thousands of life documents, in this instance letters written to family members and also autobiographical data by one immigrant in particular. This work marked a key development in the work of the Chicago School of Sociology and the development of sociological thought and method by that body (Bulmer, 1984). Plummer (2001) cites the early use of life histories by Chicago School sociologists as pioneering the use of life documents within sociological research, the interest in autobiographical narratives as a way of understanding lives increasing throughout the twentieth century. Autobiographies have been used to study as diverse a range of topics as the appeal of mountaineering (Davidson, 2002), the development of sociology in America by early sociologists (Henking, 1992) and to contribute to socio-legal analysis (Rowbotham, 2007). Autobiography as a form of study is the subject of much interest, as evidenced for example by journal special collections on auto/biography in sociology (Evans, 1993). This represents the growing use of autobiographical data as just one of many sources of data that might be utilised by researchers.

50  *Autobiography*

This study seeks to continue in this tradition of research using autobiographical data constructed by white-collar offenders. The use of published autobiographical accounts in this manner is not unprecedented within criminology. Some of what are considered classic early studies of prisoner behaviour draw upon written and published autobiographical accounts by prisoners (Cohen and Taylor, 1972, 215–216; Irwin, 1980, 37–38, footnote) but more recent criminological work has also made use of autobiographies as a resource. Maruna analysed the autobiographies of 20 street offenders who had desisted from crime to identify 'similarities in theme, plot structure and character'. (1997, 61). Morgan (1999) focused on how prisoners constructed representations of themselves and of their prison experience through their autobiographies. Common themes were how prisoners actively resisted the power of the prison, the culture of violence amongst prisoners and the injustices of the penal system in general. Oleson studied the autobiographies of three 'genius' (i.e. having a high IQ, Oleson, 2003, 391) offenders, attempting to show that such work could answer questions about the way in which offending and criminal justice can impact upon 'geniuses'. Shover and Hochstetler (2006) drew upon the published autobiographies of white-collar offenders, using them to demonstrate the difficulties such offenders report with their imprisonment.

This rich tradition in sociology more generally and criminology in particular suggests that published autobiographies could be gainfully employed to study white-collar offenders. As the foregoing discussion on the nature of autobiographies makes clear, an advantage of such accounts is the subjective interpretations they provide on the nature of the author's life. The distinctive advantages in privileging the author's interpretation of the significant events of their life that autobiographical data provide will be used to investigate processes of the experience of criminal justice and resettlement amongst white-collar offenders. The intention is to understand white-collar offenders' own worlds and the way they make sense of their punishment and resettlement. Drawing upon their autobiographies is a particularly effective means of doing this, free as their books are from a particular research context. The reading of such autobiographies will be done so as to take account of how white-collar offenders made meaning of their experiences and how they account for changes in values and beliefs as part of their desistance.

The previous chapter introduced a conceptual framework that draws upon the tenets of existentialism and existentialist sociology to inform this study of desistance from white-collar crime. Existential sociologists, while not privileging a particular methodological stance over any other, have tended towards understanding humans in 'natural' environments and through methods that aim to capture their everyday life (see for example Kotarba and Johnson, 2002; Farrall, 2005). Individuals are encouraged to highlight the relevant aspects of existence for them to convey the uniqueness of their experience and how the context of the life as a whole influences the emphasis placed upon particular experiences (Farrall, 2005). There is therefore a clear commitment to privileging the subjective nature of existence. Drawing upon autobiographical data is a particularly apposite way of satisfying such concerns.

*Autobiography* 51

## Methodological issues in studying autobiographies

In drawing upon published autobiographical accounts as a means of contributing to current criminological knowledge it is necessary to be aware of the potential problems with such data. Most significant are issues surrounding the lack of 'tailoring' of data to the specific focus of the research and issues of 'truth' in offenders' accounts.

It might be considered problematic that the researcher who wishes to use published autobiographical data for the investigation of a particular phenomenon has no means of controlling what is written and how adequately it pertains to the topic of study. However, while this may be problematic for some studies, where the issue of investigation is individual experience (as is the case here), data that have not been 'sullied' by the researcher's opinions and preconceptions is a boon. As Maruna (1997) observes, the written autobiography reflects what the author wants the reader to know and does so better than any interview. In using a published autobiographical account we can be sure that what is recounted are the writer's significant experiences, the encounters that impacted most profoundly upon them and shaped their life, and how they feel about these. This is important for understanding how individuals construct meaning and make sense of what has happened to them (Maruna, 1997). They are constructed entirely separate of the research context. A further advantage of this is identified by Shover:

> the life histories and interpretations contained in published accounts in many cases profit from the extended length of time the subjects have invested in sorting out and making sense of their lives. Unlike responses to questions, which are given without time for reflection, the insights and interpretations presented in these materials were not developed hastily. Consequently, they often contain sharper and more impressive descriptions and interpretations.
> (1996, 190–191)

These particular strengths are unique to the use of published autobiographies, thus making them a valuable resource in investigating individual lives.

There may be concerns over the 'truth' of autobiographical accounts. However, Maruna (1997) observes that the knowledge that those close to them will be likely to read it may make it more likely that a published autobiographical account is factually accurate. Many events that will be described are externally verifiable and there may also be legal reasons for ensuring that what is told is factually accurate. There also seems little a priori reason to believe people would lie more in an autobiography than in a research interview and if authors were to do so their publishers would have a vested (legal) interest in rooting out such falsehoods. Even if this were not the case, however, as has been noted above, what is relevant is the writer's 'truth'. Beyond this, the current research's focus upon what was significant for individuals and the 'internal' experiences they had is well served by these accounts. Such research is in the tradition of what has been termed 'The narrative study of lives' (Josselson and Lieblich, 1993), the emphasis being upon the meaning individuals place upon events that they encounter (Maruna, 2001).

## 52 *Autobiography*

Related to whether autobiography represents what is 'true', we might add that it is important to understand the extent to which the authors have ownership over what is written. Ghost-writers sometimes assist in the construction of 'autobiographies' and editorial influence may both have a bearing on content and presentation. Both Maruna (1997) and Katz (1988) identify the concern that the drive to publish a marketable book may have a significant bearing on what is written, hiding the author's intentions beneath a wave of prose designed to sensationalise. Ultimately, however, it must be expected that at some level what is produced is the author's own story, approved by them. In addition to this, Maruna (1997), following Sutherland (1932) suggests that such challenges are likely to be no more relevant than with oral histories collected by sociologists.

### White-collar offenders' autobiographies

The predominant source of data used was the published works of 23 individuals who had been convicted of a white-collar offence. The sample was theoretically driven, the intention of the research to identify significant aspects of white-collar offenders' resettlement and desistance and link these with directions for future research (Strauss and Corbin, 1998, 202). Books were included in the sample if at least one named author was a white-collar offender and the time period of the book covered the offender's offence and/or some period after their arrest. The decision was made not to restrict the sample to books from any particular time period because a decision to focus on one time period over another would have been arbitrary. The final sample consisted of 23 offenders and 34 books. A bibliography of the final sample of books is listed in the Appendix.

Table 3.1 contains basic information on all the offenders in the sample, their nationality, the year of their conviction, the year of publication of their book or books and whether or not any book was written with a co-author. Where more than one book was written, all years are included. Table 3.2 provides a summary of the focus of each offender's book or books listing those subjects covered in the autobiography. *Release* refers to a description by the offender of the actual moment they left prison and the following 24 hours, including their impressions of this time. *Post release* covers a description of what offenders did after punishment had ended. For a subject to be 'covered' the offender had to make extensive reference to it, including a description of their feelings about the subject. For example, 'I was released from prison' did not constitute 'extensive' coverage. However, a description of release and the anticipation and feelings this engendered did.

As Tables 3.1 and 3.2 show, the books published by these white-collar offenders represent a range of contrasting styles and emphasis of account. Some books are truly accounts of the whole life, while some focus exclusively upon the period of imprisonment. Some include very little description of the offence while others make this the almost sole focus of the book, with a few pages dedicated to the aftermath of conviction. In these latter cases it was particularly important to attempt to establish desistance through other sources. The majority, however, focus at least to some extent upon what happened to offenders after their punishment.

*Autobiography* 53

*Table 3.1* Summary of sample, year of conviction and year of book publication

| Offender | Nationality | Convicted | Publication year | Co-author? |
| --- | --- | --- | --- | --- |
| Jonathan Aitken | British | 1998 | 2000; 2004a; b; 2005 | No |
| Jeffery Archer | British | 2001 | 2002; 2003; 2004 | No |
| Jim Bakker | American | 1989 | 1996 | Yes |
| Jordan Belfort | American | 2003 | 2007; 2009 | No |
| Robert L. Berger | American | 1998 | 2003 | No |
| Alan Bond | Australian | 1996 | 2003 | Yes |
| David Bullen | Australian | 2006 | 2004 | No |
| Nelson Christensen | American | 1998 | 2005 | No |
| Charles Colson | American | 1974 | 1976; 1979; 2005 | No |
| John Dean | American | 1974 | 1976; 1982 | No |
| Darius Guppy | British | 1993 | 1996 | Yes |
| Clifford Irving | American | 1972 | 1972 | No |
| Joseph Jett | American | 1997 | 1999 | Yes |
| William Laite | American | 1969 | 1972 | No |
| Stephen Lawson | American | 1979 | 1992 | No |
| Nick Leeson | British | 1995 | 1996; 2005 | Yes (1996 and 2005) |
| Dennis Levine | American | 1987 | 1991 | Yes |
| Jeb Magruder | American | 1974 | 1978 | No |
| Barry Minkow | American | 1987 | 1995; 2005 | No |
| Walter Pavlo | American | 2001 | 2007 | Yes |
| Pete Rose | American | 1990 | 2004 | Yes |
| Joseph Timilty | American | 1993 | 1997 | No |
| Tod Volpe | American | 1997 | 2002 | No |

Two offenders are worthy of special mention. First is Clifford Irving. Irving finished his account before his punishment began. However, when his autobiography is added to interviews and similar media coverage of his offence, we can begin to understand his experience of resettlement and desistance. This recognises that processes of change are not simply tied to specific events such as imprisonment. Second is Barry Minkow. Media archive searches indicate that Minkow was reconvicted of two further offences (Fortune, 2014), six years after his most recent biography and nearly 20 years after the prison sentence he served for his initial offences. It cannot therefore be said that Minkow has desisted from crime. However, Minkow's autobiographies give detailed accounts of his attempts to resettle and take on new endeavours in the wake of a conviction, and it appears that for a while he was successful. His case is included for these insights (and as a possible warning of the difficulties in asserting any offender has desisted!).

Some books, while not written as autobiographical accounts as such, had autobiographical sections within them. Jonathan Aitken for example, in addition to writing two autobiographies, published two books containing prayers and psalms that have helped him cope with adversity. These latter books contain descriptions by Aitken of how and when particular prayers/psalms were useful to him.

54  *Autobiography*

*Table 3.2* Offenders and subjects covered by their books

| Offender | Subjects covered by book | | | | |
|---|---|---|---|---|---|
| | *Offence* | *Arrest* | *Prison* | *Release* | *Post punishment* |
| Jonathan Aitken | Yes | Yes | Yes | Yes | Yes |
| Jeffery Archer | Yes | No | Yes | Yes | No |
| Jim Bakker | Yes | Yes | Yes | Yes | Yes |
| Jordan Belfort | Yes | Yes | No | No | No |
| Robert L. Berger | Yes | No | Yes | No | Yes |
| Alan Bond | Yes | Yes | Yes | No | Yes |
| David Bullen | Yes | Yes | No | No | No |
| Nelson Christensen | Yes | No | Yes | No | Yes |
| Charles Colson | Yes | Yes | Yes | Yes | Yes |
| John Dean | Yes | Yes | Yes | Yes | Yes |
| Darius Guppy | Yes | Yes | Yes | Yes | Yes |
| Clifford Irving | Yes | Yes | No | No | No |
| Joseph Jett | Yes | Yes | N/A[1] | N/A | Yes |
| William Laite | Yes | No | Yes | Yes | Yes |
| Stephen Lawson | Yes | Yes | Yes | Yes | Yes |
| Nick Leeson | Yes | Yes | Yes | No | Yes |
| Dennis Levine | Yes | Yes | Yes | Yes | Yes |
| Jeb Magruder | Yes | Yes | Yes | Yes | Yes |
| Barry Minkow | Yes | Yes | Yes | No | Yes |
| Walter Pavlo | Yes | Yes | No | No | No |
| Pete Rose | Yes | Yes | Yes | No | Yes |
| Joseph Timilty | Yes | Yes | Yes | Yes | Yes |
| Tod Volpe | Yes | Yes | Yes | No | Yes |

[1] Joseph Jett did not serve a prison sentence.

Offences committed by these offenders include insider trading, perjury, obstruction of justice and securities fraud. The offenders themselves are former politicians, corporate executives, lawyers, a television evangelist and a former baseball player. Publication dates of the books range from 1972 to 2009 and ten were written in conjunction with a named co-author. In all cases, this co-author was a literary professional i.e. someone with experience of writing books.

In addition to the books, use was made of media archives as a way of tracing individuals' lives after the events they describe in their accounts. This was done in part to confirm where possible that individuals had as far as could be discerned desisted from crime and also as a means of locating other information given by the individual that could supplement their autobiography. Primarily, this other information took the form of media interviews that offenders gave and provided a further means of understanding how they made sense of and recounted their experiences. All the offenders whose books were sampled had desisted from crime as far as could be ascertained (with the exception of Minkow, noted above).

## Analysing autobiographies

White-collar offenders' accounts were analysed to consider common themes in authors' experiences of punishment and their life in the aftermath of this. Plummer terms this 'systematic thematic analysis', where:

> the subject is more or less allowed to speak for him or herself but where the sociologist slowly accumulates a series of themes – partly derived from the subject's account and partly derived from sociological theory.
>
> (1983, 113–114)

The analysis was guided by existential sociological understandings of the self, particularly the way in which the self is constituted within social encounters, through action and with regards to the future. In keeping with this, it was also done with a regard for the fact that although each individual's existence is unique, a broadly shared experience is still identifiable when similar situations are encountered.

Books were read with a view to identifying which experiences the writer identified as being significant during their offending, punishment and resettlement. The ex-post analysis sought to bring out the relevant dimensions of desistance for white-collar offenders, as identified by them. Having noted these, comparisons were made across books to explore whether there were commonalities across different offenders' accounts. Although the primary focus of the analysis was on the punishment and resettlement period of offenders' lives, writers' early lives were taken into account where the experiences they had related to realisations and important experiences later in life. For example, many of those who converted to a new religion (Chapter 8) contrasted the feeling of wellbeing they took from their religion with feelings of emptiness they had experienced in their lives previously, in some cases decades earlier. The ability to cover large periods of offenders' lives in this way and listen to accounts that are informed by sustained reflection on the whole life illustrates an advantage of drawing upon autobiographical data.

Some themes offenders identified are integral to issues of desistance and resettlement and frequently chapters of books concentrated upon the experience of imprisonment, release, and the aftermath of punishment for white-collar offenders. Each of these 'grand themes' contained smaller organising topics for analysis, including how offenders related to changes in their identity, how they dealt with reactions from others regarding their offence and their experience of time in prison. These chapters capture what it was like for offenders to experience particular aspects of the criminal justice system and then resettle.

Further themes were of less obvious importance in studying desistance from crime, but were suggested by the wider criminological literature. For example, the role of becoming a professional-ex and its relationship to desistance – the focus of Chapter 7 – is present in criminological work more generally (e.g. Brown, 1991; Maruna, 2001). Other themes were suggested as relevant after books had been analysed to identify commonalities amongst them. Such was the case with the study of religious conversion and its relationship to desistance from white-collar

## 56  *Autobiography*

crime. This became the focus of Chapter 8 following the realisation that a large number of white-collar offenders' accounts made reference to the adoption of religion in their lives as a significant moment for them. Chapters 7 and 8 include a subsection of offenders drawn from the main sample and the emphasis in these chapters is on understanding in some detail the processes involved in managing a change in identity when that change has particularly strong symbolic connections.

## Comparing accounts

In as much as this study explores an area that has received little attention, direct comparisons with other studies are not possible. The experiences of white-collar offenders as they attempt to resettle are an area about which little is understood. However, with its focus on desistance the present study parallels this substantial body of work and specific comparisons are made explicit throughout the analysis. White-collar offenders' experiences of resettlement are placed within the context of processes associated with desistance more generally and the similarities and differences of their accounts compared to those of other offenders are noted. Similarly, the analysis complements the work cited above which has drawn upon autobiographical accounts for a consideration of offenders' behaviour. More generally, it relates to the growing corpus of work that has sought to understand offenders on their own terms and highlight the salient aspects of their existence for them (e.g. Katz, 1988; Morrison, 1995; Farrall and Calverley, 2006; Lippens and Crewe, 2009; Hunter, 2009, 2011).

That white-collar offenders' experiences are drawn from written and published accounts does not automatically render irrelevant comparisons with other offenders' experiences. Comparisons with other work (which have predominantly used interviews to collect data) are possible based on an understanding that both methods of data collection have a shared interest in the subjective aspects of social experiences. That both approach the collection of data in different ways does not preclude the comparison of such data. It would be foolish in the extreme to dismiss out of hand the use of a potential source of data for studying a little-researched group of offenders about whom little is understood precisely because they are a difficult group to gain research access to (Shover and Hunter, 2010). Even the claim that the methodology adopted here might be considered unorthodox is increasingly hard to sustain given the previous criminological uses published autobiographical accounts have been put to as noted above.

A glance at Table 3.1 shows that offenders whose books make up the sample are heterogeneous in terms of their nationality and also that there is substantial variation in terms of when offenders were convicted and consequently when they wrote their books. The influence of cultural and historical context is undoubtedly important for any consideration of human experience. These white-collar offenders had to find ways to live within specific cultures. Given the difference in time between the periods in which different offenders were attempting to resettle it is reasonable to think that specific cultural mores would be unlikely to be the same for more than a handful of the sample. However, disentangling the way in which desistance from crime and resettlement differs from 1970s United States of America (Colson, Dean) to turn-of -the millennium Australia (Bond) to twenty-first-century United Kingdom (Aitken) is not a task this study purports to undertake.

The purpose of the current research is to understand offenders' lives on their terms and identify what is important to them. Offenders, at the time they tell their stories, are too closely placed to the events they are describing to be aware of any historical context for their resettlement. Similarly, it is perhaps unsurprising that offenders do not comment on the broader cultural context of their resettlement. In having experiences that are personal to them, the specific cultural milieu that shapes them is, if not something they are unaware of, perhaps taken for granted. If this is a price to be paid for accessing the subjective experiences of offenders then so be it.

Existential sociology undertakes to understand individuals' lives in worlds that are unique to them. To hold cultural and social context as a mediating factor for individuals' experiences is to deny them the uniqueness of their existence and their ability to constitute themselves i.e. to choose one existence over another (Craib, 1976). Craib makes this point explicit in considering Sartre's early life. Disagreeing that Sartre's early work was a product of his living in a France experiencing great social upheaval in the post-Great War period, Craib observes that Sartre was only one of many 'intellectuals' who lived during this time, yet was unique in producing the work that he did (Craib, 1976, 4). What is more relevant to understanding Sartre is how he as an individual attended to what he was experiencing.

The same could be said of those offenders whose experiences are considered here. A set of social and cultural influences that differs from one offender to the next cannot be sufficient grounds for locating differences between those offenders' experiences, because the implicit assumption then is that in the absence of any difference the experiences of both would be the same. Existence within a specific cultural context will not be uniform for all those who share that context. It will be mediated by the particular experiences, a particular past and a particular future that are unique to a particular individual. It is not that cultural context is not relevant, but understanding differences between offenders in terms of it is hardly sufficient and is the sort of cultural determinism that existential sociology eschews.

This does not mean we cannot attempt to identify similarities across individuals' experiences however. In fact, rejecting a uniform influence of a specific cultural time period makes it more interesting that a shared experience of desistance and resettlement is demonstrable for these white-collar offenders. As the later chapters indicate, there is much common ground between offenders, notwithstanding the different time periods in which they were negotiating their resettlement. This is perhaps best exemplified through a consideration of the religious conversion experiences a number of these men describe. Differences in cultural context do not invalidate the notion of a general process of religious conversion, nor do they obfuscate the fact that it appears these white-collar offenders each approached the process of conversion in a similar way. One of the key assertions of the religious conversion literature (Rambo, 1993; McKnight, 2002), of existential sociology

## 58   *Autobiography*

(e.g. Kotarba, 1984; Johnson and Kotarba, 2002; Farrall, 2005) and this study is that individuals make their own way in the world, finding ways to live that are specific to them. Religious conversion satisfies needs that are specific to individuals, but the presence of specific needs does not invalidate the notion of a general process of conversion. Within this framework, cultural context becomes one more factor that has a bearing on the specific ways individuals undertake the process of conversion. It would doubtless be interesting to identify the role culture and history play in differentiating the minutiae of the conversion experience (for example), but that is not the goal of this research.

There was great similarity between offenders' accounts in terms of the ways in which they discussed conversion experiences and the also in the resemblance they have to conversion experiences as identified more broadly despite the differences in time of writing and of offenders' nationalities. This suggests that, within this particular sample cultural and historical differences were not sufficient to markedly distinguish the resettlement of white-collar offenders.

Nor would it be possible to locate individualised cultural and historical differences if we purport to use autobiographies to accept offenders on their own terms. In attending to writers' own experiences of their lives, it is asking a great deal to expect them to reflect on 'their' culture and the specific practices of it in a national sense. Offenders do show an awareness of the specific backgrounds they come from and how these impact their experiences of punishment and resettlement (Chapters 4 and 6). Several cite the difficulties of coming from 'privileged' lives to prison and locate their difficulties in the contrast between what they had and lost. However, none locate difficulties within the struggle of being 'an American' for example.

### Are these unusual accounts?

A further potential issue with this sample of white-collar offenders is how they compare with other offenders, both white-collar and otherwise. Some of the sample are atypical when compared to offenders more generally and perhaps also the 'average' offender convicted of a white-collar offence (Weisburd *et al.*, 2001). The sensational nature of the crimes some committed is undoubtedly part of the marketability that they display to publishing houses. The 'high lives' of some of these offenders are also a prominent part of their accounts. These lift the veil on worlds of power and intrigue and serve as an interesting counter point to the nadir of a prison cell, the low seeming all the lower because of where these men came from.

It could therefore be argued that this makes this group rather unrepresentative because they had the opportunity to write a book that other offenders lack. The atypical nature of their lives and offences that makes them so attractive to publishing houses and (they would hope) the buying public is precisely that which makes them unsuitable candidates for a criminological study that seeks to generalise findings.

A few points are relevant here. That all had the opportunity to write a book is seemingly indisputable, but this does not inevitably mean all these offenders' offences were atypical or particularly noteworthy. Nick Leeson's offences were of such a magnitude and the backdrop (i.e. the Watergate conspiracy) for Charles Colson's actions relevant nationally and internationally that they can be considered exceptional. In contrast however, what separated Dennis Levine from any number of inside traders was that his arrest led to the arrest and prosecution of more high-profile offenders.[2] It is not so much then that their offences were worthy of publication, but that their lives were.

This in itself may be an issue and it may therefore ultimately be the case that the observations made here only apply to 'celebrity' white-collar offenders, but that seems unlikely. Particular issues of celebrity may have mediated the resettlement experiences of these white-collar offenders, but they represent a particular facet of their unique existence. We must also be careful not to assign a uniform level of 'celebrity' to these men. Without attempting to quantify notoriety or infamy, we can perhaps say that some of these men are – or were – more famous than others. To Colson and Leeson who are noted above we could add Bond, Aitken and a number of others in the sample who lived their lives in the public eye and whose convictions therefore had a certain marketability. Equally however, there are those who could not make claim to such notoriety. Berger, Lawson, Laite and Christensen are notable for the unremarkable nature of their offences, that had no discernable far-reaching consequences (as did Lesson's for example) or even attracted much attention. The themes of these four offenders' books support this idea that it was not their offences that made them interesting. All four focus upon their time in prison and the life they led while there, with only cursory mention of their offending, suggesting that this was not the main 'hook' on which to 'hang' their story. Also relevant to issues of notoriety and therefore the atypical nature of these offenders is that it appears not all offenders' books – in the opinion of publishers – were suitable for publication. Christensen and Berger published their own books with self-publishing support companies. Their stories were not, it seems, interesting enough to attract an advance from a publisher or to have their publishing costs covered.

Further, in considering issues of the typicality of these white-collar offenders, we return once again to the notion of individuality and uniqueness of experience. These white-collar offenders, as individual existents, by definition had experiences and lives that were not like anyone else's. They had to deal with experiences others did not. We know where these experiences were deemed important by them because they tell us so. This is a central tenet of the methodology employed.

The less than typical nature of these offenders might be more of an issue if this thesis was not advocating a similarity between this apparently highly unusual group and offenders more generally who desist. However, what is apparent is that there was much that white-collar offenders did share with offenders more broadly.

In any event, this study does not purport to be the final word in white-collar offenders' desistance and resettlement. Triangulation of findings is needed. Part of this is the observation that the accounts given by these white-collar offenders have much in common with desistance 'stories' as told by offenders more generally. The 'next step' perhaps would be to study white-collar offenders using more conventional means. The issue then however is that of gaining access to this group, a

## 60  *Autobiography*

problem that plagues investigations into white-collar offenders more generally (Shover and Hunter, 2010).

A related issue when considering the atypical nature of these offenders concerns the ease with which it might be thought these men would be able to resettle and desist from crime following their punishment. It might be expected that the nature of these offenders and the high lives they led prior to their arrest means many are in possession of resources that give them a distinct advantage with regard to their resettlement. These resources might be expected to take the form of finances that meant offenders and their families were not 'on the bread line' after release from prison. However, they could also take the form of less tangible assets such as the knowledge and skills built up over time in business and the network of contacts formed over the working life. The presence of such social and cultural capital (Schuller *et al.*, 2002) might be expected to ease the resettlement of these white-collar offenders. Determining the presence or absence of such capital and particularly whether they make this group of white-collar offenders 'stand out' from white-collar offenders more generally is difficult. Nevertheless, within the analysis that follows, a consideration of the potential advantages these offenders had will be included within the general conclusions made in each chapter.

## Notes

1    Although it should be recognised that, occasionally, an 'autobiography' will be written by a ghost writer following an interview with the person whose life is committed to text.
2    The names of Michael Milken and Ivan Boesky, who Levine's evidence helped to convict, are synonymous with Wall Street excess in the 1980s. Levine, in contrast, seems rarely mentioned (e.g. Time Magazine, 2001).

# 4 Imprisonment and the assault on the self

It might seem curious to start a study of white-collar offenders' desistance with a discussion of prison. After all, efforts to chart desistance and resettlement are difficult to pursue while offenders are still incarcerated. However, the experience of imprisonment is important because, as will be shown, the process of resettlement begins in prison, as prison is the venue for thinking and planning for the future and coming to terms with changes in the self that impact on later efforts to resettle. The experience of imprisonment was therefore quite significant for those white-collar offenders subject to it. The reasons for this are explored below, but all relate to the way offenders understood themselves and what was happening to them. This chapter outlines the literature that has considered the impact of prison on offenders generally, highlighting particularly the 'damage' prison can do to offenders. Following this, the prison accounts of those white-collar offenders who spent time in prison are outlined, organised along several broad themes that emerge from offenders' accounts. The focus of inquiry is on how the experiences of the white-collar offenders who make up this sample differ from the experiences of prisoners more generally and white-collar offenders in particular. Under this somewhat sweeping investigation, observations of prisoners suggest several distinct aspects of the prison experience that will help to direct investigation. Therefore, the concerns of the analysis here are the effects of prison on white-collar offenders, the way time in prison is spent and the potential threats that a prison sentence introduces to a sense of who one 'is'.

## Prisons and prisoners

The experience of prison and its impact upon the resettlement and desistance of offenders generally has been considered frequently. Such work invariably concludes that the experience of prison, rather than encouraging desistance from crime, can (if it has an impact at all) only increase the likelihood of further offending (e.g. Visher and Travis, 2003; Burnett and Maruna, 2004; Cullen *et al.*, 2011). Prison reduces ties to family and is associated not just with the loss of employment but also a reduction in the chance of gaining employment once incarceration ends, as skills are degraded and knowledge is lost during the sentence (Laub and Sampson, 2003, 291; Visher and Travis, 2003; Farrall and Calverley, 2006).

62 *Prison*

Sentence length may be a major determining factor of the extent to which imprisonment damages the chance of desistance (Adams, 1992; Irwin, 1980). Indeed, Irwin (1980) suggests that a short prison sentence affords the offender the opportunity to take stock of their life and plan a means to change it, involving as it does offenders' removal from the influence of criminal peers (although Flynn 2010, 177 argues that those with longer sentences are more likely to take up the offer of prison programmes designed to rehabilitate). Too long in prison, however, and the offender is likely to become influenced by the prison environment to the extent that desistance is unlikely for the reasons noted above. Farrall and Calverley (2006), however, reject the notion that time spent in prison may serve as an opportunity for thinking about one's future. They follow Meisenhelder (1985) in noting that, for the prisoner, experience while in prison is frequently predicated on the past and present, i.e. that the individual committed a crime and is now a prisoner. Absent in the prison experience – at least until the end of their sentences – is any consideration of what the individual may become and of what their future prospects are. It is also possible that prisoners themselves will avoid 'looking ahead' too far into their future as a means of coping with their period of extended confinement (e.g. Sapsford, 1978). This may especially be the case for those prisoners who are serving long sentences (Sapsford, 1978; Meisenhelder, 1985).

Lack of opportunity to 'look forward' is important because being able to envision what one's future may be and feeling that this is achievable is linked to successful reintegration into the community upon release from prison (Maguire and Raynor, 2006). The observation that wanting and being able to espy a future in which they can 'be' a non-offender is crucial in aiding efforts to desist is one that is not without precedent in the literature on desistance, emphasising the importance of individual agency driving attempts to desist (Maruna, 2001; Giordano *et al.*, 2002; Farrall and Calverley, 2006; Laub and Sampson, 2003). Prison reduces opportunities for agency by failing to provide the privacy that Irwin and Owen assert is necessary for prisoners 'to plan reasonable, productive, and rewarding courses of action and projects, and to perform many personal functions' (2005, 101).

This is perhaps why, despite the abundance of time in prison, incarceration does not represent an opportunity to reflect productively on one's life, realise the 'error of one's ways' and change. Reasoning that prisoners might take time to consider their future while incarcerated runs counter to Meisenhelder's (1985) suggestion that prison time is not future oriented and also Farrall and Calverley's (2006) dismissal of the notion that prison may provide an opportunity for prisoners to in some way take a 'time out' from their lives and consider their past:

> Prisons are not monasteries, tucked away on sunny hills in Tuscany or the Pyrenees. Prisons are places where crime is common… and where people are far from being in a situation in which they can 'kick back' and reflect on their lives so far. They are noisy, 'bustlely' places that many people find 'dehumanizing'. Boredom, not reflection, characterises many peoples' experiences of imprisonment.
>
> (Farrall and Calverley, 2006, 71)

*Prison* 63

Jose-Kampfer (1990, 110) likens the experience of prison to a form of existential death suffered by prisoners, particularly for those who serve long sentences. The women in Jose-Kampfer's sample keenly felt the 'timelessness' (see also Meisenhelder, 1985) of their situation, suggesting a limbo period during which they were removed from their life in the outside world. Some released prisoners, especially those who have spent significant periods of time incarcerated, experience a sense of 'dislocation' from the world (Jamieson and Grounds, 2005[1]). They may be estranged from relationships which have moved on in their absence and which need to be reforged (Cohen and Taylor, 1972, 67; Jose-Kampfer, 1990). Cohen and Taylor emphasise this with the observation that prisoners must start a 'new life' in prison, based on the realisation that their 'previous life' will not wait for them:

> The prisoner cannot reassure himself that each of these domains [e.g. home, job, social life] is merely being held in cold storage until his return – a life cannot be reassembled twenty years after its destruction. He has been given 'life' – a prison life – and somehow he must learn to live it.
>
> (1972, 43)

Prison is therefore noted as 'damaging' those incarcerated there, an assault not only on their subjectively experienced present, but also on their future.

As the foregoing discussion indicates, perhaps more than anything else, the experience of imprisonment is characterised by the concept of time and the way time is 'spent' in prison. Prisoners spend much time considering their lives prior to prison and the world outside. The impact of prison time on relationships with their family (e.g. Shover, 1985) is brought home to them through a realisation of (for example) birthday celebrations they may be missing (Farrall and Calverley, 2006). There is also the awareness for some that their life is ebbing away, 'wasted' in prison due to their involvement in crime (Farrall and Calverley, 2006). Such reflections add to the feeling that the world outside is moving on without them (Meisenhelder, 1985; Farrall and Calverley, 2006). Such reflections, however, are not related to behaviour change.

The oppressive nature of time in prison is something that must be managed by offenders. The prisoners in Meisenhelder's sample (a combination of those serving sentences in medium-security US prisons and those who had published writings on their time as prisoners) adjusted to the problem of prison time by creating disruption to the routine of prison life where possible in order to imbue themselves with a sense of agency, which, subjectively, would make them experience time as passing quicker. They also 'marked' time, identifying regular events such as Christmas as representing the countdown to release. Whatever strategy was used however, time in prison, rather than being experienced as a boon, was an encumbrance (Meisenhelder, 1985). Time must therefore be managed to make the prison sentence more bearable. Irwin (1980, 14) outlines how prisoners do the best they can to manage the time they have to spend in prison through taking on as many activities as they can. Others orient themselves more completely with the prison administration e.g. through attaining jobs from which they can gain prestige or

64    *Prison*

resources they can barter. In Irwin's term they 'made a world out of prison' (1980, 15). That is, they took what comforts they could from their environment.

Beyond the problem of time, the various deprivations prisoners are subjected to have been the focus of several oft-cited studies. Physical environments that provide no stimulation (Cohen and Taylor, 1972, 62) and the fear that a deterioration of mental faculties will be a result of prolonged incarceration (Cohen and Taylor, 1972, 104–105) are constant pressures on the prisoner. Such deprivations are perhaps most infamously described as the 'pains of imprisonment' (Sykes, 1958, 64–76). Sykes identifies a number of deprivations prisoners suffer, including the loss of their ability to act autonomously as a result of various prison regulations and feelings of insecurity because of the potential for attack by other inmates. These act on prisoners' sense of wellbeing by being a threat on an ontological level, denying the prisoner the opportunity to constitute him/herself through their own action and also presenting a risk to a sense of personal security. Prisoners also fear the degradation of who they are as a result of their incarceration. They worry about the deterioration of their faculties and the gradual eroding of themselves as individuals, suffering angst that any uniqueness they possess will be swept away by their institutionalisation (Cohen and Taylor, 1972).

Such an ontological threat is further emphasised when the symbolic content of these deprivations is highlighted. Sykes and Messinger suggest that the replacement of the prisoner's name with a number and them being made to wear a prison 'uniform' communicates that the prisoner is somehow 'less' than 'normal' (1960, 15). Cohen and Taylor characterise being sentenced to prison as one example of a shattering experience that individuals might suffer. Shattering experiences 'break the web of meaning we have built up around ourselves' (1972, 43). For Cohen and Taylor, however, the unique aspect of prison as a shattering experience is that whereas such experiences generally only impact upon one area of the individual's life and can have their impact lessened via retreat to others (e.g. where someone has lost their job they may decide to concentrate on their family), prison impacts all areas of the life. There is therefore nothing for a prisoner to 'fall back on' and, consequently, starting prison represents the start of a 'new life' (Cohen and Taylor, 1972).

The true power of these deprivations is their ontological rather than physical peril. As Sykes argues:

> The individual's picture of himself as a person of value – as a morally acceptable, adult male who can present some claim to merit in his material achievements and inner strength – begins to waver and grow dim.
>
> (1958, 79)

As a response to this coercion into a particular way of living, prisoners rely on a code to guide their behaviour – largely centred around the notion that you help other prisoners and resist 'the system', as personified by prison guards and governors – and which forms the basis for an 'inmate social system' (Sykes and Messinger, 1960; see also Cloward, 1960). Having a code for behaviour makes time in prison easier by imposing structure and meaning on prison existence and provides prisoners with a network of support in the form of their fellow subscribers to the code (Sykes and Messinger, 1960). Crewe (2011) revisits the pains of imprisonment, noting that the traditional pains have become supplemented with different burdens upon prisoners that deny them the chance to realise their own identity and ask them to govern their own conduct without making the rules that govern such conduct explicit.

More recent prison studies have emphasised the shock of incarceration, observed among both white-collar (Shover and Hochstetler, 2006) and 'street' offenders (e.g. Farrall and Calverley, 2006). This work emphasises the unusual nature of the prison environment for those who are thrust into it. Farrall and Calverley note that among their sample the shock was short-lived as offenders became accustomed to their surroundings. However, a focus upon the shock of incarceration is far more prevalent in the literature that considers white-collar offenders who are sentenced to prison. The contrast between the offender's life outside prison and the one inside in terms of the environment and the people who inhabit it is thought to be far more marked for white-collar offenders and, consequently, more 'painful' (Mann *et al.*, 1980):

> For the first time in their lives [white-collar offenders] are processed and surrounded by those who do the dirty and low-paying work of the world. Jail brings them into close contact with men who are openly flatulent, whose fingers are indelibly stained from years of cigarette smoking, who seem incapable of omitting 'fuck' from the conversation or whose bodies show unusual scars or tattoos.
>
> (Shover and Hochstetler, 2006, 137)

Such accounts are in keeping with the notion that, for white-collar offenders, the process of being punished (i.e. their contact with the criminal justice system) is more important than the actual punishment itself (e.g. Wheeler *et al.*, 1988; Weisburd *et al.*, 2001).

Indeed, white-collar offenders have therefore been suggested as suffering from a 'special sensitivity' to prison (Mann *et al.*, 1980), i.e. that because of their relatively privileged backgrounds they face peculiar difficulties when incarcerated. These difficulties are hypothesised to be grounded in their lack of experience of the hardship of prison conditions after leading comfortable lives and the forced association with society's 'criminal element' (Benson and Cullen, 1988). Benson and Cullen (1988), however, argue that far from white-collar offenders suffering unduly while in prison, they are actually well equipped to deal with the challenges that prison presents because they have greater resources to do so:

> due to their class backgrounds, many white-collar offenders are likely to possess the personal traits and social ties that research has suggested reduce the impact of incarceration on offenders. If these factors correlate with successful adjustments among low status offenders, presumably they operate in a similar manner among high status offenders.
>
> (Benson and Cullen, 1988, 210)

66   *Prison*

Benson and Cullen's comments are theoretical in nature and, as far as is known, a study of how white-collar offenders cope with prison has yet to be conducted. It seems appropriate, however, to follow the research on prisons more generally and identify how the important aspects of prison for offenders more generally impact upon white-collar offenders. The extent to which white-collar offenders found prison difficult is therefore one of the key themes explored here. Other aspects of the analysis consider the important aspects of white-collar offenders prison' experience, including the effect of prison on their self-identity.

## White-collar offenders' prison accounts

Nineteen of the 23 offenders whose books are considered here wrote about their prison experiences. Table 4.1 summarises these individuals and the length of time they served in prison. As can be seen from Table 4.1, some offenders served lengthy sentences even though the majority were first-time offenders. All, with the exception of Bond, served one prison sentence. Bond's first sentence of 30 months was ended by a successful appeal after he served three months in prison, but his time is included because of his prison experiences.

The extent to which each offender devoted space in his account to describing time in prison varies. Timilty, Christensen, Berger, Archer and Laite's accounts are almost exclusively confined to describing their prison experiences while Volpe dedicates a little over one short chapter (of 25) to his two-year sentence. The majority of accounts fall somewhere between these extremes. Most accounts were written after the prison sentence had been completed, the exceptions being Archer, Timilty, Christensen and Berger, who wrote while in prison. Archer and Timilty's

*Table 4.1* White-collar offenders' prison sentences and length of time served

| Offender | Length of sentence in months (time served in months) | Offender | Length of sentence in months (time served in months) |
| --- | --- | --- | --- |
| Jonathan Aitken | 18 (7) | William Laite | 12 (5) |
| Jeffery Archer | 48 (24) | Stephen Lawson | 96 (18) |
| Jim Bakker | 540 (reduced to 96) (58) | Nick Leeson | 78 (42) |
| Jordan Belfort | 48 (22) | Dennis Levine | 24 (15) |
| Robert L. Berger | 36 (38) (Served extra due to new conviction while in prison) | Jeb Magruder | 10–48 (7) |
| Alan Bond | 30 (3 after appeal) and then 120 (44) | Barry Minkow | 300 (88) |
| Nelson Christensen | 60 (36) | Pete Rose | 5 (5) |
| Charles Colson | 12–36 (7) | Joseph Timilty | 4 (4) |
| John Dean | 12–48 (4) | Tod Volpe | 24–30 (24) |
| Darius Guppy | 60 (35) | | |

accounts are taken from journal entries kept on a day-to-day basis throughout the length of their sentence. Berger's and Christensen's accounts were written while they were in prison, but not on a day-by-day basis.

There are several noteworthy aspects to the prison experiences of white-collar offenders. There is the shock of entry into prison, grounded in the dehumanising process and the contrast with offenders' previous lives. There are also the challenges of how to spend prison time and the changes concomitant with incarceration. Some of which are welcome, some less so.

## First impressions

White-collar offenders were united in the reference to prison induction. Pronounced in these accounts was the shock of induction, grounded chiefly in the contrast with former lives. Despite such shocks however, white-collar offenders learnt to cope with the prison environment.

### *Shock*

'Total institutions', of which prison is but one example, are those institutions which separate inmates from the outside world and control the contact had with that world (Goffman, 1961). They have the effect of stripping an entrant of the conception of self they had prior to entry. Previous points of reference no longer apply because such institutions curtail access to life outside them (Goffman, 1961). Exacerbating the stripping of the self are the entry procedures such institutions force entrants to undergo. Such a degradation ceremony (Garfinkel, 1956) includes removal of possessions and the requirement to wear prison issue clothing, all adding to the feeling that the self is threatened, part of a process of the mortification of self (Goffman, 1961, 24). The characteristics of the prison preclude the opportunity to partake of other aspects of the life and for the person who experiences it to be uniquely 'themself'.

Among white-collar offenders, feelings of shock and disgust were prevalent, couched particularly in terms of the 'alien' nature of the environment they entered. William Laite, who spent five months in prison for perjury and making false statements to avoid paying employee wages while he was owner of a building company emphasises this with his account of his first impressions upon entering prison:

> The others in the cell looked miserable, and most of them appeared to be either drunk or on drugs. The cell echoed with their begging and hollering. I could not believe the scene, which was completely foreign to anything I'd ever experienced before.
>
> (Laite, 1972, 36)

Other aspects of induction into the prison way of life exacerbate these feelings. Nelson Christensen, a lawyer imprisoned on three counts of securities fraud was

## 68 *Prison*

assigned a prison identification card at his induction:

> A bar code! The ultimate stroke of dehumanisation! I was as significant as a box of corn flakes. Everything there was to know about me could be viewed on a computer screen by scanning my bar code.
>
> (Christensen, 2005, 32)

Such shocks have their origin in the sudden loss of a previously taken-for-granted 'world'. The removal of everything that was familiar and its replacement with a completely novel situation and an uncertain future signalled an unprecedented threat to prisoners' ontological security: their very existence (Yalom, 1980). This is not because of the loss of these things per se but because their continued presence was always taken as a 'given' that could be relied upon (Kauffman, 2002).

Christensen's 'dehumanisation' threatened his identity. In this way then, prison threatens to remove any semblance of offenders' individuality. This is perhaps particularly pronounced for these white-collar offenders, emphasising where they had 'come from' (as per Shover and Hochstetler, 2006). They were important (or at least, 'worthy') men in their previous lives. To be given a barcode, to be subjected to the same treatment as any other prisoner marked them as no longer special, removing the status that they previously enjoyed. Robert Berger, who served 38 months in prison for corporate income tax evasion and bribery while CEO of Royce Aerospace Materials was still aware of this half way through his sentence:

> I lay here thinking about all the years that I was eminently successful and then look around this cell, and can't believe where I am.
>
> (Berger, 2003, 28)

Comparing the previous life to the 'now' of prison also underlines what offenders have lost. They cannot help but contrast the environment of the prison with the lives they had. Through all that it takes away from them, prison puts their successful pasts into stark relief and reminds white-collar offenders of their previous place in the world, emphasising the change in their identity.

Added to these feelings was the threat of violence from their fellow inmates. On his first night in prison, former politician Jonathan Aitken, sentenced to 18 months in prison for perjury, was subjected to chanting from the prisoners in his cellblock:

> they would then ask a question, 'What shall we do to effing Aitken [or effing Aitken's private parts] tomorrow?... I was terrified.
>
> (Aitken, 2005, 29)

Such threats underline the horrors of prison, confirming offenders' worst nightmares and negative stereotypes. One again, they emphasise that offenders are in a very different world.

*Prison* 69

### Adjusting to prison

The above notwithstanding, white-collar offenders adjusted to prison. Finding points of common reference between incarceration and past life experiences helped them cope with the shock they experienced. Former Boston politician Joseph Timilty, sentenced to prison for conspiring to commit fraud had been a United States Marine before he became a politician. He drew on this experience to make sense of his situation. Writing on his first morning in Schuykill prison:

> I must keep a routine to keep from going mad. Having been at Parris Island [US Marine recruitment base], I know how to move in this environment ... One way to survive here, in terms of the administration, is to accept the sense of powerlessness. Now, having come from politics, the journey from power to powerlessness might have been longer for me, but there is no more powerless experience than arriving as a Marine Corps recruit. I am able to reach back and remember that.
>
> (Timilty, 1997, 51)

Although prison initially represented an environment quite unique in the difficulties it presented, given time, offenders came to understand it in terms they could make sense of. Like Timilty, Jeb Magruder and Pete Rose came to liken prison to experiences they were familiar with. Rose could relate to the sense of power-lessness, deciding that he would approach prison life as he had being a rookie (first year) baseball player:

> It's like they say, 'You gotta get along to go along,' which was pretty much the same advice that I got from my dad just before my rookie year. 'Do your job, obey the rules, and don't complain,' said dad.
>
> (Rose, 2004, 192)

Former politician Magruder, convicted of obstruction of justice in relation to his role in the Watergate conspiracy used his experience of bureaucracy to cope with prison:

> I already knew how the system worked at the top; now I was finding out how it worked at the bottom. There really isn't much difference. In Washington and in the business world, if you want to get things done you have to find out who makes the wheels turn, and it isn't always the person whose name is lettered on the door... In prison it was the same.
>
> (Magruder, 1978, 129)

Being able to make sense of the present in terms of the past placed structure upon the experience of prison, lessening its foreign nature by making it comparable to other, equally distressing situations. There is hope to be drawn from this. If that experience was survived then prison can be as well. Further, understanding the 'rules' of institutions removes much of the ambiguity of prison, again reducing what is happening to something that can at least be related to an experienced past.

70   *Prison*

Even those prisoners who could not draw upon anything similar managed to work out the world within prison. For example, Nick Leeson, convicted of fraud for his part in the collapse of Barings Bank, found his experience of prison – three years in a maximum-security prison in Singapore – harrowing, but eventually developed strategies for coping with the deprivations he encountered, such as through a regular exercise routine (Leeson, 2005, 102).

In sum then, entry to prison was a shocking time for these white-collar offenders and this shock was constituted in part by the previous lives they led. However, these lives also gave them a point of reference for coping with the shock of prison. Eventually, prisoners came to understand that they were not in immediate physical danger from those they shared their confinement with (notwithstanding that Laite and Bond were both attacked), they began to understand the way in which prison 'worked' and they then turned their thoughts to how they would spend their time there. A final facet to coping, as will be seen later, was through association with those inmates they identified as 'like me'.

## Prison time

Prison and the concept of time are inextricably linked. Central to one's incarceration is the idea that they will 'do' time (Goffman, 1961) and that while they are 'doing' prison time, time in the world outside prison continues unabated (Jose-Kampfer, 1990). To combat this and also the futureless nature of their period of incarceration prisoners may attempt to adopt strategies to make prison time more bearable.

### *Using time*

These offenders lived what might be termed 'fast lives'. Their employment was time consuming and – with the possible exception of Pete Rose who enjoyed his baseball career – stressful. They worked long hours, were responsible for important decisions and often dealt with large projects that required management. For some, the need to act to conceal their offence added to this pressure. Five of these offenders – Aitken, Bakker, Berger, Christensen and Levine – came to realise that there were benefits to being in prison, which, relative to the hectic lives they had led, represented some time for tranquillity. Such was the case for Dennis Levine – convicted of insider trading – after entering prison for the first time:

> Despite the accumulation of aggravations, I came to see that this physical prison could be a disguised blessing. For too many years I had raced through life, too busy to lift my head and either contemplate the past or gaze towards the future. Prison slowed the pace of my life long enough for me to see how I had trapped myself.
>
> (Levine, 1991, 362–363)

Relatedly, accompanying imprisonment were feelings of relief for individuals that their period of offending was over, as was the case for Nick Leeson:

*Prison* 71

The three years of lying and rogue trading, the pretending to everybody, the role-playing, were over. The end was in sight at last, even though I knew I would have a prison sentence to get through.

(Leeson, 2005, 276)

Prison could be also a source of protection from the outside world for prisoners. Such was also noted by Tod Volpe, who realised the benefits of being sheltered from legal proceedings:

For me, being able to wake up without having to face the day to day nightmare of the legal battle was a relief. I also made friends with people I would never otherwise have had the opportunity to meet, and this brought me hope and reassurance for the future.

(Volpe, 2002, 254)

Robert Berger, concurs with Volpe. Reflecting back on his prison sentence and on what his imprisonment meant for him led him to draw conclusions about the benefits to his health that accrued from his being 'totally isolated from the outside in every way' (Berger, 2003, 184). In doing so, Berger therefore points to the possible benefits of being part of a total institution (Goffman, 1961).

Once again, the busy, stressful lives led by many of those considered here contrasted sharply with their lives inside prison. The need to conceal offences would invariably have added to this stress and the consequent removal of this need was quite welcome. Even those who do not give an account of their prison time feel relief over the removal of the need to conceal their offences as soon as they are arrested (Belfort, 2007, 512; Pavlo, 2007, 257).

There were, therefore, emotional benefits to incarceration, a sense of wellbeing to be had in the removal of malign outside influences. White-collar offenders were cocooned within the prison walls. Therefore, the curtailment of contact with the outside world to some extent worked in both directions for offenders who had outstanding business with legal agencies. Recognising this was part of making the most of prison time, seeing the 'good' in the situation they were in.

Therefore, for white-collar offenders, time in prison provided the opportunity to reflect on their lives so far. Although forced into the prison environment, they engaged with the opportunity it offered. For Levine having time to spare was a welcome anomaly:

I could not remember a time when I had time. At Smith Barney, at Lehman Brothers, and most of all at Drexel [all investment companies], there was never enough of the commodity. Here, the universal goal was to do time, to get it out of the way, to kill it. I discovered very quickly that one of the things you do with time is to think. I took long, isolated walks on the prison grounds, and asked myself painful questions.

(Levine, 1991, 369, emphasis in original)

## 72    *Prison*

Consequently, although the prison environment may have been considerably disruptive, it was significantly less 'pressured' than the life they were used to. To be certain, prisoners did experience disturbance, disruption and discord while in prison, as some attest to experiencing. They missed their families (Lawson, 1992, 128), experienced moments of 'terror' (Laite, 1972, 12) and at times found that time moved with agonising slowness (Volpe, 2002, 255). However, they also found comfort in prayer groups (Lawson, 1992, 131), deciphered the way prison 'worked' (Laite, 1972, 194–196) and found time to themselves to contemplate their past and their future (Volpe, 2002, 254). In some cases, (e.g. Timilty, Archer) they also made the notes that would later become their prison memoirs. Jonathan Aitken appreciated the privacy of his single cell:

> This privacy was such a bonus that I soon came to see the long hours of bang-up [i.e. confinement to one's cell] not as a curse but as a blessing.
>
> (Aitken, 2005, 75)

In summary then, for some, prison did serve a useful function in terms of providing the opportunity to reflect upon their life. It allowed offenders to take stock of their life, locate where it went 'wrong' and from this identify possible directions in which they wish to proceed. Nine – Aitken, Bakker, Berger, Christensen, Colson, Leeson, Levine, Magruder and Volpe – came to see prison time as something positive, even if it just sheltered them from the outside world.

So rather than imprisonment representing the end of their lives as a meaningful enterprise as some white-collar offenders express (Hunter, 2011) imprisonment may give time to plan what comes next in the life. The activities undertaken by these men in prison included consolidating a burgeoning faith in Christianity (e.g., Aitken, Lawson, Colson), attaining qualifications to pursue a career (Minkow) or making notes that would become autobiographical accounts of prison (Timilty, Berger, Archer). These activities all suggest a perspective on the future and a sense of who one wants to become (Hayim, 1996; Giordano *et al.*, 2002; Hunter, 2011). It is this sense that helped prisoners cope with the issue of prison time because it helped them to identify meaningful activities that were predicated on a future self (see also Cohen and Taylor, 1972, 95).

Although the noise and disruption of prison is an inevitable element of prison life, these white-collar offenders did still appear to find time to themselves, whether it was during recreation time or, as Jonathan Aitken did, during time 'banged up' in their cells. Companionship was available when prisoners wanted it, but so too was solitude. More than this though, the way in which many spent their prison time arose from the forced cessation of their 'normal' life and the opportunity to take some time to consider their future in terms of their past and what it meant for them. They could reflect upon their past and their future and evaluate their life. Prison provided them with the opportunity for this.

*Prison* 73

### Structuring time

One means used by white-collar offenders to cope with the problem of time involved forging a routine to impose order on the prison day, much as Meisenhelder's (1985) and Irwin's (1980, 14–15) participants did. Jeffrey Archer, convicted of perjury and perverting the course of justice, coped with long periods spent in his cell by ordering his day as if he were at home, working as a writer (which he did professionally). Writing at the start of his prison sentence:

> I resolve to spend the time that I am locked up in my cell writing, sticking to a routine I have followed for the past twenty-five years – two hours on, two hours off – though never before in such surroundings.
>
> (Archer, 2001, 20)

In the absence of meaningful activity being placed upon the day, white-collar offenders imposed their own. Note that this was not intrinsically about structuring their time. The prison routine is frequently highly structured, with set times for eating, working, attending to personal hygiene and recreation. What was lacking was purposeful activity from which they could derive meaning. Archer's example was a way for him to extract a sense of purpose from his incarceration, making his prison experience into something recognisable by following a routine special to him. Coping with the problem of prison time by imposing one's own order is a means through which prisoners might preserve their 'true self' (Jose-Kampfer, 1990).

A further way to structure prison time was to put it to good use through meaningful pursuits. Through such a process, time, rather than being a 'punishment' (Cohen and Taylor, 1972, 89), came to be viewed positively. Nelson Christensen considered his prison time a benefit because of how he employed it:

> Time is the punishment, and time is the gift. I doubt that I would otherwise in life have had the leisure time – eons of it! – to study the entire Bible in detail. Not only did I read from Genesis through to Revelations, and many books many times; I read a great deal of biblical history and interpretations of the text.
>
> (Christensen, 2005, 68)

Taking advantage of previously unavailable opportunities gives some meaning to the prison experience, protecting the self from an otherwise stultifying experience that denies the chance to grow. Television evangelist Jim Bakker, convicted of fraud and conspiring to commit fraud came to view his incarceration in these terms around two years into his five-year sentence:

> I am convinced that God did not send me to prison to punish me for my sins, even though I deserved it. God put me in prison so I could study His Word, get to know Him, and learn the meaning of forgiveness.
>
> (Bakker, 1996, 350)

74　*Prison*

Making use of prison time is therefore a way to survive the assault on the self that prison time represents and imbue the prison experience with some relevance, putting it into the context of the rest of the life rather than simply being 'lost' time. White-collar offenders took the period of incarceration as an opportunity to underscore changes that had begun prior to prison and would continue after. Barry Minkow, convicted of Securities and Exchange offences relating to his fraudulent company *ZZZZ Best*, began his conversion to Christianity prior to his incarceration and after prison became a pastor. However, it was while serving his sentence that he began the college courses that qualified him to do so:

> Throughout my life, I had never accomplished anything honestly. Completing a legitimate college education would change that.
>
> (Minkow, 1995, 218)

For Minkow, prison time meant having the opportunity to show himself that he could change, that he could have a future in which he was 'honest'. The ability to view their otherwise distressing situation in a positive light and make use of their prison time allowed prisoners to draw some good from their experiences. Prison time was not an ordeal to be endured, but taken and put to their advantage. These strategies for survival within prison were also a rejection of the prisoner identity as it was given to them by the prison system. They would not sit and go 'stir crazy'. Instead they would use the time they were afforded to their advantage.

## Change and the self

The above strategies for coping with imprisonment may be interpreted as efforts calculated to resist a change to the self, preserving who prisoners were. Regardless, given the enormity of the prison experience, the prospect that prison would change them was ever present for white-collar offenders. Prisoners reported two aspects to the experience of change in prison. There was change that came about as a result of reflection on what prison meant, and there was change that was 'threatened' by the more troublesome aspects of incarceration.

### Reflecting on the self

'Change' did not necessarily mean 'desistance'. Many felt they were not offenders and others felt they had in fact changed prior to prison. However, 'changing' did mean focusing on the past and the differences the future would herald. Approximately one month before his release Robert Berger was asked how he viewed his prison time. His reflection on this and his response indicates his belief that he was sent to prison for a purpose because it helped him identify what is relevant in was life. A result of this was a desire to be someone who lived differently:

> Not as before, when I was driven by greed and money, leaving relationships in the dust and ignoring the emotional requirements of those around me. In

prison I have been given time to think about the past and the mistakes I've made.

(Berger, 2003, 159)

Like Berger, Bakker, Levine and Volpe argued that prison gave them a different perspective on life. One that made them realise that change was necessary, as in Berger's case. In relation to individuals' rehabilitation, what is prevalent here is the notion of a change in outlook that an experience such as prison engendered. Prison forced a reconsideration of what they knew because the environment was one that was so different for them relative to other experiences. Former art dealer Tod Volpe, convicted of five counts of fraud in relation to the selling of art, was grateful for the new perspective prison gave him:

I didn't understand the dynamic of team playing until I'd been to prison... Prison is a good place to see the true nature of people... A person learns the greatest form of love in prison. It's self-love, and from that, true love for others evolves.

(Volpe, 2002, 258)

He also contrasted his prison experience with his 'previous' life:

I had been spoiled rotten in my luxurious life, sleeping until ten, travelling around the world, having breakfast in bed, depositing millions into my bank accounts, enjoying the greatest art in the world, surrounded by the most beautiful people, but in a flash my reality was changed. That's how fragile life is. By realising this I was starting to *transform*.

(Volpe, 2002, 256, emphasis added)

So the experiences prison forced offenders to endure, combined with the time to think about what had happened to them, resulted in a gradual shift in perspective. The encounter with prison left their lives ineluctably altered. The remainder of the sample do not make reference to these types of realisations. This does not mean they did not change, but suggests they did not come to such realisations while in prison. Several changed as a result of new religious beliefs, their faith strengthened while they were incarcerated (e.g. Colson, Magruder), but such shifts in self-identity were part of more general processes of change rather than those prompted by prison. The role of religious conversion is considered in Chapter 9.

### Assaults on the self

As has been noted, where time in prison led to reflection on the life, change was welcomed. However, changes in the self could also be recognised as a threat. As noted previously, entry to prison represented a change in status and a shift in prisoners' identity. They were in danger of being reduced by their prison sentence. There were the twin threats of a deterioration of themselves and the possibility of

76 *Prison*

being made somehow less by their association with other prisoners. The prison experience was therefore an assault on their subjectively viewed self.

Part of who one is is derived from the company that one keeps, which, depending on how that company is viewed, may or may not be a threat to the identity (Goffman, 1963). Some prisoners fear being contaminated by contact with deviant others (Sykes, 1958, 77; Cohen and Taylor, 1972, 63) which affects their approach to their fellow inmates. Particular individuals or groups will be avoided, partly out of a desire for self-preservation, but also because of the connotations suggested by association with them (Cohen and Taylor, 1972). Fourteen white-collar offenders – Aitken, Archer, Bakker, Berger, Bond, Christensen, Guppy, Laite, Lawson, Leeson, Magruder, Minkow, Timilty and Volpe – felt they were very different people compared to those they shared their captivity with; different in both values and character.

White-collar offenders were aware of the differences between themselves and their criminal peers. Their age frequently set them apart, but this was only a small part of their prison experience. Sometimes other prisoners were used as a 'benchmark', a warning as to what can happen to those unfortunate enough to be incarcerated. For Timilty, the danger was lethargy:

> Among the most dangerous habits to fall into in prison is napping. Some inmates here are yielding to a lifelong ambition to sleep all day ... This cannot be healthy ... In the four months I am here, I am not going to take a nap during the day, or even lie down.
>
> (Timilty, 1999, 64–65)

Timilty determined to preserve who he was, not allowing his true self to be altered by the prison system; thereby making it through his prison experience ontologically 'intact'. What other prisoners provided then was an example of the dangers of incarceration, living proof that prison can change individuals, adding to feelings of insecurity over prison time. More than this, other prisoners may actually be perceived as a source of threat to the sense of self and therefore directly responsible for the deterioration of the self that white-collar offenders experience. Such was the case for Robert Berger, who was certain that being around 'minorities' had impacted his mental acuity such that he struggled to converse with more intellectual prisoners (Berger, 2003, 74).

Christensen, Laite and Timilty echo an awareness of the 'minority' status of other inmates and an understanding that they are different from the majority of their criminal peers. Descriptions of these prisoners are prefixed by information identifying them as part of a 'minority' group, e.g. 'a 21-year-old black kid' (Christensen, 2005, 101) 'three blacks have entered the laundry room' (Berger, 2003, 75). These descriptors demonstrate white-collar offenders' awareness of their difference from other prisoners, such awareness once more indicating the hypersensitivity prisoners had to their surroundings.

Prevalent is the notion that offenders may suffer the eroding of the self while in prison, not just because of the prison environment, but also because of their new companions. Other prisoners highlight, once again, the very different nature of the prison environment relative to previous experience. For Jeffrey Archer this happened during a conversation with another prisoner on his second day in prison:

> 'Don't talk to me about the press,' he screeches like a tape recorder you can't switch off. 'They always get it wrong. They said I shot my lover's boyfriend when I found them in bed together, and that he was an Old Etonian'. 'And he wasn't an Old Etonian?' I probe innocently. 'Yeah, course he was,' says Gordon. 'But I didn't shoot him, did I? I stabbed him seventeen times'. I feel sick at this matter of fact revelation, delivered with neither remorse nor irony... I shuddered, despite the sun beaming down on me. I wonder just how long it will be before I'm not sickened by such confessions. How long before I don't shudder? How long before it becomes matter-of-fact, common place?
>
> (Archer, 2002, 18)

This adds another element of uncertainty to the experience of prison. The awareness of white-collar offenders is that they might be changed subtly and in ways distressing to contemplate. For Archer the fear that he might be changed became something of a reality when, after 17 days in prison, he had a conversation with another prisoner about the violence that takes place within prison:

> Only two weeks ago I would have been appalled, horrified, disgusted by this matter-of-fact conversation. Am I already becoming anaesthetized, numbed by anything other than the most horrific?
>
> (Archer, 2002, 207)

Encounters with other prisoners provide further example of the ways in which the self may be stripped away by the environment of the prison (Goffman, 1961). It was not enough to be fearful of the effects of the monotony of the prison routine and the dehumanisation it threatened. Companions had to be chosen carefully lest they remind individuals of the way they had changed or are a direct cause of a shift in the self. That prison represents an assault on the self is a feature of other prison studies (Sykes, 1958; Cohen and Taylor, 1972, 104–105; Crewe, 2011), but such is often constituted in the impact of the prison regime and the broader conditions of confinement. The difference for white-collar offenders is that they feared other prisoners would be a source of such self-degradation.

Perhaps because of this there was a tendency by white-collar offenders to gravitate towards other prisoners who were 'like them' and to seek out 'appropriate' companions. Irwin (1980, 14) outlines how prisoners do the best they can to manage the time they have to spend in prison through taking on as many activities as they can. Others orient themselves more completely with the prison administration e.g. through attaining jobs from which they can gain prestige or resources they can barter (see also Irwin 1980, 15). That is, they took what comforts they could from their environment. Even within prison there is the opportunity to choose

78  *Prison*

who one spends time with and white-collar prisoners wished to spend time with people they perceived as similar to them. Associating with others who are perceived by the offender as white-collar (identified in terms of their social status) prisoners helps to send a message to others regarding who one is (Goffman, 1969) but also, perhaps more importantly, confirms for white-collar offenders that they can still 'move' in the circles they are used to and can associate with others who they perceive as like them. In contrast to the way 'outsider prisoners' are described, prisoners considered appropriate for interacting with are introduced in terms of their occupation (e.g. Volpe, 2002, 251) or their high standing e.g. '[He was] obviously from money' (Berger, 2003, 75), emphasising the 'qualities' such individuals had.

Further reinforcing the differences between white-collar offenders and other prisoners was the opportunity taken by some white-collar offenders to utilise the almost unique (compared to other prisoners) skills they had for the benefit of other prisoners. Jonathan Aitken wrote letters on behalf of semi-literate inmates, while former businessman Alan Bond ran an education programme to teach prisoners about business and finance. Doing so was possibly a means of ingratiating themselves with fellow prisoners but also enabled white-collar offenders to capture something of who they were prior to their prison sentence. This is most obviously exemplified by former lawyer Nelson Christensen's 'prison based practice', which saw him advising other prisoners on matters of criminal law (2005, 37). For Alan Bond, sentenced to prison for failing to act honestly as a company director, his classes were 'a great opportunity for both the prisoners and me to get some self-esteem back' (Bond, 2003, 298). Taking on such roles also highlighted further for white-collar offenders the difference between themselves and their fellow prisoners. This was important for maintaining their distance from the majority of the prison population, to avoid the implication that they were 'just another prisoner'. Their abilities set them apart in a manner that was easily demonstrable, allowing them to show their different character. Utilising these allowed them to achieve some measure of status once again, marking them as 'better' than many of their fellow inmates.

A further part of prison interaction are those relationships offenders had with prison personnel. Generally, these are described as cordial affairs but only Archer and Bond describe having more than fleeting contact with prison staff. Most appeared to recognise that excessive contact would be viewed negatively by other prisoners and moderated their relationships accordingly. Archer's more regular and familiar contact was a consequence of his job as an orderly in the prison hospital.

## A unique experience?

The foregoing discussion of white-collar offenders' prison experiences is used as a basis for comparison between them and research observations on prisoners more generally. The most relevant aspects of prison for white-collar offenders are the shock of prison, their use of time and the possibility of change.

Accounts of the horrors of induction support the notion that the shock of prison is, for white-collar offenders, grounded in the contrast with their old life (Shover and Hochstetler, 2006; Mann *et al.*, 1980). White-collar offenders were quickly made to feel as if their status had been lessened by their incarceration. The literature that has considered the potential effects of prison on white-collar offenders has been concerned on the one hand with their 'special sensitivity' to incarceration (Mann *et al.*, 1980). Contrary to this is the assertion that given their greater 'life experience', white-collar offenders are better equipped to cope with prison (Benson and Cullen, 1988). As is indicated, white-collar offenders eventually settled into the prison routine once the shock of incarceration wore off. In part they were able to cope because, as Benson and Cullen (1988) suggest, they had experience of 'surviving' in large institutions that they were able to make reference to. Time was needed to learn the rules and to become accustomed to prison routines. Despite such shocks then, and, as seems to be the case for non white-collar offenders sentenced to prison (e.g. Toch, 1992), such feelings were for the most part transitory. Eventually, white-collar offenders became inured to the deprivations of prison life, the humiliation of strip searches and the bureaucracy of the prison world (Benson and Cullen, 1988) and began to assess how they would spend their prison time. In this way, they appear to be little different from Farrall and Calverley's (2006, 69–70) participants, who found that they slowly became habituated to prison life. Some did this by drawing upon past experiences to make what was happening meaningful to them. Although they did not appear to suffer from a special sensitivity however, nor did white-collar offenders seem particularly well placed to cope with the rigours of prison, as Benson and Cullen (1988) suggest. Prison was still difficult.

As prison studies focusing on non-white-collar offenders have identified, the issue of time within prison was one that occupied these offenders (Cohen and Taylor, 1972; Irwin, 1980; Meisenhelder, 1985). Part of coping with prison meant using time effectively. Strategies for utilising prison time were centred upon ensuring that such time was not 'lost' to prisoners. Productive endeavours were undertaken or the 'positive' aspects of prison were identified as a means of giving incarceration some purpose within the life as a whole and also to preserve something of the individual's 'true' character. Related to this, prison time allowed the opportunity for reflection upon the past, for offenders to consider their lives and also to plan their future. In contrast to the way prison has been conceived of more traditionally (Farrall and Calverley, 2006), for these men it did represent an opportunity to take a 'time out' from their busy lives and this added to the feeling that the prison experience might be construed in more positive terms than they had first anticipated. Prison, although constituting a mass of deprivations, provided sufficient 'quiet time' for them to marshal their thoughts and plan their lives. For these white-collar offenders, prison time was not as futureless as it has been characterised (Meisenhelder, 1985).

Above all, what appears to be the difference between these offenders and Meisenhelder's (1985) prisoners was that the former looked 'inward' for solutions to the problem of prison time. They made the best of their situation, attempting

80  *Prison*

projects that would better them or simply viewing their time in prison as of benefit rather than detriment to their life. Examples of such projects included obtaining qualifications (Minkow) or developing a burgeoning religious faith (Lawson). The positives they drew from their prison time included using it to plan their future or recognising the importance of being able to have a break from the outside world. Prison acted as a 'cocoon', shielding them from potentially distressing situations.

This difference in the way white-collar offenders used their prison time originates in the contrast between the 'fast lives' they lived and the sudden abundance of time in prison. Prison provided sufficient 'quiet time' for them to marshal their thoughts and plan their lives. One further reason that white-collar offenders may have been afforded some time to think compared to Meisenhelder's (1985) and Farrall and Calverley's (2006) participants is that in the main they were sent to low-security prisons, commensurate with them being first-time, non-violent offenders. It is possible that such locations offered more in the way of solitude and 'quiet time'. Finally, an unwillingness to associate with other prisoners who are not considered to be of a similar standing (as alluded to by Berger, 2003, 74 and also suggested by Benson and Cullen, 1988) may create more time where the white-collar offender is alone.

What is apparent from both a consideration of the shocks of prison and also the way time was spent, is that change was an integral part of white-collar offenders' prison experiences. Having time to think about the past and plan for the future led many to think about themselves differently. The future selves they envisioned were concerned with 'betterment', often grounded in particular ways of viewing their past (Levine, 1991, 362–363). Prison was not a stultifying experience that prevented the growth of the self, but for some actually became an opportunity for growth and a way of obtaining fulfilment through worthwhile pursuits (Kotarba, 1984).

This need was a result of the change which the prison environment forced upon offenders' sense of self, making existing ways of being 'themselves' ineffectual (Kotarba, 1984). As Fontana (1984) notes, the difference between one's own sense of self and the identity that the world ascribes to one is always likely to be a source of tension. Greater mismatch between self and identity is likely to lead to strategies to preserve who one truly is. The dehumanisation that prison can engender was indicated above, the prisoner identity removing any chance of individuality. Survival strategies were pursued that enabled white-collar offenders to maintain their status and therefore their overall sense of who they were. White-collar offenders rejected the 'prisoner' identity they were presented with (Messinger and Warren, 1984) and made the experience of being a prisoner something individual to them.

Change was also a threat in prison, however, constituted in other inmates. As others have highlighted (e.g. Shover and Hochstetler, 2006) white-collar offenders who enter prison find themselves surrounded by people who are very different from those they are used to associating with. Such differences are, in part, perceived as an attack on the sense of who one is. The threat to the self-

*Prison*   81

identity was always present, with other prisoners representing a source of 'deterioration' that had to be managed. These white-collar offenders were mindful of the differences between themselves and those they shared their prison time with, some gravitating towards other 'white-collar' prisoners as a way of protecting who 'they' were.

Much has been made, both in this chapter and more generally where white-collar offenders' experiences of prison are concerned (e.g. Shover and Hochstetler, 2006) of the contrast in offenders' lives before and during their time in prison. None of the resources or previous life experiences white-collar offenders had prepared them for the initial shock of prison. Knowing how to deliver a political speech or organise a boardroom meeting was not useful information for their induction into prison, nor was the great wealth some enjoyed relative to other prisoners.

Once over the initial shocks however, past experiences did become useful for white-collar offenders, who drew on sources of knowledge that other prisoners perhaps could not to make sense of their surroundings. It is perhaps as well that white-collar prisoners could make use of past feelings of being powerless (e.g. as Timilty did) or relating their understanding of bureaucracy (Magruder) to cope with the shock of prison, because social support networks were not immediately available to them. This was partly a result of a desire to distance themselves from the 'contaminating' influence of other prisoners.

The threats offenders perceived while in prison were a result in part of their cultural backgrounds, which marked them as very different from the majority of other prisoners. A potent worry while in prison was the possibility that they and their lives would be altered by their time there, leaving them 'less' somehow than when they entered. As much as their previously successful lives gave them resources to cope with the shocks of prison and the threat prison presented, these lives were also the source of their angst because it was these that prison threatened. Coping with the threats of prison was done to maintain a semblance of who they had been.

White-collar offenders were better able to deal with prison because they had access to skills and knowledge that other offenders lack (contra Mann *et al.*, 1980). However, it is also clear that these resources were required simply to maintain the very specific sense of self white-collar offenders held and that therefore prison was not easy (contra Benson and Cullen, 1988). Their previous lives were at once the source of and the solution to their prison angst.

There are similarities in the prison experience of these white-collar offenders when compared to other offenders. The preoccupation with time and the dehumanisation of prison induction as it threatened their sense of self has echoes with the prison literature cited throughout this chapter. Where these white-collar offenders appear to differ from other prisoners is in the source of the 'threat' that prison represented to them and their reaction to the large amounts of time they were forced to organise for themselves. That many embraced their period of enforced inactivity says much about the lives they led prior to their incarceration. They also, more than other prisoners it seems (Farrall and Calverley, 2006), took the time to think

## 82 *Prison*

about their lives and how they had 'arrived' at prison. Once again, the fact that some did use their prison time to reflect on their past is perhaps indicative of the sort of fast paced lives that other prisoners cannot make reference to.

## Note

1　Jamieson and Grounds' sample was comprised of wrongly imprisoned and politically motivated individuals. Nevertheless, the authors note that some problems 'were a function of long-term detention *per se*' (2005, 37, emphasis in original).

# 5 Who am I?

## Self and identity in the post-punishment world

Almost invariably, those who are sentenced to prison are released at some point. The white-collar offenders in this sample who were sentenced to prison were no exception and their attempts to establish themselves in society once again are the focus of this chapter. Following a review of the literature that has detailed offenders' resettlement experiences, the peculiar challenges faced by white-collar offenders are examined. This chapter asks how white-collar offenders viewed the prospect of release, whether release from prison matched their expectations and how they worked out who they 'were' in the world they found themselves in once they had exited prison. The analysis begins with prisoners' anticipation of their release and the anxiety this engendered. This anxiety gave way to concerns over the course their lives would take following release, but stigma and a curtailing of opportunities were significant obstacles for white-collar offenders to overcome.

### After a prison sentence

A number of questions are likely to occupy ex-prisoners in the period following their incarceration. These questions might centre broadly on how the life will be lived or have more specific concerns such as where employment might be found or where the next night will be spent. The backdrop for such questions however will be the expectation that the newly released prisoner will not return to offending and will subsequently make a new life for themselves, their resettlement success measured by whether or not they desist from crime.

Traditionally, work on the aftermath of imprisonment has highlighted the importance of ex-prisoners fashioning a new pro-social identity – one that sees the offender taking on roles that benefit others – if their attempts to desist are to be successful. Visher and Travis (2003) note that post-release circumstances should allow and encourage the ex-prisoner to form a new identity, centred upon changes in work practices and familial relationships, but ought also to include a civic role in which the individual comes to see themselves (and be seen by others) as a responsible citizen (see Farrall *et al.*, 2014 for examples of this). Uggen *et al.* (2004) also underline the importance of ex-offenders being able to establish a new pro-social role as part of attempts to create a stable identity that is incompatible with further offending. Part of this is the identification of oneself as someone who

84 *Coming home*

is either a conforming or deviant citizen and having this identity confirmed through interaction with others (see also Meisenhelder, 1982). Pro-social identities help offenders recognise a new future self that can replace a deviant identity (Giordano *et al.*, 2002) and also put a deviant past into context (Maruna, 2001; Maruna and Roy, 2007). In short, desistance is about making a new way to live that is incompatible with a continued commitment to deviant activity. It indicates the importance of offenders' desires to desist from crime as driving attempts to succeed and an identification of a way to achieve this desire as a first 'step' towards change (Giordano *et al.*, 2002).

Pro-social identities may be achieved in part through commitment to family or work roles (Visher and Travis, 2003), long associated with a reduction in the likelihood of re-offending (e.g. Laub and Sampson, 2001). In addition, a key part of achieving and maintaining a pro-social identity is engagement in roles that the individual identifies as holding a civic function, such as roles that enable something to be 'given back' to the wider community e.g. through working to help others (Maruna, 2001; Uggen *et al.*, 2004; Farrall *et al.*, 2014). This is because identity is created by reference to others, thus attributing to it a social aspect that reflects interpersonal relationships (Fontana, 1984, 11).

At any point, the 'fit' between identity and self is dependent on the similarity between the self-conception and the identity society attributes the individual. As Fontana (1984) indicates however, identity is not passively accepted, but can be manipulated. Common themes in the control of identity are the importance of places (Goffman, 1961; Meisenhelder, 1982; Ebaugh, 1984; Farrall and Calverley, 2006; Farrall *et al.*; 2014) and people (Goffman, 1969; Ebaugh, 1988; Fontana, 1984) that can be employed to aid the construction of a particular identity. The social situations actors find themselves in and the ways in which they act and are reacted to are therefore an important part of understanding 'who' one is (Goffman, 1969). Specific others such as supportive peer groups or family members may aid the transformation of identity by helping the ex-offender create a self-image of someone who is no longer 'deviant'. These relationships also work by providing encouragement to the would-be desister as they attempt to lead their new life (Visher and Travis, 2003).

It is therefore through interactions with others and reflecting on what these interactions 'mean' that ex-offenders come to feel their own attempts at change are successful (Meisenhelder, 1982; Maguire and Raynor, 2006). Consequently, it is important that their close relationships support and provide motivation for change. A key part of achieving such change is feeling that goals are attainable and that attempts will be successful (Maguire and Raynor, 2006). The above therefore suggests that post-release circumstances should contain structures that endow ex-prisoners with the ability to live lives consistent with their prevailing self-conception and assist them in making their aspirations a reality.

Recently released prisoners are generally in a poor position regarding the availability of such support structures, however.[1] Some may feel the offender 'label' is too big a liability in their attempts to desist and thus it undermines their motivation to try to forge non-offending lifestyles (Uggen *et al.*, 2004, 283–286;

Hunter, 2011 explores this with white-collar offenders). For example, they may be unable to find employment due to their conviction and the associated travails such as the degradation of employment-relevant skills, stigma and attenuated ties to the labour market (e.g. Visher and Travis, 2003). Further to these impediments are legal restrictions that bar those with a criminal record from entering certain types of business (Petersilia, 2003, Chapter 6; Richards and Jones, 2004). Similarly, many recently released prisoners may lack a stable family to go back to (Visher and Travis, 2003), hampering attempts to live up to positive roles centred upon the family. Soon-to-be-released prisoners are likely to be mindful of these potential pitfalls and consequently an air of pessimism may cloud the context of release from prison (Richards and Jones, 2004).

Although individuals may influence the way in which others consider them through the disclosure of information, this is likely to be only a part of how their social identity is constructed (Goffman, 1963). As has been noted above, identity is also constructed through social interaction, the assertion being that who one 'is', is related to the particular setting one finds themselves in and the other social actors the individual must relate to while in that setting (Goffman, 1963, 1969; Lofland, 1969; Farrall *et al.*, 2014). Others may infer the character of a person based upon this information and so the social actor can signal to them the 'sort of person' they are. Thus, one way to highlight that a change has taken place in the individual's life is through involvement in situations and interaction with individuals who are consistent with the change being made (Ebaugh, 1984, 1988; or see Meisenhelder, 1982 for an example of how ex-offenders attempted to show they had desisted from crime by associating with 'respectable' others and engaging in 'normal' practices).

What the foregoing highlights is that ex-prisoners' resettlement is carried out within a world that is personal to them; a world that in part constitutes their identity. Some aspects of this world will be under the control of the ex-prisoner, some will not, and these have to managed as best they can be.

## White-collar offenders' resettlement

White-collar offenders are typically thought to be in a better position than the majority of ex-prisoners when it comes to resettling. Shover and Hochstetler suggest that white-collar offenders are likely to have greater access support networks that promote law abiding behaviour than other offenders and that such networks ease their reintegration into the community and therefore their desistance (2006). The skills that white-collar offenders hold as a result of their education and work backgrounds are thought to aid them in gaining employment to smooth the transition from prison to the 'legitimate' world (Visher and Travis, 2003). Observations that white-collar offenders are more likely to be married than other offenders (Benson and Kerley, 2001) suggest a stable home life that will ease resettlement (Visher and Travis, 2003).

The presence of such networks does, however, raise a different issue that may be unique to white-collar offenders. Specifically, the loss of social status and

## 86  *Coming home*

reputation is particularly acute for them (Shover and Hochstetler, 2006, 143). The notion that arrest and imprisonment create a stigma for white-collar offenders that is hard to get rid of is oft-cited (Benson, 1999; Weisburd *et al.*, 2001; Benson and Kerley, 2001; Shover and Hochstetler, 2006). Weisburd *et al.* (2001, 93) suggest that we might expect the stigma of a prison sentence to manifest itself in further offending because once white-collar offenders have been sentenced to prison and suffered stigma they have nothing to lose by offending again and indeed this has been noted as being a feature of white-collar offenders' accounts (Hunter, 2011). However, Weisburd *et al.* did not find a statistically significant relationship between imprisonment and recidivism (Weisburd *et al.*, 2001, 113, although see Jolliffe and Hedderman (2012, 6) for further consideration of Weisburd *et al.*'s results).

If white-collar offenders do experience stigma, then this may make it difficult to establish a pro-social role, as is the case for other ex-prisoners attempting to resettle (Uggen *et al.*, 2004). However, based upon the above theorisations it is possible to conclude little regarding white-collar offenders' resettlement experiences. It is therefore the goal of this chapter to explore how white-collar offenders viewed the prospect of release, how their post-release experiences match their expectations and how they made sense of who they were in the world they found themselves in after their release from prison.

Table 5.1 contains details of those white-collar offenders in the sample who served a prison sentence and whose accounts detailed their release from prison and the aftermath, along with the length of their sentence. The one exception in the table is Jeffrey Archer. Although Archer's *Prison Diary* ends as he leaves prison, it is possible from media interviews and other archives to determine his experiences after he was released.

The length of time given to describing resettlement varies between these accounts. For example, Christensen's account covers a short period after he leaves prison and while he is still resident at a halfway house for offenders, while from Colson's several autobiographies it is possible to understand 30 years of his life after his sentence ended. The majority of offenders, however, cover a period that is around six months to a year after their release. These accounts describe the challenges that were faced in the post-prison world and the endeavours these men undertook.

One observation of note is that all of these ex-prisoners considered themselves non-offenders at the time of their release from prison. This was either because they denied any initial wrongdoing or had changed as a result of their post-offence experiences. Their concerns were on determining their identity and how they would live the lives they wished.

### Anticipating release

Much of white-collar offenders' prison time was spent anticipating the end of incarceration. Reunions with family members and friends were imagined, the return to old haunts was planned and the start of the 'rest of the life' was considered. However, with such anticipation came anxiety regarding what the future may hold.

*Coming home* 87

*Table 5.1* White-collar offenders' time spent in prison

| Offender | Time served (months) | Offender | Time served (months) |
|---|---|---|---|
| Jonathan Aitken | 7 | William Laite | 5 |
| Jeffery Archer | 24 | Stephen Lawson | 18 |
| Jim Bakker | 58 | Nick Leeson | 42 |
| Robert L. Berger | 38 | Dennis Levine | 15 |
| Alan Bond | 44 (second sentence) | Jeb Magruder | 7 |
| Nelson Christensen | 36 | Barry Minkow | 88 |
| Charles Colson | 7 | Pete Rose | 5 |
| John Dean | 4 | Joseph Timilty | 4 |
| Darius Guppy | 35 | Tod Volpe | 24 |

Six prisoners cited feeling anxious about their future when they left prison. These prisoners are presented in Table 5.2 along with those who felt no anxiety worth noting in their accounts (termed confident prisoners). Anxiety about the future was indicated by accounts describing fears of the life that would be faced upon the release from prison, difficult challenges that would be encountered or worries over what would happen to the individual upon release from prison.

### *Anxious prisoners*

The six who expressed anxiety regarding their future emphasised worry over being branded 'a criminal' and the realisation that, as a result of this, life would be difficult when they were released. Robert Berger's thoughts were on what life after prison might hold for him. Thinking about the future led him to:

> work myself up into a scared, paranoid state of mind. I wind up walking around upset.
>
> (Berger, 2003, 121)

Such anxiety may focus upon specific problems that are anticipated upon release from prison such as the fear that the criminal past will be a source of stigma.

*Table 5.2* Anxious and confident prisoners

| Anxious prisoners | Confident prisoners | |
|---|---|---|
| Archer | Aitken | Lawson |
| Berger | Bakker | Levine |
| Bond | Christensen | Magruder |
| Laite | Colson | Minkow |
| Leeson | Dean | Rose |
| Timilty | Guppy | Volpe |

## 88   *Coming home*

Berger's concerns were that his prison sentence might impact upon his interactions with others, that he would be stigmatised as a result of his incarceration accompanied by questions about the treatment he would receive from those he knew (Berger, 2003, 100).

This was also the case for Joseph Timilty, sentenced to four months in prison for conspiring to commit fraud:

> It's hard to believe, but two weeks from tonight, I'll be at a halfway house in Boston. That's when the real challenge starts. It's been easy here I guess in comparison to what life will be like when Joe Timilty goes home as an ex-con.
>
> (Timilty, 1997, 220)

As the previous chapter indicated, while within prison contact with the outside world is greatly reduced. Prison shields the prisoner from outside influences in a manner that may be beneficial if these influences were to be a source of stress e.g. investigations by credit agencies/government organisations or the weight of negative opinion from others. Prisoners acknowledged that they were, to an extent, protected. As William Laite expressed:

> After all those days and weeks, I had become adjusted to prison life. It was regimented, it was dehumanizing, it was nerve-racking, but in prison at least you were protected, sheltered from the criticisms and expectations of those on the outside.
>
> (Laite, 1972, 227)

The thought that this 'cocoon' was soon to be shattered by release from prison alerted prisoners to the fact that the various pressures that have been held at bay will soon be placed upon them again. Release made action an obligation. Added to this complication and subsequent anxiety was uncertainty over the future. There was no reference point in the individuals' biographies that would help them make sense of what would happen to them, i.e. they had not been a released prisoner before.[2]

Concomitant with an awareness that their status had changed was the anxiety that this status would prevent the return to the life they once enjoyed and that the prison experience would have changed them. As he considered leaving prison Robert Berger was both 'sad and afraid' but also at time excited about his future (Berger, 2003, 134). The uncertainty of the future could at times be welcome then. From this positon the future represented the promise of a new start (see Hunter's 2011 consideration of white-collar offenders in prison for an example of how an uncertain future may be welcomed). Equally, however, there was concern when thought of in terms of action, when practicalities were considered and thoughts turned to the problems that would be faced. Laite felt a growing unease as his prison sentence neared completion:

*Coming home*  89

> As the day of my release approached, I found that my thoughts were not at all what I had imagined they would be... a feeling of uneasy dread rooted in me, and nothing I could do... could dislodge it.
>
> (Laite, 1972, 226)

His institutionalisation and his tacit acceptance of the prison regime were the root of this unease. He became aware of the consequences of his conviction, which prompted doubts about his ability to succeed:

> Now I had to go home bearing that stigma [of his offence] ... It was a frightening prospect. I was uncertain how I would be accepted. And beyond that was the overwhelming task of rebuilding my life again from rock-bottom. I had to re-establish myself as a man – as a family man, and as a man involved in the business and social life of the community ... I had serious doubts about how successful I might be.
>
> (Laite, 1972, 227)

Prisoners therefore had existential concerns over their place in the world and a lack of certainty regarding what life would hold after prison. Ebaugh (1984) noted a similar fear of the unknown for those nuns who realised they would leave the convent but had no notion of what such leaving meant in terms of what would become of their lives. Leaving an institution forces one to consider what such a transition means in terms of the self. The future for anxious prisoners was difficult to frame in any terms but negative ones, with stigmatisation easy to imagine but positive experiences less so. The realisation was that challenges would have to be faced as the temporary suspension of the life that the prison sentence imposed came to an end. Laite's concern – and those of others studied – was focused upon his ability to regain what he 'had' before he was sent to prison and speaks to concerns with citizenship that other, non white-collar offenders have experienced (Uggen *et al.*, 2004; Farrall and Calverley, 2006). Laite exemplifies the challenge white-collar offenders may face: it is not enough to merely leave prison, it is important to become who one was and to enjoy conventional success once more. As noted above, these white-collar offenders enjoyed successful lives prior to their imprisonment and wanted to do so again. Re-establishing themselves meant realising goals that ex-offenders more generally may not hold (Farrall, *et al.*, 2014).

Therefore as release from prison approached and offenders began to think about their future they began to realise what awaited them, the way their life had changed and, consequently, how they had changed. The worry these anxious prisoners had was that their existence as they once knew it and took for granted was in jeopardy. Jeffrey Archer questioned the extent to which he would be able to pick up his life where he had left off:

> For the first time I consider the future and what it holds for me. Will I have to follow the path of my two heroes, Emma Hamilton[3] and Oscar Wilde,[4] and choose to live a secluded life abroad, unable to enjoy the society that has been

90  *Coming home*

so much *a part of my very existence*? Will I be able to visit old haunts – The National Theatre, Lord's, Le Caprice, The Tate Gallery, the UGC cinema in Fulham Road – or even walk down the street without people's only thought being 'There's the man who went to jail for perjury'? I can't explain to every one of them that I didn't get a fair trial.

(Archer, 2002, 87, emphasis added)

Archer's reference to his 'very existence' exemplifies the importance anxious offenders placed upon their former lives and the fundamental relevance of being able to return to the life they had before. Routines become part of the identity (see Goffman, 1969; Douglas, 1977 or, for examples focused specifically on offenders, Farrall *et al.*, 2014). To be denied the opportunity to act as they wished and engage in familiar comforting routines denied them freedom to express fundamental aspects of what make them, 'them'. Related to this, anxiety over a return to the old life is a result of knowledge that offenders may not be able to return to their former careers. Robert Berger was aware that he was unlikely to be able to achieve business success in a manner analogous to his former post as CEO of Royce Aerospace Materials. Instead, he worried about his ability to find work: 'I have a strange cold feeling that humiliation will be the order of business once I'm released' (Berger, 2003, 186).

Within the context of realising that their place in the world had changed, what made such fears of the future particularly acute was the inability to envision a viable positive alternative that would define who they were. For all social beings, the question 'who am I?' is answered by looking to the future rather than the past (Kotarba, 1979, 358; Hunter, 2011). These anxious prisoners were unable to answer this question adequately because they had no way of conceptualising their future.

The pessimism of these accounts are resonant with the way in which prisoners more generally view their future (Uggen *et al.*, 2004; Burnett and Maruna, 2004; Farrall and Calverley, 2006). What unites the accounts of these white-collar offenders and other prisoners is an awareness of the difficulties that await them after prison. Such uncertainty over the future direction of one's life and, consequently, the chance to realise a particular self-project highlights the ontological anxiety an uncertain future presages.

### *Coping with anxiety*

Planning for release to impose some definition on the future by identifying a particular 'world' that they could go to alleviated some offenders' concerns (Irwin, 1980 identifies this as happening amongst prisoners more generally). Two of the anxious prisoners – Berger and Timilty – made reference to preparing for life after prison. Such plans provided them with goals to work towards, filling the void of a future in which the old structures they identified with might no longer be applicable. For Joseph Timilty, the future was based upon his experience of prison and what he had identified as the flaws in the prison system. He intended to lobby Washington for prison reform (Timilty, 1997, 218).

*Coming home* 91

Planning for the period after release is a means of wresting back control of the future, choosing and investing in a particular self over others. Timilty's desire to return to politics was also a means of capturing as closely as possible the life he had prior to his offence. The same was true for former businessman Berger, who planned to start a town car service once he left prison, as this would help him provide for his family while remaining autonomous (Berger, 2003, 151). Pleased he had 'concrete plans for the future' (Berger, 2003, 152), Berger began to invest his time heavily in planning for his new business. Having such a goal and realising it was attainable gave him hope that he had a future after prison and might still achieve success. This in turn acted to assuage worries about his post-release world. Being able to envision a future self in a positive light is important in driving attempts to regain a 'normal' life. The successful life that Berger – a former CEO of a billion dollar company – had led gave him some optimism in these plans:

> I'll have to rebuild all over again, but I'm certainly not the only one who has been in that position. Allenwood [prison] is full of formerly successful businessmen with similar stories.
>
> (Berger, 2003, 10; see also, 161)

Drawing upon his past success was therefore a source of optimism for Berger, aiding his attempts to cope with anxiety. Both Timilty and Berger had blueprints for a 'future self' (Giordano *et al.*, 2002) they could try to become. In hoping for and investing in a future self, however, there was the risk that plans may not come to fruition and that the 'lifeline' that would enable them to live again would prove to be false. In Berger's case, as much as he was committed to his potential future business he was aware of the potential for it to fail and the consequences of that for him:

> I have become a driven man when it comes to this new interest. I hope all of my predictions and calculations eventually prove to be true … Failure cannot be an option. If I am released and wind up as a failure I know I'll be absolutely devastated.
>
> (Berger, 2003, 153)

There is inevitably worry that the desired future will not transpire as intended. When plans are identified as a means of securing a particular self, their success is deemed very important, with failure attributed an equally all-encompassing gravitas (although the following chapter examines how failure may be accompanied by less anxiety than success). In Berger's case, this is the down side to his previously successful past. The anxiety over the potential failure of his plans was a worry that he would fail to recapture the successful life he had. The irony is that his optimism and pessimism come from the same source, his successful past. What Berger's example (see also Berger, 2003, 134, above) illustrates is that in reality prisoners can move between optimism and pessimism when considering their future after prison. No future is so bleak that survival cannot be envisioned. Equally, there is awareness that challenges are inevitable.

## 92 *Coming home*

### *Confident prisoners*

As Table 5.2 indicates, 12 offenders did not express concern about their future while in prison. They described difficult aspects of their imprisonment and wistful reflections on their lives, but made no mention of a concern for what awaited them upon release. They were optimistic that all would be well and although, as will be shown below, the optimism was, for some, misplaced, while in prison the future seemed bright or, at least, fair. Denis Levine, convicted of insider trading, looked forward to a fresh start. A start he believed he would be allowed to make because he had been punished by his time in prison and was now worthy of a second chance:

> You make a mistake and [the US] punishes you. But once you pay the price, it gives you another chance.
>
> (Levine, 1991, 375)

Stephen Lawson, who was imprisoned for multiple Securities and Exchange Commission violations, although having many questions regarding what his future might hold, was buoyed by his faith in God as he left prison:

> As the bus droned out the miles toward Atlanta, I wondered what the future would bring... Time would tell. I knew that the Lord's main concern was the condition of my heart. And my heart held the knowledge that I had been cleansed and forgiven.
>
> (Lawson, 1992, 173)

Lawson was able to make reference to a firm system of beliefs. By referencing these, the questions about his future seemed less troublesome because the uncertainty of some aspects were tempered by reference to a greater overall sense of meaning and the stability of having a higher cause. For Lawson, the reactions of others, his success in business and the 'normality' of his life were of secondary concern next to his belief that he had been forgiven by God. Being able to make reference to this made future uncertainty less problematic because his concerns were subordinated to a belief he was certain of. The importance of religion in providing a sense of security regarding one's place in the world will be considered in more detail in Chapter 8.

Of these 13 men six, like Lawson, drew strength from their faith in Christianity. These were Bakker, Colson, Aitken, Minkow, Lawson and Magruder. Of the remaining non-anxious prisoners, Dean, Rose, Guppy, Volpe and Christensen, however, like Levine, considered that their acceptance of their crimes combined with their punishment meant that once that punishment was over they would be free to live as they wished. Upon receiving his sentence Nelson Christensen wanted to:

> accept what the law regarded as just deserts for my actions all things considered ... In the long run I came out satisfied that things had balanced out.
>
> (Christensen, 2005, 10)

Like Levine (1991, 375), Christensen was concerned with the 'clean sate' that he would earn with his prison sentence. In return for admitting his offences he expected to be able to live as he wished following his allotted sentence.

The acceptance of wrongdoing is the principal difference between those prisoners who expressed anxiety and those who did not. Figure 5.1 demonstrates this, showing those who admitted their guilt and whether or not they were anxious about their release. Regarding guilt acceptance, 'yes' indicates the offender accepted the illegality of their actions and also that these were 'wrong'. 'No' indicates they denied any wrongdoing or felt they were merely 'technically' guilty. 'Technical' guilt is recognition that their actions were illegal but not really 'wrong' (e.g. bribing of clients being simply 'common business practice') or that the offender was somehow tricked or 'permitted' to offend by their circumstances. For Berger, this is because bribery 'is basically human nature' (Berger, 2003, 94), while Leeson argues that security protocols at Barings bank were so inadequate that its collapse was 'an accident waiting to happen' (2005, 73) Timilty's assertion is that 'Technically I'm guilty' (1997, dust jacket).

It can be seen from Figure 5.1 that all of those except one (Bakker) who rejected their guilt expressed anxiety over their future while they were in prison. In contrast, all but one (again, Bakker) of the non-anxious prisoners admitted their guilt. As Christensen put it, their prison sentences balanced out their wrongdoing. In accepting not just their guilt, but the wrong inherent in their actions these men 'came clean', their remorse for what they had done expressed in their accounts. In return for this though they expected that they would be allowed to proceed with their lives as they had before. Consequently there was not the dissonance between their view of themselves and the way in which others might view them that the anxious prisoners felt. These confident prisoners, in acknowledging their wrong-doing and accepting punishment reaffirmed themselves and their place in the world. They accepted the 'rules' of society and agreed to live by them. Although former preacher Jim Bakker did not accept his guilt, he still felt he had been forgiven, in his case by God. In contrast, the six who rejected guilt stood against the judgement of the world and so for the anxious prisoners there was not the

| Anxiety about future | | Anxious | | Confident | |
|---|---|---|---|---|---|
| Admit guilt? | Yes | | | Aitken | Lawson |
| | | | | Christensen | Levine |
| | | | | Colson | Magruder |
| | | | | Dean | Minkow |
| | | | | Guppy | Rose |
| | | | | | Volpe |
| | No | Archer | Berger | | |
| | | Bond | Leeson | | |
| | | Laite | Timilty | Bakker | |

*Figure 5.1* Prisoners who expressed anxiety over their future and guilt

## 94 *Coming home*

prospect of forgiveness. To be forgiven would be to accept the initial wrongdoing they had been accused of. Their anxieties were focused upon their place in a wider social world that falsely branded them a criminal.

## Leaving prison

Whether or not prisoners were anxious about their release, the immediate aftermath of release from prison was an exhilarating but daunting time. 'Immediate aftermath' is characterised here as the first two weeks after the end of the prison sentence. Although this appears arbitrary, it seemed that it took approximately this period of time for offenders to come to divest themselves of an ex-prisoner (although not an ex-offender) identity and begin to look towards their future. The issues that may have troubled individuals while they anticipated their release now became very real concerns. At the same time, there was sense of a new start being made, all while trying to cope with the shock of the sudden change in circumstances as prison was left behind.

### *First impressions*

Much as entering prison was a shock for white-collar offenders, so was leaving. Irwin (1980, 114–115; Jamieson and Grounds, 2005) describes the disorientation that many prisoners feel upon release, and the same was true for white-collar offenders. Consider for example Nelson Christensen's account of the contrast between the closed world of prison and the freedom he gained upon leaving on temporary release:

> Pedestrian crosswalks through busy traffic frightened me. The idea that I was walking around in public without supervision was very troubling, and of course I thought that everyone was looking at me... I had no confidence or swagger, and in fact was glad to be back in confinement in only two hours. I did not savor my time in freedom. This was going to take a while.
>
> (Christensen, 2005, 163–164)

For others, the sudden return to 'normal' life was highlighted by specific events. Jim Bakker was faced with a difficult decision at his first restaurant meal following his release:

> The menu was so big! And there were so many selections. I read the menu again and again and I simply could not make up my mind. There were just too many choices. Tears welled up in my eyes. I could not yet adjust to life outside of prison.
>
> (Bakker, 1996, 608)

Ex-prisoners faced difficulty adjusting to the new worlds they found themselves in. Uncertain futures still lingered for them and the questions they had regarding their

Coming home 95

post-incarceration life persisted or, for Christensen and Bakker, were answered in painful ways. At this point, many offenders were anticipating first encounters with significant others. Such experiences underline that they have changed, making real the fears they may have had about being altered by their prison experience.

The magnitude of the experience of exiting prison is further encapsulated in what might otherwise be trivial details that highlight their new status as free individuals. Upon his release from prison, Jim Bakker was driven by a prison officer to an airport from which he could fly home:

> Along the way to Savannah, the [prison officer] offered me a stick of gum. I accepted it as a first token of my freedom. Inmates are not permitted to have any gum at all in prison... Consequently, when [the prison officer] offered the gum to me, I happily accepted it, popped it into my mouth, and chewed more vigorously than I had in years. The taste of freedom was in my mouth!
>
> (Bakker, 1996, 604)

Joseph Timilty began to fully realise his status as an *ex*-prisoner was brought home to him when he put on the clothes his wife sent him to wear when he left prison:

> instantly I feel my personality change. My muscles become less tense. It's a strange feeling of looseness and liberation.
>
> (Timilty, 1997, 239)

As important as the physical removal from the prison locale is the divestment of the trappings of prison life. The garments that signify membership of particular institutions have inevitable connotations and are an important part of identification with that institution (Ebaugh, 1984). They are a physical reminder that one is a member. Leaving prison was not done simply by walking out of the door; it was done by casting off the clothing that signified Timilty as a prisoner, or by Bakker chewing the gum that his previous status denied him.

All these men were aware of their ex-prisoner identity. With prison still very recent and without yet having the opportunity to move forward and become again the person they were or the person they wished to be, first encounters with others and the outside world were conducted within the context of this status as an ex-prisoner. This reinforced the 'alien' nature of the outside world and the uncertainty about what to expect upon release. The importance of leaving institutions is constituted in the change in identity that such leaving signifies (Ebaugh, 1984, 1988). To be part of an institution such as prison is to have one's identity constituted in various cues, connotations and practices that are attributed to a member of that institution (Goffman, 1961; Ebaugh, 1988). Even where removal from an institution is welcome, reference points that are used to make sense of the world will still be grounded in this previous, institutionalised self. It will take time to realise who one is, time that must be spent living within the 'new world' and building up new expectations around this living (Attig, 2002; Corr, 2002).

## 96   *Coming home*

A further potential source of difficulty was the realisation that questions regarding the future that had once simply been pondered while in prison, now required answers and action. Ex-prisoners were therefore immediately forced to act and, in so doing, choose themselves and commit to a future self. The immediate concerns that ex-prisoners had centred on this and on where their life would go from this point. John Dean was convicted of obstruction of justice following his role in Watergate. His first journal entry following release highlighted the importance of taking action and the potential difficulties of doing so:

> A chapter of my life has closed, punctuated with the exclamation that I'm free! But exclamation points pass quickly, and mine is followed by questions I cannot answer easily or hurriedly, What about the future? What do I do now? I must answer soon.
>
> (Dean, 1982, 13, emphasis in original)

Such questions were also pertinent for Dennis Levine:

> Sixty-seven pounds lighter than when I went off to prison, I was released from federal custody on September 8, 1988, pondering this question, After sky-rocketing to the top of the world and crashing down even faster, what do you do next?
>
> (Levine, 1991, 380)

Jonathan Aitken was similarly unsure about what his future might hold, recounting that his first thoughts upon leaving prison concerned his life and 'What on earth am I going to do next?' (Aitken, 2005, 174). Release from prison therefore does not merely provide the opportunity to act; it makes it an obligation, first because action is a means of sloughing off the ex-prisoner status and therefore a way of signalling to others that that is not who one 'is' and, second, it is a way of signalling to oneself that incarceration has not caused 'damage' by changing the ex-prisoner. The importance of acting for the newly released prisoner is to become who they feel they 'are' and actively create this through living (Ebaugh, 1988; Maruna, 2001).

Spending time with those who would support the conception of who they were was important to all these ex-prisoners and so answers to questions such as Aitken's in the first instance focus upon immediate post-incarceration behaviour. Following what may have been an intense if not necessarily harrowing experience in prison, the desire for a quiet life may be keenly felt, as expressed by Jonathan Aitken, who valued time at home and with his family because '[o]n the rare occasions when I went out, I felt slightly awkward and uncomfortable.' (Aitken, 2005, 178–180). Upon his release from prison Darius Guppy, convicted of attempting to defraud Lloyds of London, recalled the advice of his co-defendant:

> Ben, who had been free for almost a year, had warned me that the last thing I would feel like doing upon my release would be to celebrate with a mass of

*Coming home* 97

friends. He was right…for the next week or so, I simply stayed at home, enjoying my reunion with my wife and daughter while it snowed outside.

(Guppy, 1996, 301)

Charles Colson, who like Dean was convicted of obstruction of justice, wanted a similarly quiet return to life after his time in prison. He was keen to enjoy that which had been denied him for some time. Having come from the busy prison environment with its noise:

Now I yearned for peace and stillness. The seemingly little things most people take for granted had become terribly important.

(Colson, 1979, 22)

A desire for peace reflects not merely the opportunity to recover from prison time spent, but also provides the chance to take stock of one's situation within familiar, sympathetic surroundings. We are likely to feel most secure when we are within the home (Buttimer, 1976; Douglas, 1984, 82).

As will be suggested below, for the ex-prisoner, part of navigating the post-incarceration world is determining the place they have within it. The desire for a peaceable existence helped offenders come to terms with such issues by providing a safe place for them to answer the question 'who am I?' Rather than going 'out there', the world could come to them in an environment where they had a modicum of control. Through home-grounding, offenders began to consider more long-term aspects of their selves, answering questions on who they had become and who they would be.

It was noted in the previous chapter that despite the often harrowing experience of prison white-collar offenders adjusted to prison life. They came to learn how prison 'worked' and consequently were able to make sense of what was happening to them. In leaving prison, they once again found that they were unsure of the world they had been thrust into and had to once again work to build an understanding of the world. Prisoners eventually came to terms with the trauma of their prison experience. They formed new assumptions on what made 'sense' in prison by living the prison experience (Attig, 2002), learning and adapting to formal and informal codes of conduct. These assumptions were no longer viable once prison was exited however. They had to once again form new assumptions by living in the world, using cues that enabled an understanding of how their needs might best be fulfilled (Attig, 2002). Simultaneously, they could not return to previously held assumptions because these were predicated on a present and future in which they were not an ex-offender. Plans made in the immediate aftermath of prison were focused on the short term, as the above citations suggest, with the desire to enjoy family time (Guppy) or just not be 'in prison' (Colson). Ex-prisoners focused upon the immediacy of their situation, how their first few days would be spent. They eased themselves into the world, taking their time to identify who they were within it.

98    *Coming home*

### New starts

Accompanying the anxiety that the shock of release brought, however, was the sense that exit from prison represented a new start to life. Consider Joseph Timilty's thoughts on his journey home after release:

> The flight home this morning is an opportunity to reflect on how fortunate I am. Family and friends have stayed with me on this trip to hell and back, and now, I'm ready for the second day of the rest of my life.
>
> (Timilty, 1997, 240–241)

John Dean was similarly aware of the sense of having a chance of making a fresh start with his life. He was enthused by his release from prison:

> I was starting my life over. It was an unreal and very heady time.
>
> (Dean, 1982, 9)

Such feelings were grounded in the belief that they could have unfettered choice over their life now that prison was over. They could begin to make the choices and act consistently with the way in which they saw themselves but which an oft-cynical world may have denied them during their trial and sentence. These feelings were not lessened by their vacillation between these 'heady' emotions and worries over exactly how to exercise this choice or by anxiety over difficulties that might be faced. The importance of having choice then is that these ex-prisoners were now free to act in ways that underlined their sense of self. They could finally make choices consistent with who they felt they 'were'. For too long they had been denied this by prison. Release made it possible for them to be themselves again. This sense of renewed choice was also reflected in accounts of having regained control over the life after the powerlessness of the time spent in prison. Their lives belonged to them again. For John Dean this was emphasised by being able to act for himself upon leaving prison:

> I could feel all the pressure of uncertainty that had accumulated in my life suddenly vanish... I could stop worrying about the uncertainty and do something about it... I felt emotionally drained, yet physically charged with excitement. I began to plan everything from how to start packing and making flight reservations to what I would do with the rest of my life *now that it was mine again.*
>
> (Dean, 1982, 7–8, emphasis added)

As noted above, one of the most difficult aspects of imprisonment for some is the feeling that their life is no longer their own and that they may no longer be in control. Consequently, knowing one has regained the power to act and exercise choice is likely to be a moving experience. As Dean shows, despite there being uncertainty over the future, there was for some the sure knowledge that they may control parts of it. Where a meaningful future has been identified and potential

Coming home    99

answers to some of the questions regarding it have been planned, the pleasure of having back control originates in being able to act upon these plans although, as shall be indicated below, such feelings may only be transient.

### New lives and familiar activities

Answering the questions offenders had over their future and how time after release from prison would be spent depended on individual concerns. Dennis Levine's focus was how his arrest and time in prison had affected his family. Writing shortly after his release:

> I realized I would face each day with enormous uncertainty, feeling my way, trying to put together the scrambled pieces of the jigsaw puzzle of my life. I vowed to spend the bulk of my time with my family to help heal their – our – emotional wounds. One of the first things I did was take Adam [his son] to Disney World.
>
> (Levine, 1991, 380)

For John Dean, financial considerations were part of the motivation behind the decision, two weeks after release, to write his first autobiography (Dean, 1982, 18). Nick Leeson, convicted of fraud for his part in the collapse of Barings bank spent some time with friends in the Bahamas, but felt that the drug taking, party-going lifestyle did not represent his future:

> I had to get myself a plan... I wanted to get back to normality and that for me lay back in the UK. I have met many ex-pat Brits who have settled into a lifestyle in the tropics, but after so long spent in the oppressive humidity felt I needed to reconnect with my roots back in Watford...
>
> (Leeson, 2005, 236)

Charles Colson initially wished for a different life compared to that which he had led as a politician. On the night of his release from prison, he was ready to find a new path away from politics or business:

> I liked the sound of [a new life]. I wanted to put the hate and anger of Watergate behind me and forget the grimness of prison life.
>
> (Colson, 1979, 23)

Jonathan Aitken struggled in the first few weeks after leaving prison:

> Like many a newly released prisoner I found the period of adjustment to freedom a difficult experience. Even after my tag was removed I felt uncertain about almost all personal relationships outside my immediate family ... if people I was hoping to see did not communicate I became unreasonably disappointed.
>
> (Aitken, 2005, 181–182)

## 100 *Coming home*

What the above illustrate is the importance of normalcy in the life of the ex-offender, of trying again to be the person they once were or, perhaps, should have been (see Hunter, 2011 for further examples of these concerns expressed by white-collar offenders). In this way, the concerns highlighted here are little different from those of non-white-collar offenders who are trying to resettle in the community (Uggen *et al.*, 2004). The desire to find employment, to spend time with family and to recover community ties were all part of re-establishing oneself in society and were as germane for white-collar offenders as any other. White-collar offenders were therefore all future oriented upon their release from prison. In order to properly understand who they could be, however, they needed to make sense of who they were. The next section examines how they went about doing this and the information they drew upon to establish who they 'were'.

### Ex-prisoners in their post-release world

White-collar offenders used two 'cues' to determine their place in the world. They attended to stigma and came to terms with the realisation that some of their paths for the future were blocked, i.e. certain choices they might have had once were now denied them.

Although each of these newly released prisoners had a strong conception of themselves as a non-offender, many were to find that the world in which they found themselves did not confirm that conception. Consequently, the experience of stigma and blocked paths brought with them the realisation that their expectations might not be met.

Figure 5.2 indicates who experienced feelings of stigma and 'blocked' paths after their release from prison. The experience of stigma was measured by accounts of interactions with others that left the individual troubled in some manner due to that person's reaction towards them as someone who had a criminal conviction. The author suggesting they realised that future possibilities they had had were no longer available to them indicated a realisation of blocked paths. A 'blocked path' was one that was no longer available to offenders through no choice of their own. Former lawyer Colson for example had no desire to return to law and so he is not considered as experiencing a blocked path. As Figure 5.2 indicates, it was generally the case that where offenders experienced stigma, they also experienced blocked paths.

### *Stigma*

The questions about how the life would be lived continued for some time after release. Anticipated interactions were realised and ex-prisoners used these as sources of information as to who they now were and what this meant in terms of their future self. Sometimes they discovered that prosecution and time in prison adversely affected their relationships. Robert Berger was one who discovered that the reactions of others were such that he needed to 'restart' his life:

| Stigma | | Experienced | | Not experienced | |
|---|---|---|---|---|---|
| Blocked paths | Experienced | Aitken<br>Berger<br>Bond<br>Dean<br>Guppy | Laite<br>Lawson<br>Leeson<br>Minkow<br>Rose | | |
| | Not<br>experienced | | | Archer<br>Bakker<br>Christensen<br>Colson<br>Guppy | Levine<br>Magruder<br>Timity<br>Volpe |

*Figure 5.2* Offenders who experienced blocked paths and stigma

> The stigma of my incarceration weighed heavily on the outside, like a big dark cloud. I found myself cast adrift from old, pre-incarceration friends and associations. I finally decided to shut the door on my previous life, bury it once and for all, and begin anew.
>
> (Berger, 2003, 195)

Upon his release, John Dean received calls, letters and telegrams from well-wishers, as well requests for interviews. This attention boosted his self-esteem, which was fragile following the fall-out from Watergate:

> I began to feel strangely like a hero being welcomed home, instead of a released prisoner. While I tried to shrug it off, I liked the attention, particularly the flattery of the repeated job offers… These bolstered my self-confidence tremendously, and it needed the bolstering.
>
> (Dean, 1982, 13)

Dean's realisation that he was not being rejected by 'society' eased his concerns at first. However, just as positive encounters with others provided hope for the future, so negative encounters were taken as a barometer of general feeling. Dean's confidence was fragile, and his reaction to being asked to market pornographic films was drawn from the understanding that others saw him as the 'sort of person' who might be willing to do so (Dean, 1982, 15).

Dean was bothered by what the association with such films suggested about him as a person. The sordid nature of pornography (as he saw it) and the 'sleazy' reputation it had were being directly associated with him. Therefore, despite the initial euphoria of realising he was 'accepted', Dean was still painfully aware of how he might be judged by others and what that meant in terms of who 'he' was. Three weeks after his release he reflected on his interactions with others, making explicit the interaction between self, identity and social encounters. Dean was averse to seeing others, recognising that their perception of him contributed to who he was:

## 102   *Coming home*

I understand now that we judge ourselves to a greater extent than I've ever before admitted, through the eyes of others... *the mirror of my identity is partly in the eyes of others*, and I find I keep checking to see how I look.

(Dean, 1982, 19, emphasis added)

An awareness of who others thought they were was an important and sometimes painful source of information to offenders that helped them locate their place in the world. As the above demonstrates, offenders sometimes suffered the stigma that is often thought to accompany a conviction for a white-collar offence (Weisburd *et al.*, 2001; Benson and Kerley, 2001; Shover and Hochstetler, 2006). The painful reaction to being stigmatised was – as is the case for anyone – rooted in the contrast between a prevailing self-conception as an ex-offender and the image society imputed upon them (Fontana, 1984). Concrete situations, encounters and social interactions all contributed to an understanding of who they now were. As Maruna notes 'as social creatures we cannot know who we really "are" outside the social world of others' perceptions of us' (2012, 81) and so it was for white-collar offenders. Other information cues were more future oriented however.

### *Blocked paths*

The freedom of being able to act that ex-prisoners encountered upon their release was sometimes countered by the realisation that opportunities were denied to them because of their deviant past. These blocked paths are different from the experiences of stigma noted above because they frequently represent structural impediments upon one's actions. William Laite faced challenges in his attempts to re-establish himself as a man (see above, Laite, 1972, 227) through finding employment. Being unable to find work despite his qualifications left him distraught:

I would have taken any kind of job, I wasn't particular. I'd paid any debt I might have owed to society [in prison]. Still no luck. I could easily see how other ex-cons with less education might soon give up, turn again to crime, and return again to prison.

(Laite, 1972, 231)

Jonathan Aitken was prevented from following his plan of writing a biography of Charles Colson when he was refused a visa to enter the United States:

This development plunged me into a black mood of despair. No visa meant no book contract and no prospects of travel to a country I loved... If I could not write books for my US publishers, could I earn a living as an author? The answer was far from clear.

(Aitken, 2005, 186)

Invariably, it will be discovered that not all options are open to the ex-prisoner and that as convicted offenders they cannot engage in activities previously available to

*Coming home* 103

them. Therefore, some faced the reality that they would not be able to live the lives they wished. Because of their offence and the fall-out from it, some options were denied them.

To have opportunities denied one is difficult because such denies the ability to pursue life projects or realise particular selves. Three weeks after his release John Dean realised that in many US states he would have greatly reduced civil rights and, as a result, the confidence he had upon leaving prison that his life was going to continue as it had before Watergate might have been misplaced:

> I knew I had been deluding myself in feeling that I had come through Watergate unscathed, smelling like a rose...
>
> (Dean, 1982, 24)

Part of asking about the future necessarily involves considering the past. Dean recognised that he was no longer the man he had been upon his arrest. Dean's concerns reflected his preoccupation with his ability to be able to participate in civic activities. For Dean, formerly an active politician, an inability to participate in a valued role was particularly troubling.

Aitken, Berger, Bond, Laite, Lawson and Minkow made similar realisations to Dean. The realisation was that they were ex-offenders and being such brought with it a certain number of responsibilities and expectations as well as removing some opportunities. These opportunities were centred on returning to the lives they previously had. For Aitken, this focus was the realisation that he could not return to politics, an awareness that was brought to him by a discussion with former political colleague Michael Howard about politics.[5] Aitken lamented that:

> our conversation brought home to me he was talking about a way of life which had slipped away from me forever.
>
> (Aitken, 2005, 127)

More generally, those who found they had paths blocked experienced this as problematic because once again, it clashed with a strong sense of who they 'were' (as exemplified by Aitken, 2005, 127). All existents plan for the future, attempt to realise particular selves and strive for new opportunities to fulfil the self's need for new experience (Douglas, 1984), but such is often implicitly underpinned by a notion of unfettered opportunity. The earlier concerns expressed by offenders (Laite, 1972, 227; Archer, 2002, 87) over leaving prison and finding their way in the world indicated a desire to return to old spheres, and concerns with taking on pro-social roles. Knowing options were limited impacted upon that. Realising options are denied differs from experiencing stigma however. While stigma indicates who one is 'now' knowing what opportunities are available provides knowledge of who one can be and therefore contains a future oriented element other identity cues may lack. Despondency is a reaction to the realisation that the feelings of freedom and choice that characterised the euphoric period of release from prison have been shown to be false. Stigma and blocked paths forced a

104 *Coming home*

restructuring of the self and a reappraisal by offenders as to who they were. Further, they are denied the opportunity to achieve a specifically viewed future self, necessitating that a new self be envisioned.

## Discovering who one is

As white-collar offenders who were in prison neared the end of their sentences, their thoughts turned to what awaited them in the outside world. The majority of those white-collar offenders who did not admit their guilt experienced considerable anxiety in the period before release. Not admitting their wrongdoing put them in opposition to society's view of who they were (or we might more accurately say, put society in opposition to their view of who they were). Conversely, those who admitted their offence were more comfortable with the future, drawing upon other sources of support or content in the knowledge that having served a prison sentence they were then free to 'carry on'.

Release from prison forced offenders into making decisions and to constitute themselves through action by choosing how they would live in their post-release world. Simultaneously, white-collar offenders who were released from prison faced the need to reconcile the post release and resettlement experience with their own sense of self. Experiencing stigma and realising that paths were blocked were messages to offenders about themselves in the eyes of others. These made white-collar offenders aware of the changes that had taken place within their world, what this meant in terms of their future and how a change of their status had been forced upon them. Change was therefore frequently experienced as thrust upon offenders, making it particularly troubling. Resettlement represented a threat to the integrated functioning of offenders' selves (Douglas, 1984, 78).

That white-collar offenders experienced stigma while attempting to resettle puts them on common footing to other ex-prisoners (Uggen *et al.*, 2004; Richards and Jones, 2004). Some offenders had to reconcile the firm notion of themselves as a non-offender with the identity society presented them with through stigma and blocked paths and the place in the world that this consigned them to. It was a strong conception of who they were (i.e. a non-offender) that in part caused the angst they felt at suffering stigma. However, this strong self-conception was also the reason that many (as will be seen in the following chapter) did not identify the need for large changes in their perspective on life, in their beliefs and in the way they wished to live.

Post-release circumstances therefore provided several offenders with something of a reality-check, showing them they could not simply start their lives from the point they were at when they entered prison. The difficulty of coming into an unfamiliar world manifested itself in a desire to remain in a natural place (Buttimer, 1976) and draw meaning from sympathetic surroundings. Ultimately the rest of the world intruded on this peace, however, and white-collar offenders came to understand more fully who they now were in their post-release life. The stigma and blocked paths showing that the optimism some had regarding their future was perhaps unfounded. The following chapter will continue to explore issues of

*Coming home* 105

resettlement and identify how these offenders coped with the change in who they were, acted to 'live' in the post-release world and encountered success and failure as they attempted to do so.

In considering the possibility that white-collar offenders more generally and the offenders in this sample in particular enjoy far greater resources – both material and in terms of skills and social networks – than other offenders that help to ease their resettlement, a few points are relevant. The most obvious here is that several prisoners were anxious about their impending release from prison. Nothing in their pasts could prepare them for release. They had no stock of knowledge to help them understand their future.

The anxiety that some prisoners expressed prior to release is interesting because it might be thought that these white-collar offenders were far better resourced than the majority of their prisoner peers to make the transition from prison to the 'outside world'. For example, they might be thought to have skills that would make them attractive within the job market and increase their chances of gaining employment. Being in possession of such did not appear to be a source of comfort to all prisoners. Equally however, for some prisoners (e.g. Berger) there was hope to be drawn from past achievements, solace in knowing that they had been successful once and could be so again. The importance of being optimistic about one's future for successfully desisting from crime has been identified for offenders more generally (Farrall, 2002). Their successful pasts and the resources these gave this group of white-collar offenders might have been cause for optimism, encouraging a positive anticipation about their futures but, as is made clear, these were not guarantees of success.

Once release from prison was actually 'upon them', they may have felt, based on the skills they had and the knowledge they were in possession of as a result of previous employment, that there was some hope for the future. It is only possible to hope for something that is realistically possible (Simpson, 2004) and, if you have previously been a company owner (for example), you might reasonably hope that you will be again. Hoping for something and being able to achieve it are two different things however. Considering the observation that offenders experienced paths they wished to follow being 'blocked' also highlights this relationship between offenders' resources and their desire to achieve. Being able to identify particular routes to 'success' might be mediated by having the knowledge base from which to make a decision about one's future. That knowledge and skills base did not magically open all doors for offenders. They still faced impediments to their desires. It could also be suggested that these prisoners enjoyed financial resources and money worries were therefore not an immediate concern. This might be true of some in this sample (Colson, Archer and Levine for example), but these white-collar offenders are not uniform in this regard. Finding employment was still a concern for several and proved difficult for them to achieve (e.g. Minkow, Lawson).

To be clear, many of these offenders did enjoy success in quite a straightforward manner (as the next chapter explores) and we might suppose that this is because they were in 'fortunate' positions relative to other offenders. Equally, however,

## 106 *Coming home*

many did not and encountered trouble in establishing themselves and under-standing who they were following their release from prison. Although it is difficult to generalise too much, it seems unlikely that these experiences are a result of the peculiar characteristics of this sample and that they are are markedly different from other white-collar offenders.

It is clear from the above as well that any greater resources that these offenders possessed did not put them in an overly advantageous position compared to other prisoners when it came to considering release from prison. Pessimism and fear characterised the anticipation of release for some prisoners. Where concerns were expressed they were centred around the same issues that other prisoners report; worries over stigma that might be suffered and uncertainty over what life would hold (Uggen *et al.*, 2004; Burnett and Maruna, 2004). Upon release, the same problems that are reported as preoccupying ex-prisoners more generally were also of concern to these offenders (Visher and Travis, 2003; Farrall and Calverley, 2006). White-collar offenders were concerned with how they would live their lives so as to be active, contributing members of their communities. This urge was particularly strong for those like Laite who had been politicians prior to their imprisonment. White-collar offenders still had the same 'needs' as other offenders report.

## Notes

1   Visher and Travis (2011) summarise many of the challenges facing ex-prisoners.
2   Bond was released from prison prior to serving a second sentence. However, his first release was due to a successful appeal and as such was rather different from release for an offence he had been convicted of.
3   Mistress of Lord Nelson who, in 1814, went to France after her release from a debtor's prison, to escape creditors.
4   Playwright and novelist who went into self-imposed exile after his release from prison.
5   This conversation took place while Aitken was in prison. Nevertheless it made him realise that certain of his paths were blocked.

# 6 The journey to self

## Success, failure and change

The previous chapter explored the concerns white-collar offenders have immediately following their release from prison. However, as was demonstrated, resettlement was not something that was 'accomplished' in the immediate aftermath of release. Instead, offenders started to take a long-term view on their post-punishment lives. This chapter outlines their resettlement experiences in light of this long view. It begins by considering how many offenders returned to work similar to that they held prior to conviction. The focus then moves on to consider the goals offenders set for themselves and how they responded to the success and failure of endeavours, arguing that, for the self, success can sometimes be more troubling than failure. The chapter concludes by detailing how offenders understood how they had been changed by their experiences. Change was welcomed when they were active participants in such change, but for some the knowledge that they had been altered by forces outside their control was far more troubling.

### White-collar offenders and the post-punishment world

The autobiographies analysed here focus on different periods and to different degrees on resettlement. Some outline post-release life only briefly, and some devote considerable attention to attempts to establish meaningful lives in the wake of conviction. However, when supplemented with the media interviews many gave, it is possible to gain an accurate understanding of what resettlement was like for many in the sample. Table 6.1 shows the 23 offenders who form the sample and whether their autobiography included any account of their life once punishment (in all cases except Jett's this meant a prison sentence) was completed (*after autobiography*). It also indicates whether information on offenders could be obtained after the end of their autobiography. As can be seen from Table 6.1, there are 18 offenders whose autobiographies cover at least part of their lives after punishment, 17 for whom information about them after their book is identifiable and 12 for whom information about both their post-punishment experience and after the conclusion of their autobiography is available.

Special mention should be made of Joseph Jett, the only offender in the sample not to serve a prison sentence. In the strictest sense, resettlement is something undertaken following a prison sentence. For the purposes of this chapter however,

## 108 Success, failure and change

*Table 6.1* Offenders and information available

| Offender | After punishment | After autobiography | Offender | After punishment | After autobiography |
|---|---|---|---|---|---|
| Jonathan Aitken | Yes | Yes | Joseph Jett | Yes | Yes |
| Jeffery Archer | No | Yes | William Laite | Yes | No |
| Jim Bakker | Yes | Yes | Stephen Lawson | Yes | No |
| Jordan Belfort | No | Yes | Nick Leeson | Yes | Yes |
| Robert L. Berger | Yes | No | Dennis Levine | Yes | Yes |
| Alan Bond | Yes | Yes | Jeb Magruder | Yes | Yes |
| David Bullen | No | Yes | Barry Minkow | Yes | Yes |
| Nelson Christensen | Yes | No | Walter Pavlo | No | Yes |
| Charles Colson | Yes | Yes | Pete Rose | Yes | Yes |
| John Dean | Yes | Yes | Joseph Timilty | Yes | No |
| Darius Guppy | Yes | No | Tod Volpe | Yes | Yes |
| Clifford Irving | No | Yes | | | |

resettlement applies to all efforts offenders made to live in the wake of their conviction and punishment, whether it involved recovering from a custodial sentence or not. This recognises that, whatever form punishment takes, it is a significant event in the life and, as shall be seen, is an event that must be made sense of. The analysis concentrates on the extent to which white-collar offenders returned to familiar pursuits following punishment, how they reacted to succeeding and failing in their endeavours and how they experienced change in their sense of self.

## Returning to the familiar

Through media reports and the like, it is possible to make a comparison of how the lives offenders describe at the end of their books have changed since publication of their autobiographies. Where individuals could be traced, their activities are substantively the same as lives they describe at the end of their account. That is, they were still engaged in whatever activities they were at the time they were writing. Table 6.2 indicates this for 16 offenders who could be traced. *Pre-conviction* indicates their activity[1] before punishment. *Post-conviction* indicates their activity at the end of the individual's autobiography, with the latest autobiography used where more than one has been written, while *most recent activity* indicates their activity now as far as it is traceable through the media. The table also shows the source for this most recent profession.

As Table 6.2[2] indicates, many offenders undertook activities in spheres very similar to those they had occupied prior to their conviction. Nine[3] offenders were doing so at the time of their most recent autobiography. These nine plus a further two[4] were undertaking such activities when a consideration of more

*Table 6.2* Profession prior to offence, at end of book and recently (offenders who could be traced)

| Offender | Pre-conviction | Post-conviction (publication date) | Most recent activity (year) | Most recent activity source |
|---|---|---|---|---|
| Jonathan Aitken | Politician | Author (2005) | Author/prison commentator (2014) | Personal website (Aitken, 2014) |
| Jeffery Archer | Author/politician | Author (2005) | Author (2014) | Personal website (Archer, 2014) |
| Jim Bakker | Pastor | Pastor, television presenter (1996) | Pastor, television presenter, author (2014) | The Jim Bakker Show (2014) |
| Alan Bond | Business, tele-communications, property and brewing | Business (2003), mining and business consultancy | Businessman, investments | The Australian (2014) |
| Jordan Belfort | Business, stockbroker | Author (2007) | Business consultant, corporate speaker (2008) | Personal website (Belfort, 2014) |
| Charles Colson | Politician/lawyer | Author/member of Christian fellowship group (1979) | Author/member of Christian fellowship group (2012), Died 2012 | Charles Colson Legacy Fund (2014) |
| John Dean | Politician | Political commentator commentator (author) (1982) | Political commentator (author) (2014) | Justia (2014) |
| Clifford Irving | Author | Author (1997) | Author (2014) | Personal website (Irving, 2014) |
| Joseph Jett | Business, bond trader | Business (1999), hedge fund manager | Business (2013), private investment, reputation management | Website (Jett, 2014) |
| Nick Leeson | Business, futures trader | Business (2005), commercial director, public speaker | Business (2014), corporate advisory company, public speaker | Personal website (Leeson, 2014) |
| Dennis Levine | Business, investment banker | Business (1989), financial consultancy | Business (2007), financial consultancy | Fortune (2005b) |
| Jeb Magruder | Politician | Christian fellowship group (1978) | Minister, died 2014 | Lexington Herald (2014) |
| Barry Minkow | Business, company owner | Pastor/fraud investigator (2005) | Pastor/fraud investigator, Prisoner (2014) | Fortune (2014) |
| Walter Pavlo | Business, asset recovery | Public speaking on business ethics (2007) | Public speaking on business ethics, consultancy to prisoners (2014) | Etika (2014) |
| Pete Rose | Baseball player/coach | Business (2004), restaurant owner, baseball memorabilia | Business (2014), baseball memorabilia, public appearances | Personal website (Rose, 2014) |
| Tod Volpe | Art dealer | N/A (2006) | Art consultant (2006) | Personal website (Volpe, 2012) |

110  *Success, failure and change*

recent engagements is undertaken. Although, with the exception of Archer, Bond and Irving none of the activities compared in Table 6.2 is identical for any offender, it is suggested that they are similar enough for all that they suggest a return to the spheres that engaged the offender prior to their offence. Pavlo, for example, although not returning to asset recovery, is still engaged with the world of business through the talks he gives on business ethics, using his own case as an example of the potential pitfalls of business. Similarly, Dean, a politician prior to his sentence became a political commentator after it. He therefore stayed close to the political world he 'knew', although he engaged with it in a different way.

The observation that so many of these offenders returned to the spheres that occupied them prior to offending can be explained in part by a desire to recapture what they previously knew and had the skills to undertake. It also indicates that many desired to return to their previous lives. In sum therefore, what Table 6.2 indicates is punishment did not substantially impede their lives. This is not to say the transition from offence to punishment to the lives they wanted was smooth. The broader context of resettlement, as discussed here, was a time of uncertainty for white-collar offenders as they attempted to forge the lives they wanted to. The concern here is on how white-collar offenders lived in the aftermath of their punishment and how reflections on their past were related to this.

## Succeeding and failing

The previous chapter highlighted that part of the resettlement process involves deciding what will be done with life in the aftermath of punishment. This section examines how white-collar offenders responded to episodes of succeeding and failing as they tried to make an existence for themselves. Unable to simply pick up their lives exactly where they left off – notwithstanding that many eventually resettled successfully – all were faced with the challenge of achieving their desires, whether expressed in concrete terms, such as starting a new business or, more abstractly, such as having a desire to do something to help the community one 'hurt'.

'Succeeding' and 'failing' are potentially problematic value-laden concepts. While related to individuals' goals and therefore an expression of who we wish to be (Simpson, 2004), identifying what such goals may be is rarely straight-forward. Resettlement brings with it many instances of succeeding and failing. Hostile and friendly encounters with others and the realisation that the offender is able to cope (or not) in their post-release world are all examples of succeeding and failing in as much as they are related to goals individuals have and hopes about particular outcomes. Succeeding and failing may therefore come in many guises. Plans that individuals have may be expressed in rather abstract terms such as 'finding redemption', 'giving something back to the community' or 're-establishing myself'. Even seemingly concrete and easily measured goals such as 'gaining employment' are likely to bring with them a number of caveats before success can be declared. It is not the case that literally 'any job' will do for

*Success, failure and change* 111

example. It will almost certainly have to generate enough income to provide at least partial support for the offenders' family if they have one. All of those who write about the period following their incarceration, and many of those who do not, had an idea of what they wanted from their lives after their release from prison. Such plans were focused upon long-term issues regarding the life and what was to be done with it.

### *Failing*

Four offenders describe failing. That is, plans they made did not come to fruition or anticipated outcomes did not materialise. These four are outlined in Table 6.3 along with their attempted goals.

The endeavours in Table 6.3 are highlighted because they represent a concern with regaining an aspect of the life that was previously enjoyed and were an important part of who the individual was. Laite's desire to return to run for election was a result of realising how much he enjoyed the political sphere (1972, 236). Aitken's was predicated on regaining a life he thought 'had slipped away from me forever' (2005, 127). Berger and Minkow both defined themselves in terms of their businesses' success. Minkow (1995, 145) cites the pride he has in his achievements in building his company. For Berger, starting a business and making it a success was deemed necessary if he was to avoid having a 'mediocre life' (Berger, 2003, 140).

Aitken and Laite's 'failing' was their inability to gain political office once more. Aitken's desire to return to politics as a prospective Conservative Parliamentary candidate in his former constituency was preceded by a petition signed by party members, which helped to convince him that there was support for a political comeback (Aitken, 2005, 236). Laite's circumstances of his potential return to politics as Mayor of Macon County, Georgia, were somewhat different. Opinion polls suggested that he would be unlikely to be elected and yet for Laite such a realisation was not a deterrent when set against his desire to return to politics and the good he hoped it would help him achieve in his community (Laite, 1972, 236). For both Laite (1972, 236) and Aitken (2005, 127), the desire to return to politics was predicated upon wanting to recapture a part of the life that had previously been central for them. In addition, for Laite, there were other reasons for wanting to return:

*Table 6.3* White-collar offenders who cite failing and their goals

| *Offender* | *Goal* |
| --- | --- |
| Aitken | Political office |
| Berger | New business: car hire company |
| Laite | Political office |
| Minkow | New business: tyre company |

112 *Success, failure and change*

> I thought that as Mayor I could redeem myself in the public's eyes while doing all I could to repay the community that [had] been so good to me in my business and personal life before the trouble in Big Springs [where his offence took place].
>
> (Laite, 1972, 236)

Laite therefore wanted to be seen to be doing good, thereby demonstrating that he had changed. Consequently civic reintegration is a concern for white-collar offenders as it is for others attempting to resettle (Uggen *et al.*, 2004; Farrall and Calverley, 2006; Farrall *et al.*, 2014). What is also apparent is a concern with reparations, 'paying back' those hurt by the offence (Maruna, 2001). The making of amends to the community is part of offenders' attempts to redeem themselves, part of an ongoing attempt to build a positive sense of self. Election to office would also act as a form of certification for offenders (Meisenhelder, 1985), affirming that others acknowledge their change. Engagement with community based work may be identified as a way in which one can be seen to be publicly atoning for one's past. By being seen to act as reformed, such reformation may be recognised and affirmed by one's community.

Barry Minkow wanted to set up another business, aiming to learn from the mistakes he had made previously in business that had led to his imprisonment. His motivations for doing so were embedded in the context of the aftermath of separation from his wife. His focus on starting a new company was driven in part by the feeling that it would to help him rebuild his marriage but also by his concerns with the management of his reputation:

> there were the many skeptics who I was convinced thought I was a failing. I had to prove them wrong.
>
> (Minkow, 2005, 224)

Although Aitken, Laite, Berger and Minkow failed, however, reactions to the failing of such initiatives do not appear to be commensurate with their importance as described. The denial of opportunity to engage with valued roles is noted as being existentially difficult (Shaffir and Kleinknecht, 2005, 714; Brewer *et al.*, 1999) as the associated trappings and connotations for the identity may be missed for some time, leaving a large amount of 'role residual' (Ebaugh, 1988, 175–176). Being denied a return to political office like Aitken and Laite would be expected to be particularly difficult in this regard as a result of the forced removal of the associations made with their political role. Minkow is the only person to express his regret at the failure of his venture by simply stating, 'To my extreme disappointment, the tire company failed' (2005, 227).

For Laite, his failure to be elected as mayor is stated with a brief 'I lost the Democratic primary' (1972, 236). This was then followed by continued efforts to gain employment, although this time outside politics. Aitken describes his failure to be adopted as a candidate as unproblematic. His 'feelings of disappointment were fleeting' (2005, 237).

*Success, failure and change* 113

In the aftermath of failing however there was a restructuring of what endeavours meant. The importance placed upon them was lessened as the focus of the life shifted to other concerns. For Minkow, who was also pastor of a church in San Diego, an email from one of his congregation needing help made him realise what was really important and that he needed to take time to rebuild himself and take stock of his life. His attempted venture as a company owner was merely a reason to avoid focusing on his self:

> Instead of going through the normal process of healing, I had chosen to run.
>
> (Minkow, 2005, 229)

Aitken was similarly quite sanguine about his failure to re-enter the political sphere,

> I was philosophical about being rejected from my old politics because I was getting so much fulfilment from my new passions. Returning to the House of Commons might have been exciting, but then not going back to politics would allow me, as the cliché has it, to spend more time with my family.
>
> (2005, 237)

Failure then, so it seems, is temporary, with any disappointment transient. One explanation for this may be a function of autobiographical accounts. The time between experiencing failure and writing about it means that a specific incidence of failing can be viewed within the context of the life as a whole and set against a life that is identified as essentially 'successful'. Further, it is important for the self that an endeavour is not, once it has failed, conceived of as the only viable future. To do this and to have this future 'taken' by failing would present a significant challenge to the self and attempts to achieve a viable future self (Yalom, 1980). The failure of an endeavour perceived as the only viable chance for a successful life would risk being ontologically crippling. This challenge is best avoided by recasting it as something else, hence the shift in focus to other plans. New future projects are conceived in the wake of failure and such failure is then recast appropriately.

To cope with their failing offenders were, to some extent, able to recast the previously valued pursuits as not particularly important. Such 'divestment' (Brewer *et al.*, 1999) of valued roles allowed them to view other areas of their life and the roles associated with them as equally important. Failing is easier to cope with when other possibilities are identifiable and in particular when they are recognised as being viable. Aitken, Laite and Minkow[5] presented failure as a discrete event. It was something that 'happened' rather than something that was ongoing, one event in a life in which other projects were present. As a specific event, it was something that they could leave behind and move on from.

114   *Success, failure and change*

### Succeeding

The white-collar offenders shown in Table 6.2 eventually came to enjoy what might be considered conventional success.[6] Their autobiographies present themes of hardship and the ordeal of punishment by the criminal justice system but of ultimate survival and triumph against this. 'Succeeding' is celebrated in the closing pages of autobiographies, as part of the reflection on the life and also in the interviews given to the media after punishment. This section analyses how the success of specific endeavours was responded to by offenders and the reactions to the fruition of plans made as included in accounts. Table 6.4, indicates only those offenders who wrote about striving to achieve certain goals and the attainment of these. As Table 6.4 shows, these are few. This is partly a function of some offenders' autobiographies, that may not cover a sufficient period for success to emerge. Where success has been achieved but attaining it is not deemed worthy of mention in accounts it is not included. For example, former investment banker Dennis Levine, following his release from prison formed a financial consultancy. However, the formation of this agency is given nothing but the most cursory of mentions in his autobiography (Levine, 1991, 383). While success appears to have come to Levine, it is not included here because it is not apparent that it was significant (or perhaps, significantly imperilled) enough to be worthy of detailed description. The success that was worth recounting seems to be that related to ventures far removed from offenders' previous lives.

For, Minkow, Colson and Magruder, success was related to their attempts to serve God, following their conversions to Christianity. Similarly, Aitken's desire to study theology at Oxford University came about as a result of his own conversion and was accompanied by a desire to further understand the 'journey' of spiritual change he felt he was undertaking.

The four who described succeeding outline new enterprises far removed from their previous spheres. This may explain why their accounts of succeeding differ from that of others who returned to familiar practices such as Levine. Their ventures were into unknown territory and as such committed them to very different future selves and different life projects (Sartre, 1958, 147; Craib, 1976, 28–30; Hayim, 1996, 74). These projects were bound up with particular goals offenders identified and in this way success was tied to the self in a far more tenuous way than might be the case where the future project one strives for has a familiarity that is safer.

*Table 6.4* White-collar offenders who cite succeeding and their endeavours

| *Offender* | *Endeavour* |
|---|---|
| Aitken | Gain entry to university |
| Colson | Form a Christian fellowship group |
| Magruder | Employment as vice president of Christian group |
| Minkow | Employment as a pastor |

Jeb Magruder exemplifies how the success of personal goals was attended to by offenders. Following a conversion to Christianity Magruder, upon his release from prison, wanted to 'arouse that "sense of God's presence" through whatever I did for a living' (1978, 197). A key feature of any employment was that it would have to be in keeping with his identity as a Christian. He identified that the best way he could do this was by joining Christian service organisation Young Life and applied to join as a Vice President, hoping to use his skills in administration to aid the running of the organisation (Magruder, 1978, 200).

Magruder was given encouragement from his interview with Young Life, but became anxious when the directors expressed concern at a convicted offender gaining a position with them. Magruder waited three months to be offered the job with Young Life, an anxious time, because 'I had the feeling God wanted me to go to Young Life' (Magruder, 1978, 201). Magruder's new identity as a Christian was intimately related to his goal leading him to reject other offers of work (1978, 201). Attaining the job demonstrated for him that he could live his life as a Christian, that his new way of 'being Jeb Magruder' was viable 'Now I knew where I was going – and it was where God wanted me to be' (Magruder, 1978, 203). He realised that he could do work consistent with his new identity as a Christian, thereby 'arousing a sense of God's presence' (Magruder, 1978, 203).

It is unlikely to be a coincidence that all those who describe succeeding also describe experiencing radical change in their self-identity, as will be shown later. The accounts of their success suggest the anxiety present in attempting to change and in living that change. As Magruder's example demonstrates, succeeding showed that a new life could be led, different from that which they knew but fulfilling nevertheless and that therefore their future self was attainable, as is the case for other offenders who take pleasure in living a new life (Giordano *et al.*, 2002; Farrall *et al.*, 2014, Chapter 6). For those who had linked their ventures to higher goals such as serving God, succeeding also served to confirm the validity of their fledgling belief systems. What succeeding engendered was the feeling that they could again achieve their desires, providing further hope for the future.

In outlining failing as it was experienced by some offenders, the nature of it as an event was highlighted. Aitken's example indicates that succeeding is more of a process. There was no one joyous moment where 'succeeding' had been achieved for Aitken in his attempt to gain a place at Oxford University. Instead, each small success brought another test. His success at gaining entrance to Oxford brought with it anxiety:

> Would Wycliffe Hall be the right place for me? Would I get along with my fellow students? Would I be intellectually and theologically capable of meeting the required standards? Was this new chapter of my life in accordance with God's will?
>
> (Aitken, 2005, 189)

Aitken's 'failure' to re-enter politics therefore caused less anxiety than his success, illustrating that each goal attained merely brings with it the chance to progress

116 *Success, failure and change*

further and adds another goal to be achieved. In this sense, a self is never fully realised, constantly growing and projected into the future (Sartre, 1958; Heidegger, 1926). This in turn brings concerns over the self to the fore. Hopes are redirected, refocused and made relevant to a new future self. Succeeding brought about change in Aitken's life and change in the life can be unsettling, even if it is welcome (Corr, 2002). In a similar manner to failing, with succeeding the meaning of events is reconstructed as the life project is re-evaluated in the light of changes in the world.

As for all existents, the goals offenders pursued were an expression of the future selves they identified following their punishment. They were part of offenders' establishment of who they wanted to be. For those who describe success in particular, their ventures were concerned with confirming new ways of life, as if the venture represented an 'experiment' with the new identity. This is in keeping with offenders more generally who are attempting to resettle and establish themselves in the community (Uggen *et al.*, 2004). The different reactions to failing and succeeding reflect this. The characterisation of failing as an event versus succeeding as a process is in keeping with the notion of the self as future oriented and constantly becoming (Fontana, 1984). Dwelling on failing or viewing succeeding as 'the end' denies the opportunity for future growth. To dwell on failing is to condemn oneself to having no other viable future. Similarly, to dwell on succeeding would mean there is no opportunity for growth of the self.

## Responding to changes in the self

To exist is to change, to partake of experiences and to grow, the sense of self developing over the life. Therefore, being changed by the experiences they have is something that is a constant possibility for all individuals. Particularly 'extreme' events, such as punishment for an offence and the way the aftermath of this is dealt with, make change all the more possible. For these white-collar offenders, the changes that took place in their lives through the circumstances of their arrest and punishment were reflected in changes in outlook on life or their values and a shift in their sense of self.

The focus of this section is the extent to which individuals were aware of a change in the self and the way in which such change was perceived and attended to. Change was identified by the individual citing a new way of life or living compared to the period prior to their offending. It was also identified by them making reference to a new outlook on life and/or lessons learnt in prison or after reflection upon their offence that made them view their life differently to the way they had before.

Change is characterised here along different dimensions. First, there is the extent of change. That is, is change characterised as substantial or partial? Second, there is the engagement with change. Some actively sought and embraced change, making efforts to be different and committing to different selves. Other accounts present offenders as passive recipients of such change, it being something 'done to' them. Such groupings should not be taken as indicating hard and fast 'types' of change. Rather they represent a means of ordering the accounts given by those whose books are considered here. What is of relevance is tracking change as it was experienced by individuals. Table 6.5 presents those offenders for whom information about their change is known and whether change for them was substantial or partial.

One means of highlighting the distinction between those who have been identified as undergoing substantial and partial change is to say that substantial change represents a commitment towards being a different person, engaging in new activities to underscore this. In contrast, partial change represents the absence of offending behaviour, without any large commitment to changing how the life is led post-punishment relative to before conviction. The experience of offending and being punished for it may leave a sense of heightened awareness of who one is and consequently of some change in who the offender feels they are or wants to be, but in a way that can be incorporated into existing lifestyles.

### *New lives*

Of the 23 white-collar offenders, six underwent what is termed here a substantial change, taking on very different perspectives to life compared to that which they held previously. In addition, all underpinned these new perspectives with new ways of living. Substantial change therefore is change in thought that is reflected in a change in deed. Table 6.6 shows these offenders, the activities that occupied them before their change and those that subsequently did, based on the most recent information available. In some cases, the old life had a natural relationship to the new, even as it was different. Minkow's new life was predicated on 'undoing' the types of crime he had once perpetrated for example.[7] For the rest, their new lives are encapsulated in new beliefs they have that underpin who they now are. Once again, the 'lives' reported here are not meant to demean offenders by focusing on one aspect of their existence. Rather, they describe particularly important facets of individuals' identities, as recounted by them.

Charles Colson is one offender who experienced substantial change. Shortly after leaving prison, Colson spoke to former AmericanPresident Richard Nixon, to whom he was formerly. The conversation made him wish briefly that he could return to politics:

*Table 6.5* Offenders who reported substantial and partial change

| Substantial change | Partial change | |
|---|---|---|
| Aitken | Archer | Jett |
| Colson | Bakker | Laite |
| Lawson | Berger | Leeson |
| Magruder | Bond | Levine |
| Minkow | Dean | Timilty |
| | Guppy | Volpe |
| | Irving | |

118   *Success, failure and change*

*Table 6.6* White-collar offenders who cite substantial change

| Offender | 'Old' life | 'New' life |
| --- | --- | --- |
| Aitken | Politician | Christian |
| Colson | Politician | Christian |
| Lawson | Estate agent | Christian |
| Magruder | Politician | Christian |
| Minkow | Businessman | Christian, anti-fraud investigator |

> For an instant my heart skipped as the longing returned for the old relationship, to advise a President, even a discredited one.
>
> (Colson, 1979, 28)

Colson's Christian faith, however, developed and strengthened by his time in prison made him realise that he had changed too much to return to that aspect of his life:

> My affection for [Nixon] was strong; what had happened to him and his presidency wouldn't change things between us, but what had happened inside me [his conversion] would.
>
> (Colson, 1979, 28)

While in prison, Stephen Lawson addressed a parole hearing and attempted to underline the change that had taken place within him, emphasising his 'rebirth' as a Christian, his repentance of his sins and that his time in prison had been used productively to strengthen his burgeoning Christian faith (Lawson, 1992, 159–160). In identifying himself as born again, Lawson referenced not just how he felt, but how he had acted. He had studied Christianity and employed its tenets to help him live his life. He also cited his new life, asserting that the 'situational ethics' that led him to offend were no longer tenets he lived by (1992, 178).

Change is not linked to punishment in these accounts (all these offenders served prison sentences). Rather, where the role of prison (for example) is mentioned, it is in providing the *opportunity* for reflection on life, emphasising the importance of certain aspects of the life over others. At the end of the 'journey', these five men were left – at least as far as they were concerned – as very different people, different in the way they felt and thought about themselves and also in the way they acted.

Perhaps unsurprisingly, the five who are identified as experiencing substantial change within their lives changed at least in part within the context of a religious belief system. Beyond this reporting of change, all demonstrated the impact of a different outlook through their engagement in rather different lifestyles from those they had before. All engaged with activity consistent with their Christian faith. Minkow became a pastor and Aitken renounced his prideful past, studying theology at university and becoming president of Christian Solidarity Worldwide. Colson and Lawson became engaged in prison fellowship groups that aimed to teach prisoners about Christianity. Undertaking a change in the self might be rather the point of religious conversion. New belief systems provide adherents with vocabularies they may draw upon to make sense of their experiences and values systems that require new commitments. Consequently, religious conversion is considered in more detail in a later chapter.

### *Partial change*

Thirteen of these white-collar offenders are identified as undergoing what is termed here as 'partial' change. They are shown in Table 6.5. For them, the desire for such wholesale changes to their life as the above accounts suggest were deemed unnecessary. Those offenders cited as undergoing total change adopted rather different views of the world and took on activities commensurate with these. In contrast, those who changed only partially began to think differently about specific 'areas' of their lives. Dennis Levine, while still in prison, recognised that the culture of competition on Wall Street was what had led to him to commit insider-trading offences. He realised his imprisonment could be a positive event:

> Dennis, I said to myself, this is a blessing in disguise. You need this withdrawal [from the finance industry]. You were hooked, just as surely as any junkie, alcoholic or compulsive gambler. That's the answer. You overdosed on deals. And you were not about to stop until someone caught you, or until the irresistible lure of the action on [Wall] Street killed you.
>
> (Levine, 1991, 372)

Similarly, John Dean desired change in some aspects of his life. He had hoped that the process of writing about his experiences might lead to a sense of catharsis and a lessening of his feelings of guilt. He eventually realised that this would not occur:

> What had been achieved, however, was perspective. Reducing yourself to paper gives you a picture of yourself that is far sharper in focus than all those thoughts that rumble loosely in your head. Seeing myself on paper made me realize that, in many ways, I had not changed.
>
> (Dean, 1982, 85)

Dean felt he was essentially who he had always been. He did, however, have a greater understanding of himself as a person. His past was placed into perspective by this realisation of who he was.

Former futures trader Nick Leeson also made reference to a change in perspective. Reflecting ten years after his offences, Leeson felt little remorse at the collapse of Barings Bank, which his unauthorised trading had inadvertently brought about. Instead, his change was predicated on the realisation that his actions had impacted upon those close to him:

> I've drawn a very clear line now where that risk [in helping others] has become personal. I'd never overstep that, as the impact on my family would be

## 120   *Success, failure and change*

unimaginable. Throughout the collapse of the bank I was ensconced in a small cell and it wasn't until I was released that I realised quite how much impact my actions had on those people around me.

(Leeson, 2005, 111)

Leeson's change exemplifies the notion of partial change as it is conceptualised here. He cites a greater awareness of how his behaviour affects others, but does not otherwise identify himself as actually having changed (Leeson, 2005, 40). Nor does he cite a new way of living his life. Following his release from prison, Leeson stayed largely within what might be broadly termed the 'business' sphere, becoming CEO of a soccer club for six years, resigning in 2011 (Leeson, 2014). In 2013 he joined GDP, a debt advisory practice (Financial Times, 2014). From this, it is clear that Leeson did not adopt a radically new outlook on life unlike those who underwent substantial change. Those who underwent 'partial change', like Leeson were more concerned with ensuring they did not repeat their past mistakes. They were more focused on being the person they 'were' than living a new life as 'someone else'.

Clifford Irving typifies this desire to return to the former life following his offence. Irving, a writer, had attempted to defraud his publishers by claiming to be writing a biography of reclusive billionaire Howard Hughes, which was actually a work of fiction. In a radio interview on the show *Wired for Books* in 1984, ten years after his release from prison, Irving was asked if he was tired of people's continued interest in his offence:

[Laughing] Yes I certainly am. But you can't blame me. If you'd done something ten or twelve years ago that you weren't particularly proud of and everyone kept asking you over and over again for details you'd say 'for God's sakes leave me alone. It's done, I've paid my dues'. And I did.

(Wired for Books, 1984)

Although Irving viewed his offence as wrong, it was not something symptomatic of a problem with his life in general. It was instead something he was not proud of and wanted to leave in the past. Where offences are anomalous as an indication of who one is, they do not prompt a desire for wholesale change in the life or the deep soul searching that characterises accounts of complete change. The meaning placed upon it can be incorporated into a perspective that sees the person as essentially good. Irving's example highlights what unites the men who underwent partial change. They fundamentally wanted to be and felt as if they were the same people they had always been. Five of these men – Archer, Bond, Laite, Bakker, and Jett – considered themselves innocent of any wrongdoing.

Four others – Berger, Guppy, Leeson, Timilty – accepted the illegal nature of their actions but qualified them in some manner. Berger suggests that the bribery he was convicted of is common-place, occurring in all businesses (Berger, 2003, 94). Darius Guppy accepted that his attempt to defraud insurers Lloyd's of London was illegal, but felt it was justified because Lloyds' actions had previously bankrupted his father (1996, 301). Leeson accepted his part in the collapse of

## Success, failure and change    121

Barings Bank but asserted that the autonomy he was given and bank's inadequate security measures made its collapse inevitable (2005, 73) while Joseph Timilty's assertion following his conviction was that 'I may be guilty of stupidity...but not conspiracy' (1997, 31). Although sorry for the effect their actions had had on those close to them, these men felt no remorse for their offending.

The final five who underwent partial change – Dean, Irving, Levine, and Volpe – all accepted their guilt without qualification. They appeared to feel however that their offence did not represent who they 'really' were. As Irving's example shows, his offence, as far as he was concerned, was not something that defined him and Levine concurs, feeling that having served his prison sentence he was 'forgiven' (Levine, 1991, 375).

Feeling they had done no wrong – or at least, no substantive wrong – meant that there was no desire for wholesale change on the part of those who experienced partial change. They wished to be the people they had always been.

### Agency and change

In addition to substantial and partial change there is also the consideration of how change was attended to by those who experienced it. Some offenders were active in bringing about change in their lives. Change for these men was solicited and made welcome. It was embraced as an opportunity for growth. In contrast, for others, change was less actively sought or experienced as forced onto offenders. The former are classed here as experiencing active change, the latter, passive change. Table 6.7 shows those offenders who reported active and passive change.

#### *Seeking to change*

Eight of the white-collar offenders considered here sought out change in their lives. For Charles Colson, the arrest of his son for possession of drugs highlighted that he himself had been lacking as a father because of the time he had spent in politics:

*Table 6.7* Offenders who reported active and passive change

| Reported active change | Reported passive change |
| --- | --- |
| Aitken | Archer |
| Colson | Bakker |
| Dean | Berger |
| Magruder | Bond |
| Minkow | Guppy |
| Lawson | Irving |
| Levine | Jett |
| Volpe | Laite |
| | Leeson |
| | Timilty |

## 122  *Success, failure and change*

> Remorse flooded me as I realized how much four years in the White House, two years of embroilment in the Watergate upheaval and seven months in prison had kept [my son and me] apart. I had not been the father I should have been. *That would have to change.*
>
> (Colson, 1979, 25, emphasis added)

Dennis Levine realised change was necessary when he identified how he had become drawn by the lure of money on Wall Street. This desire to make more than other traders was something he had not recognised in himself at the time and he felt that it had led him to commit insider trading:

> I burned with anger at my own blindness. *I had to change my priorities.* I had to regain control of my own life.
>
> (Levine, 1991, 372, emphasis added)

In seeking change, former offenders sought to be someone 'better'. Those who desired change all noted aspects of their lives which led to them to 'fall'. Negative aspects of the self, such as problems with their view of the world or the impact their life might have had on relationships with significant others, may suddenly be thrown into light in the aftermath of a conviction. The feelings elicited might have served as the catalyst for change and where this occurred it resulted from such negative feelings of anger provoked by previous actions. What accompanied such feelings was a notion of how the person might be redeemed, made 'better' in their own eyes. As Colson's and Levine's examples show, they identified where they had gone 'wrong' and wished to rectify that. Part of committing to a better future self was also a way of reconciling the shame that they felt at having been responsible for the way their lives had impacted others, as Colson indicates above (1979, 25).

The identification by these actively changing offenders of the 'wrong' aspects of their lives links their reflections on their offending to the experience of shame and its importance as a catalyst for change (Manion, 2002). Those offenders who were active in seeking change, to a greater or lesser degree all felt ashamed of their pasts. This prompted them to attempt to take steps to bring about change in who they were, either by identifying completely new ways of living like Colson (who, it should be recalled from earlier, changed substantially) or eradicating those 'deficient' aspects of themselves, as Levine did. This allowed them to show that they were not 'that sort of person' any longer, creating space between themselves as an offender and the person they wished to become.

### *Receiving change*

To this point the discussion has focused on change that was sought and welcomed by offenders. It was a means of making the individual better by changing their 'faulty' thinking or giving a new focus to their life that would prevent them from repeating the mistakes of the past. In contrast, ten offenders, as shown in Table 6.7, describe their relationship with change as rather passive, with change thrust upon them.

*Success, failure and change*   123

What, by and large, unites the offenders who experienced change as a passive experience is a denial of any wrongdoing on their part, either because they themselves felt they had done nothing substantially 'wrong' or because they denied any offence had ever taken place. Only Irving accepted his guilt but, as already noted, felt he had 'done his time'. Of the remaining nine Berger, Guppy, Leeson and Timilty's justifications for their offending are noted above, while the final five – Archer, Bakker, Bond, Jett and Laite – denied any offence on their part. It was indicated above for those who actively sought out change that negative feelings regarding past actions – frequently their offence – were the motivation to actively seek change. Conversely, and as these ten offenders suggest, feeling that no wrong has been committed – or in Irving's case feeling that on has been punished – means that little attempt will be made to change who one is. These offenders displayed no shame at their pasts.

The uniqueness of the experience of conviction and punishment, however, would inevitably have changed offenders in some ways. A change in identity that is not actively sought may only be noticed retrospectively, acknowledged after some time. Passive change, although not anticipated is not always unwelcome. Instead, the experiences that have been lived contribute to a new perspective on the world that is construed as beneficial and giving a sense of greater importance to the life, as is evidenced by considering Alan Bond. Businessman Bond was sentenced to prison for failing to act honestly as a company director and although he pleaded guilty for financial and health reasons (Bond, 2003, 285–290) he denied wrongdoing. Notwithstanding that prison was 'brutal' (2003, 299), Bond reflected on his life three years after his release, and in particular how his experiences related to his new work as a business consultant:

> The big bonus for my clients is that I am a better businessman today because I am now able to temper my views of the business world with my more recent experiences – I've got the yin and the yang, the experience of succeeding and failing.
>
> (Bond, 2003, 313)

It is important that what Bond had learnt had relevance to what he wished to do with his life i.e. returning to the business sphere, which he was involved in prior to his imprisonment. The changes he reports were assimilated by his self and could be made consistent with the way he wished to live his life. His experiences of conviction and imprisonment, although distressing, were made meaningful and simultaneously consistent with his overall sense of self in this way.

Similarly, Darius Guppy reported feeling he was an 'improved' person as a result of his experiences. Reporting a conversation with his co-defendant Ben Marsh in the first week after his release from prison:

> 'Darry' he told me, 'although I wish it had been a shorter experience, in many ways I'm almost grateful for what happened. I'm far less concerned with the trivial things in life that used to occupy so much of my time and I feel a

## 124 *Success, failure and change*

stronger person'. 'I agree', I replied. 'Although like you, I wish it hadn't been for quite so long'.

(Guppy, 1996, 300)

Guppy's example demonstrates that the offenders who viewed passive change as positive did so to make sense of the experiences they had undergone and identify a purpose within them relative to their lives as a whole. Not all who experienced passive change found it to be such a positive experience however. Some characterised their change as inflicted upon them, making them somehow less than they were. These are shown in Table 6.8, and the four offenders describe the changes they underwent as representing a threat to their self.

For these four offenders, the threat originated in the prison environment they were forced to endure during their sentence. They feared they would be changed by their time in prison, becoming somehow 'less' than the person they were when they entered. Deterioration of their faculties or the notion that they will become like 'other' prisoners was a source of worry, as was the concern that the life they had prior to their sentence was now unattainable, as was explored earlier. Such concerns may persist after the prison sentence has ended. Joseph Timilty considered this on his flight home from prison:

It is a lifetime since the day four months ago when I left Boston... it's never going to be the same, not for me, anyway. They [the department of corrections] have made sure of that. Everyone in jail changes. But how have I changed, and how much?

(Timilty, 1997, 240–241)

For Robert Berger, the realisation that change had taken place was underlined by the contrast between the life he had before prison and that after it:

Often, I think about the past... and of the once powerful and wealthy man I once was. It all seems like such a long time ago, much more than a lifetime.

(Berger, 2003, 195)

*Table 6.8* Offenders who experienced passive change and their reaction

| Change reported as positive | Change as negative |
| --- | --- |
| Bakker | Archer |
| Bond | Berger |
| Guppy | Laite |
| Irving | Timilty |
| Jett | |
| Leeson | |

*Success, failure and change* 125

Timilty's concern was that he had been changed from within by the experiences he had endured while incarcerated. The realisation that the world had changed around them also had a bearing on change as it was experienced passively. The previous chapter showed that leaving prison was viewed as representing a fresh start to life. However, as Timilty and Berger indicate, there was a less positive aspect to such a feeling. The notion that a lifetime separates the man they were from the man they are emphasises the significance of their experience, underlining that life will now be different. The place of these men in the world had changed without them wishing it to and, in this, their identity failed to fit with their sense of who they were (Fontana, 1984).

### *Healing wounds and the passage of time*

It may be that the passage of time diminishes punishment's threat to the self. The four who write about change as a deterioration of their self all have accounts that finish as their prison sentence does. Given time, the majority – if not all – of these four might come to see their experience in a more positive light, in much the same way that the other cases did. This possibility is suggested by considering Jeffrey Archer. Archer's prison diaries show an acute awareness of the possibility of change, the fear that he may become like 'other convicts' and also the difficulties of prison life, devoid of any positives he may be able to take from his situation. Writing 19 days into the 14 months he served in prison, he expresses an awareness of the possibility of being changed by his time in prison (Archer, 2002, 207). However, in an interview two and half years after his release from prison he was asked if his incarceration changed him:

> I think if you live in that situation for two years it would be fairly remarkable if you weren't changed. I think I came out realising how very privileged and lucky I was.
>
> (BBC Sunday AM, 2006)

Archer was ultimately able to draw something positive from his experience, relating it to what at the time was described in rather different terms. Although his feelings of horror (Archer, 2002, 207) are described at a time relatively near the beginning of his sentence, no change occurs in them that Archer deems worthy of description. Given sufficient time, even the most harrowing of past experiences will be assimilated into the life narrative in such a way that they can be referred to in a positive manner, contributing to the growth of the self.

The anxiety of those considered here was grounded in recognising a threat to the integrity of the sense of self that could not be coped with (Douglas, 1984). The prison experience was so alien to some and so all-encompassing in terms of its impact upon the lives of individuals that it was recognised as irrevocably upsetting their 'place' in the world and presented a challenge to the security of the sense of self.

Given enough time however, the threat to the sense of self faded. Prisoners returned home and, despite meeting some resistance in the form of stigma towards

126    *Success, failure and change*

them and limited opportunities (see previous chapter), they discovered that they were able to re-establish themselves after prison. As a consequence of this re-establishment that operates on a social, civic and familial level there was the re-establishment of a coherent self i.e. one where who they were in the present made sense in terms of their past experiences (Douglas, 1984; Maruna, 2001; Vaughan, 2007). The immediate aftermath of release from prison was unlikely to be conducive to this narrative restructuring as there was still the need for offenders to identify who they were socially and the manner in which this related to their sense of self. This is reflected in the sense of insecurity that is present in some accounts, manifested in the desire to spend time in and around the home upon release from prison. To be part of a sympathetic environment they could feel secure in (e.g. Colson, 1979, 22; Aitken, 2005, 178–180). Only with the passage of time and the gradual establishment of who they could be after prison could the past be put into some sort of meaningful context that acknowledged it but simultaneously construed it as beneficial.

This is not, therefore, intrinsically a function of the length of time. Rather, it relates to the way the passage of time relates to actors' own sense of self (Kenyon, 2000). The sense of self needs time to cope with threats to its integrity and become secure once more. Part of this is constituted in the restructuring of the past. What was once experienced as threatening and debilitating is still recalled as such but is cast in positive terms. This is a result of recognising that we are our past and that in this regard our future self is already determined (Douglas, 1984). To fail to identify any positives in the experience of punishment would be to accept a future self as irrevocably changed, institutionalised by the prison regime, dehumanised by the treatment of the justice system and 'spoilt' by the interaction with 'common criminals'. Better to recast the experience so that the self might gain from it. As others have noted, a deviant past cannot be disavowed but it can be reconciled in terms of a current conception of self as a 'good person' (Maruna, 2001; Maruna and Roy, 2007; Vaughan, 2007).

White-collar offenders' reconstructing of the past is somewhat different from this process of narrative reconstruction however (Maruna and Roy, 2007; Vaughan, 2007). A deviant past contains actions that were ultimately something the deviant themselves chose to do, even if 'driven' to offend by circumstance (Maruna, 2001). In contrast, the negative change amongst white-collar offenders was seen as inflicted, originating from 'outside' the individual during their punishment. In drawing strength from this experience and learning from it they forged a meaningful sense of self in spite of and not because of certain aspects of their past. Joseph Jett, a former bond trader, drew strength from his 'persecution' by the Securities and Exchange Commission and his 'false' conviction on books and records violations:

> When all except your family have turned their backs on you and all that you had has been taken from you, you must reach within yourself. How many of us know if there is anything there to draw upon? Few people are granted the opportunity to truly see what they are made of, to be tested by fire before the world. My wealth was not in my bank account. It was within me.
>
> (Jett, 1999, 373)

*Success, failure and change*  127

For Jett, the past was given meaning by relating it positively to the future. He now knew the 'wealth' that he had and this gave him hope that he could survive similarly taxing experiences. His past therefore had implications for his future.

## Life after punishment

Resettling following punishment can take a significant amount of time. Long-term issues of resettlement such as encounters with succeeding and failing and realising that change in the self has taken place are all part of coming to terms with what life holds after punishment. White-collar offenders were, after punishment, left with a sense of how they had changed and none were unscathed by their experiences. For some offenders, only large changes in the way they lived were sufficient to make them feel they had properly resettled, with aspects of the old life giving way to new ventures. The role of shame at their actions and feeling they had 'done wrong' was important in prompting the desire for such large-scale change. Failure to achieve goals and regain some aspects of the old life were not, in the main, problematic for those who tried and failed because they had identified other priorities and other ways to live their lives. Conversely, succeeding was attended to keenly within accounts of resettling, particularly where it represented the attempt to undertake new goals and a new life. Despite all that had happened, these men were happy with their life as it now was, the past constructed in terms that made it, if not 'necessary', then an important part of the self now.

This chapter began by noting that the majority of these offenders were living very similar lives now to those at the end of their books and a large number had returned to what occupied them prior to prison. This does not mean resettlement was a straightforward process for these offenders however. It is particularly important to make this clear within the context of considering what advantages these offenders had when it came to resettling relative to other prisoners.

In considering the potentially privileged lives of these men and the impact of this on their resettlement, it is more accurate to say that their resources were an important source of mediating their decisions regarding their futures, but did not make success inevitable. Of course, some did succeed seemingly unproblematically and we can locate this success within the context of their knowledge base and other skills they might have, as was the case for Dennis Levine who formed his own financial consultancy, apparently without trouble. Not all were able to pick up their lives where they left off as Levine did however. William Laite, based on his previous involvement in politics understood how he might run for mayor and therefore achieve something meaningful with his life. He had knowledge of how to canvass public opinion and run a political campaign. Nevertheless, these 'advantages' could not help him overcome an unfavourable public opinion towards him on polling day. For Berger and Minkow, their business knowledge and skills encouraged them to try to start new businesses, but it appears they were not sufficient to ensure such businesses could be successful. The resources that white-collar offenders have compared to other released prisoners might be best thought

# 128  *Success, failure and change*

of as a source of hope for the future, as identified in the previous chapter, but not a guarantee of success.

To be sure, these white-collar offenders do not, on the whole, report the same problems with resources that other prisoners did, problems that are frequently financial (Richards and Jones, 2004). They still had problems achieving that which they wished though. We can suggest then that being better 'resourced' than perhaps other newly released prisoners are was useful for these white-collar offenders but it was also as much a source of angst as contentment. Previous success may have helped some get to where they wanted to be, but was also the source of their discontent at not being 'there'. In short, in wanting to return to something meaningful for them, they had further to go than other prisoners. They needed to use their 'resources' to try and find some measure of contentment.

## Notes

1   The activities cited in Table 6.2 largely relate to individuals' professions. These are cited as an indication of what offenders spent a considerable portion of their time doing, noting that frequently this was activity related to employment. This is not to essentialise offenders by attributing to them only one sphere of activity. Offenders were far more than just their job. However, the attributions included in Table 6.2 represent aspects of their lives that were key to them as indicated by the emphasis placed on them in offenders' accounts. Further, it is not unreasonable to place an emphasis on employment given the importance of this for many of the sample.

2   Berger, Bullen, Christensen, Laite, Lawson, and Timilty could not be traced through the media.

3   Archer, Bakker, Bond, Dean, Irving, Jett, Leeson, Levine and Pavlo.

4   Belfort and Volpe.

5   Berger gives insufficient information to determine his reactions to his failure.

6   Notwithstanding that Minkow was eventually reconvicted, he spent the majority of 16 years as a fraud investigator and pastor.

7   As is noted earlier and explored in more detail later, Minkow was subsequently reconvicted. This conviction came ten years after the period he describes and six years after the publication of his most recent autobiography (2005).

# 7 Becoming who one was

## Professional-ex roles

One difficulty for offenders in attempting to resettle is how to manage a deviant past and the 'spoilt' identity they now hold as a consequence of their offending (Goffman, 1963; Harding, 2003). But identities are constantly in flux and also malleable, with strategies available to help confirm or deny perceptions of the individual. Previous chapters indicated the general difficulties of identity management that white-collar offenders experience. The aim of this chapter is to consider a specific way in which deviant identities are managed by white-collar offenders by identifying white-collar offenders who took on the role of professional-ex (Brown, 1991). That is to say that they drew on their previous deviant identities to perform socially desirable roles that underscored they had reformed. The chapter begins by summarising the literature on roles and role exit and the impact of role exit. This literature has indicated that when it comes to deviant roles (e.g. offender), instead of such roles being abandoned upon exit they can in some instances be incorporated into a new, 'legitimate', role that emphasises the deviant past rather than seeking distance from it.

The chapter then details the white-collar offenders whose accounts indicate they adopted professional-ex roles after their punishment. The analysis concentrates on two of these men – Charles Colson and Barry Minkow – and the process through which they adopted professional-ex roles. Underlying a common experience, each man realised his professional-ex role in very different ways, utilising different aspects of their deviant past. The chapter concludes by contrasting Colson and Minkow's professional-ex roles with the way such roles have been conceptualised more generally.

### Ex roles and professional-exes

The leaving behind of particular, highly salient roles has been termed role exit (e.g. Ebaugh 1988; Drahota and Eitzen, 1998; Shaffir and Kleinknecht, 2005), with the exiter then becoming an 'ex' e.g. ex-teacher, ex-doctor, ex-prisoner (Ebaugh, 1988). To be an 'ex' presents a unique perspective because having been engaged in a particular role is different from never having held it (Ebaugh, 1984, 1988). Roles have their own conventions and social expectations that contribute to one's sense of self and in leaving the role the self must take account of who one was as well as who one will – or might – become.

## 130   *Professional-ex roles*

The roles we hold make an important contribution to our self-identity and so leaving a role behind has significant implications for how we identify ourselves (Ebaugh, 1984; Goffman, 1969). Exiting a role creates something of an identity vacuum and is subsequently likely to be an anxious and uncertain time for the exiter as behaviours associated with the role are no longer appropriate. Instead, the self must take account of the absence of this previously taken-for-granted aspect, adjusting to fit the demands of a new role while simultaneously leaving behind patterns and behaviours associated with the old one (Ebaugh, 1984, 1988; Ford, 1996; Shaffir and Kleinknecht, 2005). Any anxiety adjusting to the loss of a valued role may be exacerbated by lack of certainty over what the future holds. This is particularly likely to be the case if exit from a role has occurred without warning as there will have been no opportunity to prepare for role exit e.g. by considering suitable alternatives (Drahota and Eitzen, 1998). Shaffir and Kleinecht (2005) demonstrate this with ex-politicians who likened removal from office to death, while Drahota and Eitzen highlight the emotional, mental and social difficulties of forced role exit with their sample of professional athletes (1998).

Inasmuch as roles are enacted in front of or with respect to other people, they have a social component to them. This includes the way others react to the role holder, and sometimes these reactions may outlive the departure from the role (Ebaugh, 1984, 1988; Brown, 1991). Although responses from others may be based upon the stereotyped ideas associated with the role, such responses still serve as reminders of what has been left behind in the transition out of the role. Consequently, attempts to leave a role and the associated identity behind may be made more difficult by society's constant preoccupation with who the individual 'was'. Conversely, and where exes are trying to leave particular roles behind, responses from others that confirm or deny the transition are likely to be of particular importance in underscoring change (Ebaugh, 1984, 175).

To transition to being an ex is less problematic when the role held was socially desirable, assuming the change was voluntary. Where the role held was deviant however, the preferred strategy may be to avoid disclosure. Ex-offenders, for example, may be at pains to hide their criminal past for fear of the reaction against them and the consequences for attempts to resettle (Harding, 2003; Hunter, 2011). Such a strategy is fraught with its own difficulties however. Most employers take a dim view of lying in job applications for example. In some instances, however, complete abandonment of a role may not accompany role exit. Individuals who have previously been engaged in deviant roles may draw upon them, even as they attempt to lead a non-deviant life. This has been termed becoming a 'professional-ex', where a deviant past is acknowledged and even touted as an occupational strategy (Brown, 1991, 227; Maruna, 2001).

Professional-ex roles are commonly associated with therapeutic settings (e.g. Brown, 1991; Klingemann, 1999; White, 2000). Those who have previously been addicted to drugs or alcohol for example may become counsellors upon the completion of their own treatment program. A comparable example would be organisations set up and run by ex-offenders to aid those who wish to desist from

*Professional-ex roles* 131

crime such as Unlock – the National Association of Ex-Offenders. In such settings, instead of abandoning their former role, the professional-ex draws upon it as they seek to succeed in a new role, frequently centred around employment (Brown, 1991). Drawing upon a previous deviant identity has several advantages. Initially, within a new occupation, being able to cite a previously deviant identity affords the professional-ex an authority to carry out the role that they feel non-exes lack (Brown's 1991 participants argued that having lived the experience of substance abuse only they could understand it), while identifying with a previous deviant role – even while attempting to leave it behind – allows an ex to continue to draw on sources of support (Howard, 2008).

More importantly for a consideration of desistance from crime, however, is that the adoption of a professional-ex role helps individuals with their own attempts to desist (Maruna, 2001; Howard, 2008). Becoming a professional-ex satisfies a desire to undertake generative pursuits i.e. those that will benefit subsequent generations (e.g. Erikson, 1965, 240). A professional-ex role may be construed as generative because it allows the individual to feel they are helping others avoid the ex's own mistakes.

For Maruna (2001), generative pursuits, offer four 'advantages' for the ex-offender: fulfilment, exoneration, legitimacy and therapy. *Fulfilment* is gained through having a sense of meaning and purpose in one's life, provided by the professional-ex role. Simultaneously, the generation of a professional-ex 'script' provides the deviant with a means of highlighting their own change by fulfilling a role that is widely recognised in society i.e. as the ex-offender who helps others avoid the mistakes they made (White, 2000; Maruna, 2001). *Exoneration* is gained through 'making good' the deviant past, giving something back to a world 'hurt' by the individual's deviant behaviour (reports that feelings of remorse were a strong predictor of ex-prisoners taking on helper roles, 2007). A professional-ex role can help alleviate feelings of shame and guilt felt by previous actions, proving to the world that the ex is not a bad person (Brown, 1991).

Becoming a professional-ex also provides evidence of the *legitimacy* of the change the ex-offender has undergone. The activities associated with professional-ex status are likely to be viewed by others as incompatible with further deviance. To be a professional-ex is not just about doing good. It is about *being seen to do good*, thereby showing the world change has taken place.

Finally, associating with legitimate others in the course of their occupation provides the professional-ex with a means of furthering the *therapy* they have been given (Maruna, 2001). In undertaking their duties, professional-exes are frequently surrounded by those who will help them reaffirm a commitment to their own change. Being a drug counsellor involves working with other drug counsellors for example. These others will provide an informal code of conduct for the professional-ex that may guide their behaviour further, increasing their chance of avoiding deviant behaviour (Brown, 1991). By dedicating themselves to providing help for others then, professional-exes reaffirm their own commitment to change. This new role is one they will not be able to reconcile with continued deviance (Brown, 1991; LeBel, 2007). To this last point Sharp and Hope sound a note of

## 132  *Professional-ex roles*

caution however, observing that professional-ex roles may on occasion facilitate deviant behaviour (2001).

Perhaps above all a professional-ex role allows a virtue to be made out of what has previously been a stigma. A life narrative can be constructed that makes the deviant role a prerequisite for a law abiding life, the implicit assertion being 'only because I experienced that can I effectively do this' (Lofland, 1969; Brown, 1991; Maruna, 2001; LeBel, 2007).

Professional-ex statuses afford those who hold them a particular strategy of information disclosure regarding a deviant past and how much of this past to reveal (see Goffman, 1963; Harding, 2003). Trading on a previously deviant status as a professional-ex not only permits the individual to fully disclose their deviant past, but actually requires them to do so in order to afford them credibility (as they perceive it) in their new occupation. An undesirable past thus becomes a *necessity* for them to act effectively in their new role.

Professional-ex statuses have tended to be associated with drug and alcohol addiction and 'street' offending more generally. However, nearly one third of this sample of white-collar offenders took on what might be considered professional-ex roles, and this chapter considers what might be unique about the professional-ex experience as it applies to white-collar offenders. The analysis below focuses on two members of the sample – Charles Colson and Barry Minkow – chosen because they discuss their engagement with a professional-ex role in some detail. The analysis investigates the type of professional-ex roles adopted by white-collar offenders, how such roles are formed and how professional-ex roles are situated with regards to the general context of offenders' lives.

### Professional-exes in the current study

Of the 23 white-collar offenders in the current sample, eight became what might be termed professional-exes for at least some period after their punishment. Although the majority undertook other activities as well, all eight spent time in a professional-ex role, drawing upon aspects of their deviant past to serve particular ends. Table 7.1 shows the eight professional-exes and their activities. Each man, with the exception of Minkow (see below) was engaged in their role at the point of the most recent information available.

Amongst the eight offenders noted in Table 7.1, there are differences in the way offenders realised a professional-ex identity. Minkow spent time after his punishment to help prevent the types of fraud he perpetrated while Pavlo and Leeson give talks about their offending and Belfort sells advice on 'how to ethically persuade anyone to take any action' while cautioning potential customers 'I once used these same tactics for the wrong reasons' (Belfort, 2014). For these four, their ex-identity was one of ex-offender. The remaining four – Aitken, Berger, Colson and Lawson – undertook activities where they could employ their ex-identity to focus upon their time in prison i.e. they were 'ex-prisoners'. For example, Colson was co-founder of prison ministry group Prison Fellowship, where his ex-prisoner status was used to convince other prisoners of the validity of his work. The majority

*Professional-ex roles* 133

*Table 7.1* White-collar offenders' professional-ex roles

| Professional-ex | Activity |
|---|---|
| Jonathan Aitken | Prison ministry (part time) |
| Jordan Belfort | Speaker, business ethics |
| Robert Berger | Counsellor to white-collar offenders |
| Charles Colson | Prison ministry |
| Stephen Lawson | Regional governor for prison ministry |
| Nick Leeson | Speaker: his offence and prison |
| Barry Minkow | Fraud investigator |
| Walter Pavlo Junior | Speaker: his offence and business ethics |

gained or attempted to gain some income from employing their past, but it is unclear whether Aitken and Berger's activities garnered them any profit.

As a means of highlighting how professional-ex roles may be taken on by white-collar offenders and how they relate to attempts to manage the deviant past, the experiences of two members of the sample are considered in some detail. Case summaries 1 and 2 provide a synopsis of Barry Minkow's and Charles Colson's cases respectively, with particular emphasis on their professional-ex roles.

Minkow and Colson were chosen for further analysis because their accounts contain large amounts of information regarding how they took on their particular professional-ex role. Little can be gleaned about the professional-ex roles of the other offenders in Table 7.1 other than their presence in offenders' lives.

---

*Case summary 1:* Barry Minkow

Minkow was sentenced to prison for 25 years (serving seven and a half and leaving prison late 1994) for defrauding investors in his company *ZZZZ Best* by presenting an inaccurate picture of the company's value. While his case was under investigation he converted to Christianity and went on to study theology at first-degree and postgraduate level. After his release from prison he hosted a radio show for several months (ending October 1996), giving advice to potential investors. In this, Minkow drew upon his conviction to demonstrate that he had knowledge of business failure. This radio show became subordinate to his desire to be a pastor, however he founded the Fraud Discovery Institute in 2001. The FDI investigated possible fraudulent activity to protect potential investors. Beginning in 1995, Minkow also gave talks to law-enforcement agencies, most notably the FBI, on how to detect fraud, drawing on his experiences as an offender. In March 2011, Minkow pleaded guilty to conspiracy, relating to attempts to manipulate the stock of Lennar Corporation, a building company. Minkow hoped to profit by a drop in the Lennar's share price. He was sentenced to five years in prison and ordered to pay restitution of $583 million (see Fortune, 2014). In January 2014, he was sentenced to a further five years in prison (to be served consecutively with his first sentence) for embezzlement from his church and parishioners and ordered to pay restitution of $3.5 million.

134 *Professional-ex roles*

Additionally, Minkow and Colson's cases are used because they represent two different ways of employing a professional-ex role. Minkow used his past as an offender in his role as a fraud investigator while Colson drew upon his ex-prisoner identity when establishing Prison Fellowship. Minkow's case is of further interest because he subsequently was convicted twice, in 2011 and 2014. He was sentenced to prison each time. His case is therefore a reminder that professional-ex statuses are not mutually exclusive with continued deviance (as per Sharp and Hope, 2001). His case is included here however because it demonstrates the uses to which a deviant past can be put as part of efforts to desist from crime and resettle following a conviction and indeed there is nothing to suggest that Minkow took on his professional-ex activities with the intention of further offending.

---

*Case summary 2:* Charles Colson

Colson was special counsel to American President Richard Nixon from 1969 until 1973. Although Colson was involved in Watergate, it was not for his role in the scandal that he was imprisoned. Instead, motivated by his Christian faith he pleaded guilty to spreading defamatory information about someone who was under federal investigation. This did not constitute an offence under US law until Colson pleaded guilty (Colson, 1976, 222–224). Colson was sentenced to between one and three years in prison but served seven months, being released early because of family problems (the conviction of his son for possession of drugs). While the Watergate investigation was taking place, Colson converted to Christianity. His Christian faith was consolidated while he served his prison sentence and after his release he set up a prison ministry, Prison Fellowship. The fellowship's work involved taking groups of prisoners out of prison temporarily and training them as 'disciples'. Disciples learnt the tenets of Christian faith before returning to prison to teach other prisoners about God. Colson himself, as part of the fellowship, visited prisons to give talks about his faith, drawing upon the fact he had been in prison to give himself the legitimacy to communicate with potential disciples. Prison Fellowship was established in 1976. Colson was part of the organisation until his death in 2012 aged 80.

---

## Becoming a professional-ex

The adoption of a white-collar professional-ex role is conceptualised here as a series of 'stages' that Colson and Minkow progressed through. Figure 7.1 illustrates these stages. This is not to say that becoming a professional-ex is a series of discrete events. Instead this conceptualisation is a means of illustrating a broadly shared experience.

The starting point for the analysis is that both Minkow and Colson were open to taking on the role of professional-ex, based on the changes each had undergone following their convictions. From this point, both had a vague idea of the desires they had but no immediate way to fulfil them. The next significant point for them

*Professional-ex roles*   135

was how they came to find their particular professional-ex role, and how it was taken up. Becoming a professional-ex was not straightforward, however, and both men had some hesitation in fully embracing the role. Finally, however, there was the acceptance that becoming a professional-ex was the only way to achieve that which they wished and they began to fully 'live' the roles they had developed for themselves.

### Initial idea

For Colson and Minkow, the origins of what would become their professional-ex roles lay within the desire to achieve quite specific goals. However, neither explicitly set out to utilise their past deviant identity. Upon his release from prison, Minkow wanted to make amends for the harm he felt he had caused:

> What possible good could I do that would ever make up for the evil I was responsible for causing?
>
> (Minkow, 2005, 142)

Minkow's future self was therefore uncertain, clouded by anticipated reactions from others but keen for redemption, albeit he wanted to do 'something' with his life after prison that would relate positively to his deviant past. Colson's concerns were similarly future oriented:

> the most shattering thing about prison was the thought that I would never again do anything significant with my life... I could never fulfil my dreams.
>
> (Colson, 2005, 22)

Colson's prison time represented the end of a chance to achieve what he wished and the chance to have a meaningful existence was therefore beyond him. The dreams Colson makes reference to are unspecified, but his broader concern was that nothing was possible. At this point then, both men knew, in abstract terms, what they wanted to do with their lives, Minkow to do some good and make amends, Colson to do 'something significant'. However, each was unsure as to how their desires might be achieved and concerned with how this would be possible. They were open to possibilities regarding the future, but lacked the opportunity to envision anything definite.

| STAGE 1 | STAGE 2 | STAGE 3 | STAGE 4 | STAGE 5 |
| --- | --- | --- | --- | --- |
| Initial idea | Finding the role | Taking up the ex role | Hesitation | Embarkation |

*Figure 7.1* Stages in becoming a white-collar professional-ex

136  *Professional-ex roles*

### Finding the role

From having a vague idea over the direction of the life, attempts were made to identify what would be done with the remainder of it. However, there were doubts regarding the best way to proceed. For Colson, the uncertainties he felt were centred on his Christian faith. Although Colson was a committed Christian, he was unsure what this meant in 'real terms':

> Jesus Christ was very real to me, but what did that mean from this point on?... What does a new believer do?... What is the *real goal* of being a Christian? I felt restless and confused.
>
> (Colson, 1979, 29–30, emphasis added)

Colson's concern with the 'real goal' was motivated by a need to demonstrate his change to himself, to act as a Christian. Bible study and other, perhaps more private, ways of being a Christian were not sufficient. He needed more. Minkow also experienced some uncertainty as to how he could proceed with his goals of making restitution to his victims, undoing the 'hurt' he had caused. Financial concerns were therefore at the forefront of his mind and although he was a pastor he felt this was insufficient for 'doing good':

> There was something else that I would need to do... I just needed to figure out what.
>
> (Minkow, 2005, 142)

Minkow's concern was at least in part for his self-presentation, for how others viewed him because of his offence. Like Colson, he was aware of the need to act to demonstrate his change because of the way such actions would be viewed by others. Where Colson was concerned with being a Christian for himself, Minkow's focus was on demonstrating to others that he had changed, on advertising the reform in his character from fraudster to law abiding citizen (Visher and Travis, 2003).

In a similar manner to Minkow, Colson found himself trying to decide what he could do with his life after he had left prison. Both Colson and Minkow's searches resulted over what they perceived as a lack of meaning in their lives (Douglas and Johnson, 1977; Kotarba, 1979). Their uncertainty over how to proceed with their lives represented a difficult time; goals had been identified, but there was no obvious way of attaining them. However, from the vague ideas expressed about doing good and having a meaningful life there was a narrowing of focus. Colson and Minkow's thinking began to orient more specifically towards what would become their professional-ex roles. Such a reorientation has some concordance with Giordano *et al.*'s (2002) notion of individuals being open to a specific 'hook for change' (in this instance the professional-ex role being the hook) as a precursor to taking advantage of that hook. Colson and Minkow both envisioned a future self but were unsure as to how that might be achieved, as the need to take account of their deviant past overshadowed attempts to identify a meaningful future self.

*Professional-ex roles* 137

After all, who one can be must have regard for who one was (Maruna and Roy, 2007; Hunter, 2011).

### Taking up the ex-role

Although holding a broad conception of their future selves, it took almost epiphany-like moments (Denzin 1989) for Colson and Minkow to take up activities as professional-exes. These experiences impacted upon their thinking, making them consider their future, particularly within the context of their past and what they hoped to achieve. For Colson, it was the continued reflection on his experience in prison:

> it gradually became clear to me that I had been in prison for a purpose. I had encountered people who had no hope, who had no one to care for them ... They needed a champion. It took a year and a half of wrestling through the decision, but in the summer of 1976 [my wife] and I realized that caring for prisoners was my calling. So out of my prison experience, paradoxically, came a challenge, which has turned out to be more fulfilling than anything I could have ever imagined.
>
> (Colson, 2005, 30)

Although Barry Minkow had given several talks to FBI agents and also produced a short film to provide guidance for those attempting to detect fraud, he had considered this to be the extent of his contributions to fraud prevention. This changed when a fraud investigator made use of his seminars to detect fraud (Minkow, 2005, 158). Minkow's decision to work to uncover financial deception followed directly from this conversation, as the incident highlighted that he was in possession of knowledge that others did not have because of his past:

> Maybe there was a way to identify points of similarity between my fraud at ZZZZ Best and fraud being perpetrated by others.
>
> (Minkow, 2005, 158)

Charles Colson's experience was of a very different kind, but of no less significance to him, as one morning his doubts about helping prisoners were expunged by a 'vision' of what his future prison ministry would look like:

> I saw sharply focussed pictures – of smiling men and women, streaming out of prisons, of Bibles and study groups, of fellowship around tables... Was it of God?
>
> (Colson, 1979, 40–41)

Both Minkow and Colson experienced sudden moments of clarity that laid out for them how they could achieve their desires. Minkow's 'elation' (Minkow, 2005, 158) and Colson's 'assurance' (Colson, 1979, 40–41) at this clarity came from

138　*Professional-ex roles*

understanding something about their respective futures. They now both had a 'blueprint' for a future self to guide their actions (Giordano *et al.*, 2002). For Minkow though, there was still uncertainty as to how he could start to help people through a career in detecting fraud. This uncertainty continued until he was given the opportunity to host a radio show in which he gave advice to potential investors:

> My motto for the show was simple, 'I am an expert at failing. Never ask me what you *should* do in business, because I failed. But I am an expert at showing you what you *should not* do'.
>
> (Minkow, 2005, 167, emphasis in original)

Minkow explicitly used his past, drawing upon his notoriety to solicit callers to his show and to provide a context to the advice he was giving. In this regard, his disclosure of his past was a necessity in order to give his advice some credibility (Goffman, 1963; Brown, 1991), although given the high profile nature of the *ZZZZ Best* case, such disclosure was almost always unnecessary. His 'expert knowledge' was important as a means of arming himself with this credibility. The role of opportunity to fulfil one's desires is also of importance here. It is not enough to simply wish for something; one's desire to act must find purchase in a suitable opportunity (Giordano *et al.*, 2002, 1001; Laub and Sampson, 2003).

### Hesitation

Initial experiences were important for indicating to Colson and Minkow how they might specifically achieve their goals. However, even in engaging with the professional-ex role there may be doubts over the ability to engage fully with the role. Colson attempted to resist becoming too involved with the prison ministry, despite the emotional resonance the work held for him:

> Logic warned me to keep other career options open. Inner emotions began tugging at me to get more involved. But I held them in check.
>
> (Colson, 1979, 118)

Ultimately, however, taking on the ex-role was the only way Colson could reconcile his actions with his perceived self. His faith convinced him that he had little option but to go into the prison ministry:

> It wasn't a choice, I was beginning to understand, that could be weighed out rationally and logically. My question would have to turn on the central issue of *obedience* [to Jesus].
>
> (Colson, 1979, 151, emphasis in original)

In this regard, then, Colson saw himself as having no option but to begin his ministry because this was the only way he could make his actions consistent with his emerging Christian belief. His identity as a Christian was one that he had invested much time and effort in developing. His conversion experience had begun while Watergate was being investigated and it was his faith that had led him to plead guilty to what, at that point, was a non-offence. Only by living his faith could he affirm it and become authentically 'himself' (Macquarrie, 1972; Patrick and Bignall, 1984; Kotarba and Bentley, 1988). To do otherwise would have been to deny many of the experiences he had encountered during his conversion and would have been inconsistent with the conception of self he had. In short 'obedient discipleship offers me no other path' (Colson, 1979, 152). This 'forced' choice was not problematic for Colson. It was not restrictive as it was in keeping with his sense of who he was (Douglas, 1984, 83). As Colson notes 'Freedom lies in obedience to our calling' (Colson, 2005, 30). Paradoxically, being obedient led to a sense of being free. This was the only way in which he could reconcile the 'tug' (Colson, 1979, 118) of his emotions, by 'choosing' to be who he felt he was and living in accordance with his values (Douglas, 1984, 83).

For Minkow, there was a similar realisation. Given his goals and the promises he had made to himself that he would do some good, it would have been difficult for him to reject the opportunity to act to prevent fraud. In what was to be his first active investigation into fraud (instead of lecturing on uncovering fraud) Minkow was asked to investigate the company MX Factors. Initially he was reluctant to carry out the investigation, doubting his ability to do so. However, he then began to consider how his failure to investigate would fit with his goals. His doubts were inconsistent with the future self he was striving to achieve:

> For years I had talked about wanting to help people from becoming victims of fraud... The dream was now being compromised by excuses.
>
> (Minkow, 2005, 253)

Acting as a fraud investigator allowed Minkow to fulfil his goal of doing 'some good' (Minkow, 2005, 142). Fulfilment for him was being seen to work to prevent others from becoming victims of offences similar to his. For Minkow, given his past and the hurt he felt he caused others, making some form of restitution was of great importance. To be able to do this was his fulfilment. Minkow's hesitation took place after he had identified fraud detection as a means through which he could achieve his desires (Minkow, 2005, 241). It may therefore take some time to overcome doubts that are held. Nevertheless, it was through commitment to the professional-ex role that Minkow and Colson were able to reconcile their desires with their actions.

Because taking on the role of professional-ex was a means of making their actions consistent with their desires, doing so committed Minkow and Colson to very particular future selves, but selves that nonetheless acted as a guide to their actions. Their hesitation is also explicable in terms of awareness that this commitment 'tied' them to a particular future, limiting their potential to achieve other desires (Sartre, 1958; Macquarrie, 1979). Ultimately however, the need to make their future consistent with their past meant to overcome such hesitation and fully embrace the professional-ex role.

## 140 *Professional-ex roles*

### *Embarking upon the ex-role*

For Minkow, although it was several years after he had quit his radio show to become a pastor, a friend encouraged him to go back to fraud prevention in 2001 by noting that he was especially talented in that area. It was a real way in which he could help people by protecting them from losing their life savings. These arguments appeared to have some concordance with Minkow's original reasons for taking part in fraud prevention initiatives, giving him reassurance that his life could proceed as he planned:

> One word described how I felt at that moment. *Clarity*.
> 
> (Minkow, 2005, 241, emphasis in original)

Minkow's path was 'mapped out' for him in this regard. This clarity is also representative of the relief Minkow felt at identifying that his actions could be consistent with his sense of self and also at identifying a solution to the pain he felt at recognising himself as selfish. He realised that by focusing his efforts on his church and how it related to his self-esteem he had been ignoring aspects of his life that required his attention. Colson's prison ministry was the answer to his particular concern that having spent time in prison he could no longer do anything significant with his life. Consequently, it was a chance for him to fulfil his goal, because it gave him:

> an opportunity to serve others in significant ways. In my case that service has been a ministry to prisoners around the world.
> 
> (Colson, 2005, 23)

For both Colson and Minkow, there was a direct link between their new role as a professional-ex and the goals they identified as being worthy of attainment. Being a professional-ex was the 'answer' to the question 'how may I achieve my goals?' As a result, embarking on a career as a professional-ex was an extremely exciting time, representing the beginning of the chance to achieve one's desires. In keeping with other professional-exes, Colson's and Minkow's roles drew upon their past but with a view to the future (Brown, 1991; Maruna, 2001). This relationship between past and future is explored below.

## Deceitful pasts and the management of the professional-ex role

To be a professional-ex is to draw upon a past identity as a means of giving oneself credibility. However, drawing upon a deviant identity is not without its problems. Professional-ex roles can be fragile, with their success dependent on the continued ability of the ex to perform the role effectively.

### *Professional-ex identities and credibility*

It has been suggested that exes approach professional-ex roles by framing their deviant past as a source of credibility for engaging in the role effectively (Brown,

*Professional-ex roles* 141

1991, 226).[1] Such framing was a feature of Minkow's and Colson's roles. Minkow was acutely aware of this when speaking to an audience of FBI agents:

> I had to prove that only someone who has ... committed fraud, and been to prison could speak authoritatively about the why behind the crime.
>
> (Minkow, 2005, 154)

Minkow also illustrates that he was able to use his own experiences as a fraud perpetrator to detect fraud committed by others, citing the parallels between the techniques he used to commit his own offences and the frauds he detected (Minkow, 2005, vi). Minkow also makes the concept of credibility explicit by describing how he used his past experience of committing fraud in his investigations into James Lewis, whom Minkow suspected of defrauding investors (Minkow, 2005, 16).

The relationship between Minkow's past deviance and his present professional-ex role is expressed in a similar manner to other professional-exes who, in effect, assert that 'because I have done that, I can now do this' (see for example, Maruna, 2001, 106; LeBel, 2007; Leverentz, 2010). Minkow's description of his investigations suggests that only he, as an ex-offender, could effectively do what he was doing, emphasising the importance of 'inside knowledge' (see also Minkow, 2005, 16).

In common with others who draw on deviant pasts (Maruna, 2001; LeBel, 2007; Leverentz, 2010), Minkow suggests that his deviant past was a necessity in order that he might work to help others. This was necessary for him to feel that he could act effectively as a fraud investigator, convincing him that he was able to have a meaningful impact in terms of achieving his goal of 'doing good'. Such feelings of credibility were important in helping him overcome his own self-doubts.

Colson made similar reference to his experiences in relation to his ability to be a leader of a prison ministry. He too felt he was the owner of a privileged experience that gives him legitimacy to talk to inmates:

> If you were to design a prototypical prison-ministry leader, someone who could relate to inmates and evangelize them, you might design someone just like me ... I've been in prison.
>
> (Colson, 2005, 323)

Colson 'traded' upon his prison status and the credibility his ex-prisoner role gave him and therefore, like Minkow, the past was forever relevant in his life. The past is therefore the starting point for the finished 'product' that the individual is as the professional-ex. The meaning placed upon the past was therefore changed. It could not be 'hidden' – both men were too well known for that – but it could be reconstructed (Maruna and Roy, 2007).

### *The fragility of ex roles*

What the foregoing highlights is the intimate connection between professional-ex roles and individuals' specific goals. Professional-ex activities were not about

142 *Professional-ex roles*

'getting by', but represented a higher calling (e.g. see Brown, 1991, 224–225). Minkow earned no money for his work at the Fraud Discovery Institute while Colson, who claimed a wage for his work with Prison Fellowship had several other job offers he refused prior to forming the organisation (Colson, 2005, 323). Both men identified their professional-ex roles as the 'answer' to the questions they had about how they could proceed with their lives. This investment in the professional-ex role makes professional-exes particularly sensitive to negative experiences that might threaten the role. Minkow expressed worries over his ability to be a fraud investigator:

> I did not relish this newfound trust, though – I feared it...I did not want the pressure of another case because if I was forced to arrive at a conclusion and that conclusion was wrong – I was done.
>
> (Minkow, 2005, 277–278)

A professional-ex position can therefore be tenuous. Drawing upon a deviant role keeps that role at the forefront of self-identity, even when it is in the past, and Minkow's experience illustrates the difficulty of keeping the deviant identity close at hand. For Minkow there was a tension in highlighting his past as a 'con man'. Falsely identifying someone as a fraudster would damage his credibility and reinforce the message that he had not changed. By using his (ex) fraudster status he kept such a status to the fore, leaving him unable to 'move on' with that aspect of his life. In fact, his professional-ex role imperilled his attempts to do work based upon it.

Colson's professional-ex role was imperilled in a different way. As part of the prison ministry and in accordance with his vision (Colson, 1979, 40–41) Colson set up a scheme to train 'disciples', i.e. prisoners who would minister to other prisoners. But the scheme itself was reliant on the good conduct of those chosen as disciples while they were being trained outside the confines of the prison, and the grace of the department of corrections, who sanctioned the programme. Colson outlines the threat to the programme as a result of possible prisoner misconduct (1979, 67). Any such threat to the programme was also a threat to Colson. For Colson there was an added dimension to any threat to his professional-ex role, related as it was to his Christian faith. His work as part of Prison Fellowship was what God had intended him to do and a threat to the fellowship also represented a threat to his faith, indicating his vision was not sent by God. From these two examples, it can be seen that there is an uncertainty to professional-ex roles as characterised here. This results from the professional-ex role being an answer to questions regarding how to live the life. A future self is imperilled if professional-ex role comes to nought.

### The professional-ex role and restructuring of the past

Colson and Minkow's professional-ex roles were not directly related to their desistance; each felt he had changed prior to taking on their role. What is of greater relevance is that the activities they undertook as professional-exes were related to their past and were also a way in which they made some meaning of their future. This is a further 'power' of professional-ex roles. They permit sense to be made of the life (Maruna, 2001; Maruna and Roy, 2007).

This 'making of meaning' also extends to considering the past and the way in which the professional-ex role 'fits' with one's personal biography, so as to be consistent with one's experiences. Colson's reflection on his experiences led him to conclude, 'Prison turned out to be one of the best things that ever happened to me' (Colson, 2005, 23). In this way then, meaning can be made of past experiences, and they can be considered in a positive light. For Colson, there was the feeling that his prison experiences were not completely (or even predominantly) about 'him', but about what God had intended for his life and what his 'purpose' was to be; that purpose was something far more important than simply changing his attitude to life (Colson, 1979, 151–152).

Minkow reasoned there was a lesson to be learnt from his experiences (2005, vi). Taking encouragement from them, even to the point of understanding that they were 'destined' to happen, or by making use of them as Minkow did to provide a lesson for others, is a means of making sense of the deviant past, constructing it as of use for a particular future (Brown, 1991; Maruna, 2001; Vaughan, 2007). Becoming a professional-ex may be the ultimate expression of this, because where the previous deviant identity is employed to give the individual some legitimacy in their new role, the negative experience is one that 'had to happen' in order for the good that followed it to be accomplished. In this way, professional-exes, including Colson and Minkow manage their sense of self (Douglas, 1984, 82). They bring together the past (deviant) self with hope and the promise of a legitimate future self.

## The professional-ex concept revisited

Maruna (2001) has highlighted four ways in which a concern for generativity may be manifested in particular work practices, frequently realised in professional-ex roles. These give professional-exes a sense of fulfilment, exoneration and legitimacy and also act as 'therapy' for the professional-ex. Minkow and Colson use their professional-ex roles in a similar manner, but neither draws all four of Maruna's 'benefits' from their role. Instead, Colson drew fulfilment and therapy from his professional-ex role while Minkow drew exoneration and legitimacy.

*Table 7.2* Colson and Minkow's ex-role 'benefits'

|  | Colson | Minkow |
| --- | --- | --- |
| Fulfilment | ✓ | ✗ |
| Exoneration | ✗ | ✓ |
| Legitimacy | ✗ | ✓ |
| Therapy | ✓ | ✗ |

## 144 *Professional-ex roles*

Table 7.2 illustrates this. The purpose of highlighting this difference is to indicate that these two men took very specific things from their engagement as professional-exes. The professional-ex role acted upon particular areas of their lives.

### *Minkow: exoneration and legitimacy*

Minkow's role as a professional-ex did not give him the fulfilment experienced by other professional-exes. He took fulfilment from his work as a pastor. Note that he was able to come and go from his professional-ex role, having had a false start when he gave up his radio show for the 'bigger' job of becoming a pastor (Minkow, 2005, 171). Nor was his professional-ex role related to therapy. Once again, this was gained through his pastor role, through which he ministered to others and preached about his own change, thereby reaffirming his commitment to this change. Instead, Minkow gained exoneration and legitimacy from his professional-ex role.

The exoneration he gained was from redeeming himself by detecting fraud equal to the amount he had committed; in this way he 'made good' his past offences. Discussing his fraud prevention work in a television interview Minkow refers to the 'skills' he employed:

> Use what I did to do evil and kind of flip it on its back and use those talents to help the very community I once hurt. And that's what I want to do.
>
> (CNN, 2005)

In highlighting his reversal of his previous role Minkow makes explicit how much he had changed since his fraud. Similar to those professional-exes who focus on being a 'wounded healer' (White, 2000) Minkow references a poacher-turned-gamekeeper script with the 'tools of evil' now being used for 'good', with Minkow repaying the debt that he accrued through the number of people he defrauded:

> Maybe proactively stopping millions of dollars in fraud, far more than I had ever perpetrated as the CEO of ZZZZ Best, would be the 'does good' part of my story.
>
> (Minkow, 2005, 158)

Minkow quantified his doing good, measuring it by the amount of fraud he prevented compared to how much he perpetrated. It is the case, however, that once Minkow had worked to prevent 54 million dollars' worth of fraud, the same amount as he had committed, he continued as a fraud investigator. This was the next 'step' in his redemption strategy, to prevent 'far more' (Minkow, 2005, 245) fraud than he had committed.

Minkow also derived legitimacy from his fraud detection activities. His investigations provided him with a means of demonstrating he had made the change from fraudster to reformed citizen. Minkow was particularly aware of the importance of his professional-ex role in this regard, concerned with how long it would take to persuade others he had changed and also fearing that he would conduct a fraud

*Professional-ex roles*   145

investigation and be wrong in his conclusions. This scenario would, in his opinion 'undo' all the good work he had previously conducted, marking him as deceitful again.

The concept of legitimacy is closely tied to notions of certification whereby change from a deviant to a legitimate identity is recognised by others (Meisenhelder, 1982). An important part of Minkow's work as a fraud investigator, was that it enabled him to gain the trust of people 'in order to get the second chance I so desperately needed' (Minkow, 2005, 151).

Minkow's concerns were focused upon conveying to others that he was an ex-offender (Minkow, 2005, 142). Positive encounters while enacting the ex-role also highlighted for him that his goal was being achieved. Minkow was 'certified' during a conversation with a Securities and Exchange Commission (SEC) official who considered Minkow reliable:

> The [American] Fraud Association may not have believed that I had changed; the reporters may not believe I had changed but a single SEC attorney in Los Angeles did, a law enforcement official of all people. I relished the moment.
> (Minkow, 2005, 319)

Minkow's emotional involvement with his ex-role is evident in the above. It was significant that certification for Minkow came from an SEC official, a law enforcement agent and previously someone who would have been on the 'other side'. This acceptance showed Minkow that he was someone who could be trusted again, at least by some. This did not necessarily indicate the end of the certification process, but it provided important validation for Minkow that not everyone viewed him as a 'conman'. The importance for Minkow of acceptance, particularly by law enforcement officials is also evident by his account of his first anti-fraud talk for the FBI (Minkow, 2005, 156). This talk led to further offers for speaking engagements, these encounters underlining for Minkow that he was becoming trusted, thus allaying the fears he had upon leaving prison that he would not be trusted. In addition to this, the encouragement he received helped him feel that he was achieving his goal of doing good. It provided encouragement that he could be successful in the manner he wished.

Although Minkow is not someone who can be said to have desisted, his adoption of the professional-ex role is still instructive of how such roles might be used by white-collar offenders. Minkow's fraud investigation activities helped him make sense of his self and the world he encountered after prison. These and his work as a pastor helped him successfully resettle. For a time.

### Colson: fulfilment and therapy

Colson, as Table 7.2 indicates, did not gain exoneration or legitimacy from his work as a member of Prison Fellowship. His conversion to Christianity had already seen him exonerated by God, while engagement in a prayer group he had joined was a means of demonstrating that his change was authentic. For Colson, his

## 146 *Professional-ex roles*

professional-ex role was one from which he drew fulfilment and therapy (to use Maruna's terms). Fulfilment came from knowing he was following a directive from God, imbuing his life with meaning and purpose. The 'therapy' he received – helping to reinforce his own change – was more subtle however. Colson's change in how he viewed himself was related to his conversion to Christianity. His forming of Prison Fellowship was an extension of this because he felt it was a directive from God. Because of this, the success of Prison Fellowship was tied to Colson's change. The success of Prison Fellowship helped underscore for Colson that his change was a viable one and that God was in support of the organisation, reinforcing the efficacy of his new way of living.

Any fulfilment at successfully doing something significant and so alleviating 'the most shattering thing about prison' (see above, Colson, 2005, 22) came about through the successful behaviour of those who went through Prison Fellowship program. Simultaneously, the knowledge that his ministry was a success was a reaffirmation of his faith in God, who had sent him his vision, and instructed him to start it. The ministry and Colson's faith were therefore intertwined. This confirmation and validation shows the value of Colson's endeavours (see Maruna, 2001).

For Colson, this was his therapy, because it confirmed his beliefs as a Christian, reinforcing his own change. Positive experiences emphasised for him not only the efficacy of his ability to make a significant contribution to people's lives, but also supported his belief that God was at work in helping Prison Fellowship. At a prison ministry dinner, Colson reflected on what had been achieved by considering the people present, both trainers and disciples:

> Here were men who represented opposite poles culturally, politically, socially… Yet on this night they prayed together, wept together and embraced – joined together by the power of the Holy Spirit in a fraternity that transcends all others.
>
> (Colson, 1979, 173)

This and other experiences e.g. one of the programme's prison disciples getting married and the acceptance of previously sceptical prison governors of the efficacy of Prison Fellowship (Colson, 1979, 278–279) provided a positive not only of the efficacy of the prison ministry, but also of the 'right' of the course of action Colson had chosen to pursue. As a result, for Colson there was a reinforcement of his faith. The positive examples he cites were for him tangible evidence of God's work and of God's will being fulfilled, emphasising the importance of wider processes that support change.

### *Deviant identities in practice*

There are further differences in the way the professional-ex role was realised by Colson and Minkow. Table 7.3 illustrates these. These differences have their origin in the particular aspects of their deviant past that Colson and Minkow drew upon: Colson as an ex-prisoner and Minkow as an ex-offender.

*Professional-ex roles* 147

*Table 7.3* Differences in the realisation of the professional-ex role

|  | Colson | Minkow |
|---|---|---|
| Means and ends | Means to an end (ex-role used to gain trust of prisoners) | An end in itself (detecting fraud) |
| Basis of ex role | Shared experience | Specialist knowledge |
| Relationship with deviants | Similarity – 'I *am* like *you*' | Difference – 'I *was* like *him*' |

Both men focused upon the aspects of their past that would have the greatest salience for their future. The differences have their origin in the particular desires each man had. For Colson to fulfil his directive from God, he needed to work to convince prisoners of the presence of God and of the efficacy of change. For Minkow, the best way for him to gain redemption was through stopping fraud. This led to him working against other offenders to stop them defrauding others. These were the best ways in which each man could envision his past being utilised to do good.

Colson's use of his previous deviant identity is largely in keeping with Brown's characterisation of the professional-ex role. He '[embraced his] deviant history and identity as an invaluable therapeutic resource' (Brown, 1991, 223). Colson is more reminiscent of the drug therapists who were previously drug addicts described by Brown (1991). This is particularly the case towards the start of his 'career' as a professional-ex, where he received the 'therapy' his role gave him outlined above. Further, Colson's use of his previous deviant identity was a means to an end. His identity as an ex-prisoner was used to gain the trust of other prisoners in order to effectively communicate his ideas regarding God. The basis of his ex-role was that it was predicated on an experience he shared with other prisoners, of the similarity between him and them. They were 'like him' (see above Colson, 1979, 60). Colson was sympathetic to prisoners and 'other-centred' in his use of the professional-ex role, working with those he identified with and using himself as a model of change. In addition, he is what might be termed desistance focused, aiming to bring about change in the beliefs of those prisoners he worked with, guiding them away from offending. Finally, in keeping with Brown's (1991, 224) observations, Colson's professional-ex role assumed something of a 'master status' for him. His status as a former sinner 'saved' by God was one that was not situationally specific but instead was relevant to all social encounters.

Minkow, for the reasons outlined in Table 7.3, represents a very different way of conceptualising a professional-ex role. Minkow's use of his deviant identity was an end in itself: detecting fraud was the only way he could achieve redemption. In contrast to Colson, Minkow's use of his professional-ex role was more adversarial with respect to offenders, as he attempted to identify fraud as it was being conducted and the basis of his role was the specialist knowledge he held. Minkow was not concerned with the desistance of those offenders he encountered and was not a model for change in the way that Colson was. His professional-ex activities were predicated upon specialist knowledge that his past gave him, putting him in fundamental opposition to other offenders. Perhaps, because Minkow's role was

148 *Professional-ex roles*

employed for a specific purpose – to gain redemption – he was not as heavily engaged in it as Colson or Brown's (1991) professional-exes were. In his employment as a pastor he was part of a separate world where his professional-ex status had little or no viability.

In drawing upon his past, Minkow simultaneously sought to distance himself from it. In working to convince others of the reality of his change, the legitimacy the ex-role gave him allowed Minkow to distance himself from those fraudsters he was investigating. He had changed from the fraudster he was and consequently other fraudsters were the sort of people he 'used to be'. What Minkow's case illustrates is that professional-ex identities may be constructed out of very different circumstances from the way in which they have been conceived of traditionally, while still allowing ex-offenders to reconstruct their past and make their personal biography meaningful in terms of their present.

## Past identities lived into the future

Traditionally, the adoption of a professional-ex role has been characterised as running parallel to other aspects of change in the life (Maruna, 2001). The desire to adopt a professional-ex role is simultaneously a precursor to change and also an example of shifts in the ex-deviant's thinking about their life and the future (Brown, 1991; Maruna, 2001; LeBel, 2007). Utilising a deviant identity as a professional-ex accompanies, and is responsible for, a gradual transition in a sense of self with respect to a deviant past (Maruna, 2001). In a similar manner to how such shifts in identity have been noted as being related to desistance (Giordano *et al.*, 2002), the 'traditional' professional-ex is one whose professional-ex role in itself helps prompt desistance, the *therapy* component of Maruna's (2001) list of 'benefits' to engaging in generative pursuits. In Brown's model for offenders more generally, part of becoming a professional-ex means to 'begin to turn the moral corner on their deviance' (1991, 222). That is, seeing deviant activities as 'wrong' and 'symptoms of a much larger disease complex' (Brown, 1991, 223). Through engagement in therapeutic practices as part of their own rehabilitation, the offender comes to identify a 'replacement self' (Giordano *et al.*, 2002) they can use to guide efforts to change. This is why professional-exes have been noted as feeling almost compelled into the professional-ex role, seeing little other choice (Brown, 1991, 223). Once a particular replacement self has been identified, it may be difficult to identify another.

White-collar offenders may approach professional-ex roles in a different way, including having doubts about the suitability of the role. For Minkow and Colson, the adoption of a professional-ex role was one that was an example of their change in values and their identity and not a precursor to it. Each reported having changed before leaving prison and before taking on the professional-ex role. It is for this reason that their professional-ex roles were not ones they (initially) felt driven to take up and should therefore not be considered as precursors to their change. Further example of this is demonstrated by the observation that both took time to come to their professional-ex roles following a 'search' for what they should do with their lives. Minkow in particular took several years to set up the Fraud Discovery Institute. Although his fraud talks and his radio show were started shortly after his release from prison, they were considered less important than his job as a pastor and it was five years after his release from prison that his professional-ex role was reprised full time as founder of the Fraud Discovery Institute. His professional-ex role was one he felt was important, but not as important as his role as a pastor.

The above shows how Colson and Minkow took on the role of professional-exes. Both Colson and Minkow had particular objectives they wished to achieve and particular notions of how they could make their existence meaningful that awaited an opportunity to act. Identities that drew upon their deviant pasts helped them achieve what they wished, their roles being particular demonstrations of their change.

Taking a deviant past role and making it a part of an ongoing 'successful' future is one means of managing a past, reconstructing the meaning of it. Coming to the professional-ex role was a process that, for Minkow in particular, was not a quick one and doubts had to be resolved before the role could be fully accepted. From uncertain beginnings, the work that Colson and Minkow undertook using their previous deviant identities was almost stumbled upon, being used to satisfy particular goals each man had. Being a professional-ex has been identified as bringing with it several advantages for the individual in terms of their own change and the 'message' that being a professional-ex sends to the rest of the world. The distinction between other professional-exes and Colson and Minkow is in the nature of the advantages drawn from the role. The advantages other professional-exes take from their roles were also present for Minkow and Colson although in a limited capacity when compared to professional-exes more generally. The professional-ex concept still has efficacy when considered in terms of white-collar offenders, although the analysis here makes more explicit the link between the exes' past and their professional-ex role. Colson and Minkow took different and rather specific things from their roles. What they have in common however is that both used appropriate aspects of their past to help their lives move forward as they desired.

A recurring consideration throughout this analysis is the possibility that this particular group of white-collar offenders are particularly well placed to draw upon resources financial, social and knowledge based that facilitate their desistance from crime. In general, previous chapters have indicated that such resources were not necessarily a significant influence aiding offenders' desistance.

With regard to professional-ex roles, the 'capital' that Minkow and Colson had might have helped them establish a professional-ex identity. Colson was able to use political connections to facilitate the establishment of Prison Fellowship. Minkow used the particular knowledge he had of business and finance to detect fraud. Despite having very different kinds of ex-role compared to the way such roles have been conceived generally however, such roles still 'worked' in a similar – if specialised – way for Minkow and Colson.

## Note

1 Brown actually uses the term *legitimacy*. However, for the purposes of this chapter the use of an ex role as providing a source of knowledge others lack is referred to as credibility. This is to separate it from the legitimacy Maruna identifies as being derived from professional-ex roles (see above), referring to them imparting a 'signal' that the offender has changed, a signal other roles may not 'send'.

# 8 Becoming who one is

## Religious conversion narratives and desistance

The story of conversion to a new religion is an easily recognised device in scripting a change in the life, particularly a change from a deviant life to a new, 'good' one. Perhaps because of the assumed power of religion to motivate change however, the authenticity of conversion is likely to be met with some scepticism. Potential ridicule did not prevent a number of the sample from converting to religion however. This chapter begins with a focus on belief systems more generally, how a belief system serves as a filter for the holder's perception of the world and the purpose of a belief system. The chapter then considers the relationship between religion and desistance as it has been explored within criminology, with particular reference to recent work by Giordano *et al.* (2008) before considering the adoption of religious beliefs by white-collar offenders. The analysis attends to the circumstances that surrounded white-collar offenders' conversion to religion and how they came to adopt beliefs that would become highly significant within their lives. The focus is also upon the way religious conversion resulted in a shift in the way they viewed their pasts within the context of a future in which they were a believer. Finally, the investigation is concerned with religious conversion as a social activity for these offenders and the interpersonal aspects of belief.

## Belief systems

To have a belief system is to have 'a stated conviction – either political or religious in nature – including all the complex human concepts about the structures and meanings of the world and human existence' (Brune *et al.*, 2002, 453). Whether religious or secular, a belief system acts as a framework for interpreting experiences (Converse, 1964; Grube *et al.*, 1994), providing an explanation as to the how and why of events, as well as an explanation of causality and an indication as to right and wrong behaviours (Frank, 1977). In addition, for Frank (1977), belief systems – religious and secular – are likely to be articles of faith, being relatively immutable even in the face of evidence that might contradict their central tenets. This conceptualisation of a belief system also emphasises the nature of it as an evaluative tool used, first, to interpret the behaviour of oneself and others, second, to order the importance of the believer's experiences and third, to consider the likely outcome of events (Frank, 1977). Consequently, belief systems are to some

## 152 *Religious conversion*

extent self-reinforcing, as experiences are likely to be interpreted in accordance with their tenets (Hersh, 1980).

These observations suggest a link to existentialist concerns. A firmly held system of belief provides the individual with a means of interpreting distressing situations and allows them to make sense of their experiences within a clearly defined framework (Rambo, 1993; McKnight, 2002). By providing answers as to the 'why' of existence, belief systems can therefore counter ontological anxiety: anxiety about the meaning of one's life (Frank, 1977). Rambo's (1993) suggestion that conversion to religion can be a route to self-worth is in keeping with this. Belief systems help believers to overcome ontological insecurity by appealing to notions of something bigger than the individual e.g. something that will outlast the transient nature of human existence. For religious belief systems it may be the notion of God and the concept of an afterlife, while for secular belief systems it might be the idea of working towards a fundamental 'truth' regarding reality or of making a contribution to society that will outlast the individual.

Frank (1977) suggests, however, that in guarding against ontological anxiety, religious belief systems are better able to help the individual cope, because they offer answers to the meaning of existence that belief systems that rely on the analysis of subjectively viewed experiences cannot (Rambo, 1993). A worldview that Frank considers 'mystical' or 'transcendental' (1977, 556), such as that characterised by religious belief, recognises that alternative realities may exist beyond the purview of measurable, observable experiences. Therefore such a worldview is able to provide satisfactory answers to otherwise 'unanswerable' questions e.g. why apparently unjust things happen. Paloutzian (1981) is in agreement, indicating that those who adopt a new religion score more highly on purpose of life measures, linking religion to the search for a meaningful existence. Further, Mahoney and Pargament (2004) associate the adoption of religious beliefs to the search for significance in life.

### Religious conversion

Paloutzian *et al.* (1999) note that religion meets a human need for meaning and identity, defining religious conversion as 'a change in the self-system due to commitment to that which the person believes to be sacred' (Paloutzian *et al.*, 1999, 1053). Inherent in this is the notion of transformation of the self. For Paloutzian *et al.* (1999), converting to a new religion may be a means of accomplishing personal growth goals. Paloutzian *et al.* also suggest that in instances of religious conversion and behaviour change, rather than the conversion being the catalyst for change it may in fact be the manner in which a desire to change is realised:

> Many of those who do convert do so as part of an effort to change their identity and self-definition. In short, many people who convert are seekers trying to find a way to change themselves in a way that they see as positive.
>
> (1999, 1061)

*Religious conversion* 153

Adopting a new religion can then be part of a commitment to change rather than being the cause of it (Rambo, 1993; see Patrick and Bignall, 1984 and also Kotarba and Bentley, 1988, for an example of how individuals make new commitments in accordance with their prevailing self-concept rather than as part of an attempt to change).

For Mahoney and Pargament (2004), the benefit of religious conversion is that it allows for a surrendering of control over one's life, relinquishing this to a higher power. This permits individuals to feel inadequately equipped to deal with problems they encounter, without such weakness reflecting a fundamental flaw in the self. Accompanying this, religious conversion is likely to herald themes of rebirth of the self and a subsequent forgiveness of the 'old' flawed self. This is particularly the case where a religion espouses themes of redemption. A reorientation of one's beliefs may therefore allow for the absolution of shame and guilt felt at past actions (Mahoney and Pargament, 2004). Conversion to religion impacts upon the past as well as the future. The former life can be re-evaluated in light of what the convert now knows. Religious conversion necessitates that the personal biography be placed in some sort of coherent narrative, the past making sense with regard to the present self. Events that were once confusing or difficult to understand are made meaningful by relating them to the will of God (Rambo, 1993).

Rambo (1993, 17) identifies religious conversion as one way of approaching a predicament in life.[1] According to Rambo, conversion takes place over seven 'stages': context, crisis, quest, encounter, interaction, commitment and consequences. *Context* is not, strictly speaking, a stage. It refers to the 'world' of the potential convert, everything social, cultural and psychological that impacts upon them, providing the setting for the start of their conversion 'journey'. It is the experience of a *crisis* that motivates individuals to explore other options. Crises can vary in their intensity from feelings of general dissatisfaction with the life to deeply rooted and very troubling feelings of angst or anguished soul searching prompted by events within the individual's realm of experience.

Experiencing a crisis can send the potential convert on a *quest* to resolve their problems. Important within the concept of a quest is that individuals are active in their search for 'something', seeking out new options to alleviate their crisis. Quest is the manifestation of the human desire for meaning and is present at all times, but becomes greatly magnified if the individual is experiencing a crisis. *Encounter* is the meeting of a questing individual with someone who can provide 'answers' to the questions they are struggling with. This is an 'advocate' in Rambo's (1993) terminology. The advocate attempts to convert the individual in crisis to their religion.

*Interaction* involves the convert learning more deeply about the religion the advocate espouses. Through friendships and the power of religious ritual the convert comes to identify more deeply with the religion, locating themselves as a follower of that religion. They gradually come to understand the interpretative framework of the religion and apply it to their life. Part of interaction also involves living the role of a convert, experiencing the new way of life inherent in such a role.

During *commitment*, the potential convert forms a 'bond' with God, a bond sometimes symbolised through particular religious ritual. The process of commitment

154 *Religious conversion*

is one of surrender to God, accepting God into the life, and it is frequently difficult because of this relinquishment of control to a superior power. A consequence of this commitment is the restructuring of the personal biography. Rambo (1993) conceptualises commitment as a specific turning point where God is acknowledged. This turning point is reached by making the decision to commit to the religion.

Finally, the *consequences* of the conversion become apparent to the convert. They may feel more complete or have a greater understanding of their life or, perhaps, may come to regret their conversion, realising it has failed to resolve the crisis as they hoped it might.

McKnight, in seeking to refine Rambo's (1993) model, prefers to discuss dimensions of conversion, feeling that Rambo's reference to stages suggests 'a deterministic march from earth to heaven' (McKnight, 2002, 49). Despite this, McKnight's (2002) analysis is largely sympathetic to Rambo's model. McKnight (2002) identifies six dimensions that mirror Rambo's seven 'stages' – the only absentee, *interaction*, included as part of the *encounter* dimension – and largely focuses upon emphasising the dynamic nature of the various dimensions and their relationship to one another. For example, a quest might be in answer to specific needs and might generate a crisis rather than being a result of one (McKnight, 2002).

Both Rambo and McKnight attempt to provide general models of conversion, seeking to capture all possible facets of the experience. As a result, their writings border on the vague at times, as they attempt to capture all possible nuances of conversion. For example, the 'strength' of an individual's crisis interacts with the earnestness of the quest, the vigour of the advocate in actively soliciting conversion, founded on a context that is likely to be highly individualistic. Rambo's (1993) account in particular lacks a full consideration of the 'reality' of conversion for particular individuals. What the following explanation of white-collar offenders' conversion to religion seeks to do is to identify the specifics of conversion for those offenders who had such an experience. The analysis has much concordance with Rambo and McKnight's models of conversion. However, the analysis below, in studying specific conversion stories, also departs from their conceptions of conversion in important ways. The most obvious difference in the way that conversion will be framed here is by situating it with regard to existential sociology. To pre-empt the below analysis, it is suggested that Rambo (1993) does not make enough of the emotional aspects of conversion, nor does the consideration of commitment allow for the possibility that relinquishing control over the life can potentially be attractive. Finally, both Rambo and McKnight identify conversion as a sometimes rather passive process, with the potential convert 'lured' to religion and 'sold' the benefits of religious belief by the advocate. While this is possible, it is important to note that here conversion was actively wanted by all of those white-collar offenders who did engage with religion.

## Religion and desistance from crime

Despite some contrary results, recent research suggests that religious involvement and participation in crime are negatively correlated. Baier and Wright (2001), in

*Religious conversion*   155

their meta-analysis of 60 studies of the influence of religion on crime noted a significant impact of religion, such that religious involvement deterred crime. Despite this, as Chu (2007) notes, there are no theories of desistance that include an explanation for the impact of religion upon criminal behaviour.

Giordano *et al.* (2008) remedy this to some extent in their study of desistance amongst 'street' offenders, asserting that religion can have an influence through traditionally conceived social control mechanisms (Hirschi, 1969), but also through acting to help reframe definitions of the offender's situation, providing a 'cognitive blueprint' for change that guides future action (Giordano *et al.*, 2002). Religion in this latter instance helps to promote a change in the conception of self. Giordano *et al.* (2008) investigated whether two indices of religiosity were related to persistence and desistance from crime, supplemented with interview data and specifically focusing upon the role of religion in the lives of 'highly disadvantaged offenders' (Girodano *et al.*, 2008, 101). This involved considering whether spirituality was related to desistance when the strength of adult social bonds such as marriage (Laub and Sampson, 2003) and the propensity towards crime of the individual's social network (Giordano *et al.*, 2003) were accounted for.

Common in the interviews conducted with participants was the notion that offenders believed their spirituality was an important influence in their desistance from crime. For Giordano *et al.* (2008) the importance of religion as a 'hook for change' (Girodano *et al.*, 2002) is that religious beliefs are frequently directly incompatible with continued deviance. Other hooks for change such as employment are not possessed of anything intrinsic that prevents involvement in deviant activity. As they observe, a job may have some desistance potential but does not preclude involvement in crime (Giordano *et al.*, 2008, 115). Religious conversion may therefore offer a greater opportunity for certification (Meisenhelder, 1982) from others that the offender has changed than other routes away from offending.

Giordano *et al.* (2008) note that, through attending to religious scripture, offenders are given a blueprint for how to act, and direct guidance for how change can take place. Beyond this, they show (2008, 117) that spiritual conversions have an emotional component. Religion did not just provide structure for how to live one's life; it made respondents feel happier, more peaceful and content with life more generally. Finally, religion was also a means through which offenders could interact with pro-social others, who in turn provided support for their desistance.

Limiting the positive effects of religion as a hook for change, however, were the extreme negative impacts of the disadvantaged areas in which individuals lived. Further, interview data indicated that only where religious conversion was reinforced by pro-social networks, i.e. was not a private affair, did it help to influence sustained behaviour change. In the absence of such networks, it is possible that offenders were able to rationalise a way for their spiritual beliefs and their deviant lifestyle to continue together. Additionally, the focus of some religious beliefs upon temptation as an external force e.g. as prompted by the devil, may allow for a rationalising of deviant behaviour (Giordano *et al.*, 2008, 123). Finally, the difficulties faced daily by some of Giordano *et al.*'s (2008) participants were often associated with 'God's will', limiting any possibility that they would attempt to

156  *Religious conversion*

deal with them. This last highlights the importance of attending to the way in which a belief system fits with the life more generally.

## Religious belief and white-collar offenders

Amongst the white-collar offenders whose accounts are considered here, six, identified in Table 8.1, converted to a religious belief system at some point after their offending began. Although some of these men had paid lip service to religion prior to their conversion, their accounts make clear that the beliefs they adopted that formed their conversion experience represented a significant undertaking in their lives. In keeping with the view that conversion is a process rather than an event (Rambo, 1993), it is neither possible nor desirable to identify a particular moment when each man converted. As shall be seen, accepting a new religion took some time for each man, notwithstanding the fact that several report highly significant 'encounters' when they engaged with God. All of these men were in the process of discovering more about their particular belief system before they were convicted. Conversion to a religious belief system was identified by an offender's account making reference to a shift in beliefs, such that they came to believe in the existence of a 'higher being' or a 'higher calling'. David Bullen's conversion was to Buddhism, while the remaining five of these men converted to a Christian belief system. Table 8.1 shows the beliefs converted to and when offenders first became aware of them.

The analysis below explores the conversion process as described by these men. It investigates how white-collar offenders come to take on religious belief systems, how religious belief related to their lives more generally and, as part of this, distinguishes between 'inner' and 'social' aspects to religious conversion.

## Adopting new belief systems

This section outlines a broadly shared 'process' through which white-collar offenders who converted to religion went. Much of the conversion experience was made up of being amenable to change and also having the opportunity to take advantage of this amenability. Although the presentation of the experiences of individuals who undergo a change in their beliefs may appear to suggest that such a change is

*Table 8.1* White-collar offenders' religious beliefs and first awareness of them

| Offender | Belief converted to | First awareness of belief system |
| --- | --- | --- |
| Jonathan Aitken | Christianity | Before offence detected |
| David Bullen | Buddhism | Before offence detected |
| Charles Colson | Christianity | Before offence detected |
| Stephen Lawson | Christianity | Before offence detected |
| Jeb Magruder | Christianity | After detection of offence, before conviction |
| Barry Minkow | Christianity | Before offence detected |

linear, this is not the case. On the contrary, belief change is a dynamic process, with continuous interplay between doubts and positive experiences and these impacting upon the way conversion is experienced.

### *The context of conversion*

The adoption of a religion must necessarily be considered within the context of the convert's life more generally. Individuals might be made open to change in response to an existential crisis. All six of these men report feelings of a 'void' in their life, with feelings of general, vague emptiness that left them ill at ease, but which were insufficiently defined to be dealt with. Stephen Lawson, for example, felt angst periodically throughout his adult life, concerned he was 'totally alone' in the world (Lawson, 1992, 88), while David Bullen, convicted of illegal trading while with the National Australia Bank, was also despondent with his life:

> I was beginning to feel that this whole merry-go-round [his life] was leading nowhere except to my death and I wondered what the point was. In a way – even though I was happier than I had ever been before – I was also beginning to be a bit despondent about life in general. I already knew what path my life was taking...
>
> (Bullen, 2004, 64–65)

Jeb Magruder had similar feelings:

> All my life there had been a sort of restlessness inside me. Something wasn't quite right about wherever I was or whatever I was doing. I was never really happy, even though I had everything supposedly necessary to make a person happy.
>
> (Magruder, 1978, 69)

Such feelings prepared offenders for the introduction of something to 'fill the void' in their lives and through such experiences they became open to change, albeit without any notion of how such could be achieved (Giordano *et al.*, 2002). Offenders made little attempt to address such lack of meaning however. In the first instance, the reason for this might be that such feelings of emptiness are temporary. Second, a search for 'something else' may entail the partial rejection of the current life, which could bring about its own existential concerns by admitting that what one may have spent many years striving for was of little use in achieving a meaningful sense of self. This could lead to a critical assessment of one's values and beliefs and consequently even greater distress if these were found to be wanting. What these accounts suggest, however, is that white-collar offenders who converted to religious beliefs felt something missing in their lives. This in turn made them more amenable to the possibility of change more generally (Giordano *et al.*, 2002). What they lacked was the ability to envision the specific form such change would take.

## 158  *Religious conversion*

### Becoming aware

Although awareness of a void in the life opened individuals up to the possibility of change, such feelings were not inevitably acted upon. Instead, these accounts suggest almost 'stumbling' across what would become a highly significant perspective on life. While Charles Colson was worrying about the revelations that would accompany the discovery of Watergate and how they might affect President Nixon's administration, a friend told him about his own personal crisis and how he resolved it by accepting God into his life:

> A prickly feeling ran down my spine. Maybe what I had gone through in the past several months had not been so bad after all – except that I had not sought spiritual answers.
>
> (Colson, 1976, 109–110)

With the exception of Bullen, offenders were made aware of the belief system by friends. Bullen was introduced to Buddhist beliefs through books. All were aware of religious tenets before they decided to pursue such beliefs. Such awareness alerted them further to the possibility of change along the quite specific lines suggested by the religion. They began to orient themselves to the possibility of adopting the beliefs of a particular system. The desire for change they had was now complemented by a means of envisioning how such change could be realised.

### Accepting a belief system

Despite being open to change, the demands of life may preclude the opportunity to attempt to resolve feelings of a lack of meaning. Jonathan Aitken learnt about Christianity from Bible study during a parliamentary retreat. This gave him some perspective on what was important in his life. However, he felt that his court case with *The Guardian*, the newspaper he was suing for libel, took precedence:

> [I had a] glimpse of a past and a future in which what really mattered was the power of God. Yet for all the assurance of Isaiah 43,[2] I was living in a present where what really mattered was the power of *The Guardian*.
>
> (Aitken, 2000, 101, emphasis in original)

It was only when the demands of life more generally were removed did offenders deal with the angst that had troubled them. With the exception of Bullen, accepting a religious belief system was done within the crucible of the detection of their offence. Their lives were thrown into turmoil, with previously anticipated futures suddenly having little or no veracity. The consequences of detection included the loss or temporary suspension of employment, negative reactions from others and the disclosure of the 'secret life' that the offence represented to their family. Concomitant with this were feelings of shame and guilt. Rationalisations offenders used during their offence to protect themselves from these emotions were rendered useless by the reactions of others who highlighted the contrast between individuals'

*Religious conversion* 159

values and their actions. The distress of this uncertain future was exacerbated by feelings of a lack of control over their lives as they awaited the result of investigation into their offence. The context created by the detection of their offence denied them a solid grounding from which to see a safe future.

This was an existentially shattering experience, with no future discernible except one couched in negative terms. The lives these men had led were suddenly and swiftly changed, impacting upon their sense of who they were (Drahota and Eitzen, 1998; Shaffir and Kleiknecht, 2005). Stephen Lawson was distraught when he discovered he was to be charged by the Securities and Exchange Commission, concerned that his life had ended (Lawson, 1992, 102). Barry Minkow's life was similarly devastated by the discovery of his offence. His company *ZZZZ Best* was central to his identity because he had used it as a means of achieving the admiration and respect from others that he desired (e.g. Minkow, 1995, 32, 38). He had founded his company at the age of 16 and had been subject to much positive media attention because of his young age as a company owner. Consequently, its collapse exposed him as a fraud and this revelation of the lie behind the Barry Minkow 'legend' represented a severe crisis for him:

> my whole purpose for living had ceased to exist. I had no identity apart from ZZZZ Best... But it was worse than that. I wasn't just a failure – I had fallen, hurting thousands of people on the way down. although I had tried for years to earn people's love, acceptance and respect, now I'd be remembered as the kid who'd conned everyone.
>
> (Minkow, 1995, 178)

Such feelings illustrate the impact that the detection of a criminal offence may have. The collapse of Minkow's company prompted strong feelings of ontological insecurity, shame and guilt. The end of his company represented the end of his identity, the end of his respect from others and consequently the 'end' of him.

Feelings of shame and guilt directly challenge notions of self-worth, being grounded in the individuals' past (Corr, 2002; Taylor, 1985). While the future is distressing because it is unknown, the past is distressing because of the realisation that one's own values have been violated, signalling a flaw in the self (Douglas, 1984; Manion, 2002). The exception in this instance is David Bullen. Bullen accepted Buddhist teachings and was on his own quest for enlightenment before his offence was detected. As will be noted below, this conversion helped him to neutralise feelings of shame and guilt that he might otherwise have felt.

For the others, although the detection of their offence was extremely distressing, it also represented the nadir of their despair. Ultimately, offenders had to attempt to look to the future and envision a manner in which they might rebuild their life. From an existential perspective, this looking forward is a given, as the self can only achieve a meaningful identity by moving forward. Remaining stagnant is not an option (Douglas, 1984; Fontana, 1984). The only remaining issue therefore, is how this rebuilding might be achieved. It was during this time that individuals begin to respond to the possibility of adopting the religious beliefs they had already

## 160 *Religious conversion*

been made aware of. Reflecting upon his *metanoia* (change of mind: Aitken, 2000, 252), Jonathan Aitken identified its origin in his distress following the collapse of his libel case:

> The starting point of my metanoia was the rock bottom I had hit in terms of despair. Was I going to collapse at this rock bottom and lie there wallowing in thoughts of suicide, self-pity and sadness? Or was I going to get up and change direction in the spirit of *metanoia*?
>
> (Aitken, 2000, 252, emphasis in original)

At the time when his offences first came to light, his company had collapsed and he faced the prospect of prosecution, Barry Minkow consulted a Christian friend:

> I felt safe in [Maggie's] small place, temporarily removed from the media and the many people I had victimised'What are you really here for, Barry?'...
> 'Peace, happiness, contentment – to be able to look at myself in the mirror without feeling guilty'. ... 'On the other hand, I don't want to go to jail. Or' Suddenly, unaccountably, I wanted to be honest with her – and with myself. 'Maybe I'm here because becoming a Christian might earn me some sympathy with the media or some future jury'.
>
> (Minkow, 1995, 182)

Religious belief therefore offered a solution to individuals' crises. Minkow began to think of the consequences of belief, not the least of which was the positive social impact his conversion would have. Potential converts are likely to have an awareness of how their conversion may be viewed (Pitulac and Nastura, 2007). Minkow was aware of the potential benefits of conversion, based upon the positive associations that he felt being a Christian would impart (Goffman, 1963; Lofland, 1969; Meisenhelder, 1982). Recall that this was early in Minkow's conversion 'journey'. Therefore, although on the surface this duplicity relates to the 'con-man' Minkow was when he was defrauding investors in his company, his desire to be 'suddenly, unaccountably... honest' spoke to his desire to change, particularly with his desire to be honest with himself.

Within the context of Rambo's (1993) model, the detection of their offences was a crisis that prompted offenders' quests. In keeping with some conceptualisations of quest, what is lacking in these accounts is the notion of an active search for 'something' that the belief system comes to fulfil (Rambo, 1993). The belief system was brought before offenders and they then responded to it. Consequently, there appears little thought given to alternatives, although it might be thought that one alternative open to all would be to reject the belief system. Given the existential crises faced, however, it seems unlikely that a serious attempt would be made to reject what seemed a potential solution. Further, the general shift towards the efficacy of a change in beliefs made these offenders open specifically to religion as a means of resolving their feelings of despair and emptiness (Giordano *et al.*, 2002).

*Religious conversion* 161

In the encounters considered here, therefore, the possibility of adopting religious belief was always attended to positively, at least in the first instance. However, for those who did consider conversion following a period of existential angst, the underlying motivation to do so was that the belief system provided a means of solving their dilemma. At this point then, these white-collar offenders began to think seriously about what it meant to be a believer and began to tentatively envision what such a future entailed.

### Doubts

Initial encounters with belief systems were a mundane experience, unaccompanied by the crashing of thunder or divine pronouncement. Such encounters introduced the possibility of a new way of living however, alerting individuals to a way out of their crisis. Feelings of ontological insecurity which ordinarily might prevent growth of the self (Yalom, 1980) could be overcome by the desire to do 'something' to solve the problem. Nevertheless, doubts were still experienced as these men struggled to accept that the belief system could do for them what others promised it could. Individuals decided to 'invest' their future in the belief system, realising that to do so meant a reshaping of their life. This meant there would be a period of transition where their sense of self would enter a period of flux as new values and beliefs were considered and adopted (Ebaugh, 1984), while the old self with its associated values and beliefs was left behind. Such a solution meant considering a future unlike any previously imagined and the start of a venture where success was not guaranteed. Barry Minkow experienced such doubts when the idea that he might get help from God was suggested to him:

> Could God really love me? Could He satisfy my deepest needs ...?
>
> (Minkow, 1995, 180)

Stephen Lawson had similar concerns, wanting to accept God but unsure his acceptance would be reciprocated. A Christian friend was of little help when he could not answer questions Lawson had regarding his new faith:

> For the first time I was asking Don questions he couldn't answer, and that upset me ... 'Could it be that I want [God], but he doesn't want me?'... God's rejection would be the final, unbearable indictment.
>
> (Lawson, 1992, 106)

Given the desperation of the circumstances of conversion, the possibility of failure in the new venture conversion represented was terrifying, signalling a return to the existential wilderness. Better perhaps not to even try, not to risk hoping one might have a meaningful life once more, than to attempt and fail. The desire for love and to be wanted, as present in Minkow's and Lawson's accounts is indicative of the shame and guilt felt at the discovery of their offences. To hope for a particular future would be to commit oneself to it and

162 *Religious conversion*

overcome such shame (Simpson, 2004). To hope for God's love and fail to achieve it would be to have the self rejected.

More fundamental doubts surrounded the actual existence of God. Three men – Aitken, Colson, Magruder – indicated the importance of coming to intellectual terms with the presence of God. As Jonathan Aitken started to explore the possibility of seriously pursuing his Christian faith he studied religious texts and devoted much time to considering the nature of redemption and how a believer might repent (Aitken, 2000, 251). Some took the further step of arguing rationally for God's existence as Charles Colson (1976, 122–128) and Jeb Magruder (1978, 67) did. However, although such approaches led individuals to believe in the existence of God, belief was not a purely rational endeavour. As Aitken conceded:

> a soul does not move to God by a logical process of conversion from the head, but from mysterious and incomprehensible changes within the heart.
>
> (Aitken, 2000, 190)

'Decisions' to believe were therefore driven by the way such belief felt. Therefore, despite the doubts expressed, all offenders reported a single significant moment where a connection was made with the belief. In these moments, the relationship between belief and life suddenly had great clarity. Existentially, this represented the realisation that there was a solution to their situation, that they might move forward with their life and that the future promised by belief was one they might 'live' in (Fontana, 1984; Hayim, 1996; Giordano *et al.*, 2002). The life could have meaning again. Barry Minkow had such a moment:

> In desperation I began to pray… When I finished, no lightning came down from above. There were no spectacular signs… But that evening, a lonely, distraught, twenty-one-year-old boy began a relationship with Jesus Christ.
>
> (Minkow, 1995, 186–187)

David Bullen's experience was equally dramatic. He read a passage from the Tao Te Ching, a Chinese spiritual text:

> *When people see some things as beautiful, other things become ugly.* From the moment I read this line something changed in me dramatically. It felt like a veil had been removed. I understood the depth of meaning in those words. From that point I understood that my life was to be devoted to the work of developing spiritually and helping others to do the same so they could realise enlightenment, and that nothing else was important unless it assisted in this.
>
> (Bullen, 2004, 67, emphasis in original)

It was not the case that these highly significant moments led to instant change in offenders' lives. Instead change was achieved gradually (see for example, Farrall, 2005; Farrall *et al.*, 2014 for this sort of gradual change amongst other offenders). What such experiences did, however, was cement individuals' motivation to change. Change was no longer part of their possible future; it was actually happening.

*Religious conversion* 163

### Learning to believe

The tensions present as the conversion process continued demonstrate the importance of individuals learning how to believe. That is, they must come to understand
what being an adherent to the religion entails. How does a believer act? What does
a believer do? These are pertinent questions, particularly within the context of an
offence, not least because it was the difficulty presented by offenders' circumstances that prompted them to think seriously about conversion. What was
necessary for white-collar offenders was reconciling their new beliefs with their
current and past actions. While under investigation for his role in Watergate,
Charles Colson came to the realisation that his denial of any wrongdoing, while
true as far as Watergate was concerned, was fundamentally incompatible with his
newly acquired Christian faith:

> My conversion would remain incomplete so long as I was a criminal
> defendant, tangled in the Watergate quagmire. I had to put the past behind me
> completely. If it meant going to prison so be it!
>
> (Colson, 1976, 223)

Although innocent of any Watergate charges, Colson did feel he was guilty of
obstructing a federal investigation by disseminating defamatory information about
a man who was under indictment. Although this was not an offence at the time,
Colson's faith prompted him to plead guilty to it, creating a legal precedent in the
process (Colson, 1976, 222–224). Ultimately, this led to his prison sentence.

Stephen Lawson felt that if he were to truly be a Christian, he must act as one
should in regard to the investigation of his offences:

> I wanted to embark on my new life in Christ with old things truly past. That
> meant I must even admit to things the court knew nothing about and would
> depend on God to watch over me as I revealed the truth.
>
> (Lawson, 1992, 118)

Jonathan Aitken recognised that his continued exploration of his faith was incompatible with his attempt to sue *The Guardian* for libel (because the allegations the
newspaper made were true):

> My spiritual posture at this crossroads in my life was ludicrous... So I prayed
> in one direction with my lips and went in another direction with my life... I
> continued to charge ahead at full throttle of pride into the furnace of the libel
> battle, fuelled by an arrogant determination to defeat my unlovable neighbours
> at *The Guardian*... The conflict between prayerfulness and pridefulness created
> within me an acute sense of tension, restlessness and, at times, misery.
>
> (Aitken, 2000, 190, emphasis in original)

Aitken took no direct action to resolve this problem however, although he did pray
for it to be resolved (Aitken, 2000, 190). Colson's and Aitken's accounts highlight

## 164 *Religious conversion*

the tension between the old self, with its accompanied beliefs and values, and the future self that they converted to, defined in part by who they no longer wanted to be (Sartre, 1958; Denzin, 1987). The transition period as the old self is gradually left behind and the new one is accepted is more difficult if the individual still doubts the value of the beliefs encapsulated in the new system.

Despite this, what the above examples demonstrate is that eventually behaviour and beliefs became aligned to one another. The values that a believer 'ought' to hold became gradually internalised and any potential inconsistency between beliefs and behaviour became increasingly acute. The presence of others helped the individuals to realise the inconsistency between their beliefs and their actions. Barry Minkow was confronted with regard to his plan to lie about his offending in a TV interview:

> 'Now, Barry, you just got through telling me that you wanted God to change you, and yet here you are taking matters into your own hands again'.... 'You're going to go on national television and lie!' Her words cut through my rationalizations.
>
> (Minkow, 1995, 188)

Internalisation of values was strengthened through following them in problematic situations that consequently had a beneficial outcome. Therefore, values became self-reinforcing as they helped with the navigation of novel situations (Douglas, 1984). Accepting the tenets of the belief therefore meant to accept a way of living the life. It was in this way that the offenders chose to make the commitment to belief. In providing a set of rules by which to live, the belief system set out a 'blueprint' for behaviour (Giordano *et al.*, 2002, 2008); tenets that could be used to interpret situations and also provide a guide for action.

### *Confirming the efficacy of beliefs*

Despite accepting the tenets of a belief system and (where appropriate) the existence of God, offenders still had doubts that their new beliefs truly represented a guide to how life should be lived. Tackling such doubts meant confirming the efficacy of the belief system as a guide to life by identifying the benefits of living in accordance with it. In some ways, this is done as has already been described, by learning how to 'be' a believer. Additionally, confirming the worth of religious belief can be done by selectively experiencing phenomena in a way that re-enforces beliefs, with particular emphasis on confirming the presence of God. Stephen Lawson was disappointed when friends initially refused to provide financial help for his wife while he was incarcerated (Lawson, 1992, 122). This was taken as an example of human frailty, rather than the absence of God. Conversely, when contributions were made these were taken to be as proving God's existence:

> Thus I learned some vitally important lessons. I learned that I must look ultimately to God, because people will let you down... And I must trust *God* to

provide for my family. I had meant to see that my family was taken care of –
by me.

(Lawson, 1992, 123, emphasis in original)

Lawson attended to the 'tangible proof ' (Lawson, 1992, 123) of God's existence
and it is in this way that the belief system becomes self-reinforcing. Events are
considered within the framework the system provides, which are then interpreted
as 'proving' the value of the system. It might also be suggested that religious belief
systems, with their emphasis on faith over proof, may be particularly easy to
reinforce in this way. Everything that happens can be interpreted as being God's
will, and consequently as proof of the validity of the system. Lawson's example
also demonstrates the resistance of belief systems to experiences that might prove
a risk to them.

A further way in which the efficacy of the belief system may be underlined is
when employing the tenets of it helps the user to solve the problematic encounters
that their situation forces upon them. Stephen Lawson describes the relief of
starting to apply the tenets of his new faith. Lawson asked those he had sinned
against by being petty and vindictive to forgive him:

Those visits were never easy, yet each time I did what Jesus commanded, I was
blessed far more than I could have expected... The moment I dropped the
letters in the mailbox a tremendous weight lifted off my heart. And I wept
there – right on the street corner.

(Lawson, 1992, 110)

Similarly, Aitken prayed to be able to forgive those in the media he felt had
persecuted him (2005, 53–54). All six men admitted their offences (although
Bullen, as shall be seen later had some qualifications about his guilt) but Lawson's
and Aitken's actions were not intrinsically about easing these feelings of guilt
related to criminal activity. Instead they were focused on a desire to undo all the
wrongs of their pasts, like Colson did when he pleaded guilty to an – at the time –
non-existent offence (Colson, 1976, 222–224).

Ebaugh (1984) notes that individuals who are considering embarking on a new
and uncertain venture that is likely to herald significant change in their self will
attempt to practise engaging in activities that would be expected of them if the
change is made. Such 'role rehearsal' permits the individual to gain a notion of
whether or not they will adapt to a new role. Experiences such as Lawson's helped
to persuade converts that their new beliefs provided a way of living life that was
viable and could help them to navigate new situations. This further emphasises
that the individual can 'be' a believer and live according to the belief system and
consequently that they do have a meaningful future.

Part of learning to be a believer means learning to trust in God. Confirming the
efficacy of religious belief is more likely to be done by what it 'feels like' to believe
in the existence of God, as touched upon above (Aitken, 2000, 190). Engagement
with a belief system is as much an emotional endeavour as it is a cognitive one.

166　*Religious conversion*

With that in mind, this chapter now turns to two specific aspects of adopting a religious belief system. These are rather roughly dichotomised as internal and social aspects of belief, while maintaining regard for the fact that internal aspects of belief will impact upon the social experience of it and that also the reverse is true.

## Inner aspects to a belief system

Focusing on the 'inner' aspects of adopting a religious belief system means to concentrate on what it 'feels like' to believe. Experiencing powerful emotions was part of religious conversion for all of those considered here. Another facet of religious belief is the way in which the belief system changes the believer's perspective on their life, both the future and the past.

### *Shame, guilt and relinquishing of control*

An example of how belief acts as a 'lens' through which life may be viewed is the way in which it allowed offenders to view their offence in such a way that guilt and shame were lessened. What made religious beliefs attractive to offenders is that they allowed the relinquishing of control over offenders' lives (Mahoney and Pargament, 2004; Giordano *et al.*, 2008). This is particularly the case with Christian belief systems, which propose notions of man as a flawed character, a sinner who must relinquish himself to God's control. Such relinquishment is not necessarily a troublesome proposition, because God will forgive all one's sins if they are admitted. This then allows for the individual to be 'reborn', to start their life afresh under God's tutelage. Confessing the past in this way helps to ameliorate shame and guilt because the past is immediately forgiven. Stephen Lawson reached the understanding that such forgiveness had taken place:

> I had been hopeless; now I experienced the power of God's grace, grounded in the knowledge provided in the previous two and a half years of reading and study. I had called out to the Lord, and he heard – and delivered me from my fears.
>
> (Lawson, 1992, 114–115)

Relinquishing control aids attempts to confront past actions. Accepting that only by relinquishing the life to God can the convert be saved is less problematic than believing one has responsibility for one's own actions and therefore could have acted differently (Mahoney and Pargament, 2004). Accepting we have mastery over our own actions has the potential to be deeply distressing, particularly when those actions are perceived as harmful in some manner or as running contrary to our values (Ford, 1996). The distress in this instance has its origin in knowing one could have acted differently if one had chosen to do so and that we are responsible for our actions (Sartre, 1963). To realise that one could have acted differently would prompt feelings of shame and guilt at the failure to live up to the self-perception, and it was better to accept the fact of one's own specific flaws and give one's life

*Religious conversion* 167

over to a belief system that espouses forgiveness. Jonathan Aitken finally came to achieve closeness with God through penitence, making the analogy of being at sea on a stormy night to describe how he relinquished control over his life:

> Whether I drowned or got back would depend on a power far greater than my own.
>
> (Aitken, 2000, 261)

Rambo (1993) touches upon this giving up of control during the *commitment* stage of conversion. Rambo emphasises the pain of commitment to God that is present in some forms of Christian worship, as the convert is encouraged to see the sins present in their own life. Commitment to God is the only way to save oneself from these sins. A final aspect of commitment is surrender, '...an inner yielding of control, an acceptance of the authority of the leader, group, or tradition...' (Rambo, 1993, 132)

Surrender is characterised by conflict within the convert. On the one hand there is the desire to convert to the new life as espoused by the belief system. On the other there is a fear of relinquishing control of one's life. Consequently, surrender is presented by Rambo as potentially problematic and a time of great conflict. In contrast, the accounts here suggest that relinquishing control makes conversion attractive because of the way in which it mitigates shame and guilt. The men considered here – with the exception of Bullen – had pasts they felt ashamed of. This is not to say that these men did not struggle over their conversion. As the above accounts testify, several did. However, the source of this struggle was a worry that the belief system was not a solution to their crisis (e.g. Minkow, 2005, 180; Lawson, 1992, 106).

Many types of Christian conversion force the convert to recognise their sins as a prelude to acknowledging the 'death' of their previous self and subsequent 'rebirth' (Rambo, 1993, 132). This is difficult and painful. The difference for these white-collar offenders however is that their 'sins' were already more public than those of most people. They, and many others, were aware how they had sinned. Confessing would therefore have been less difficult perhaps. This makes explicit the relationship between the crisis that initiated the conversion and the reflection on what the conversion 'means'.

A different example of the relationship between conversion and guilt and a further, albeit quite specific example of the manner in which a new belief system's 'lens' may be used to view one's behaviour in a positive way is presented by David Bullen, convicted of illegal trading while with the National Bank of Australia. Bullen continued to offend after his conversion, his Buddhist views meaning he saw the illegal trades he was conducting in a new way:

> After all, the law is simply made up of black markings on pieces of paper. People believe in these markings but this is also a mutual delusion that there is something of value in the markings. All those markings do is support the wealthy and powerful when they are related to money.
>
> (Bullen, 2004, 133)

168    *Religious conversion*

With his offence constructed in this way, Bullen felt no shame or guilt at his activities. He recognised that he had made illegal trades. In accordance with his new beliefs, however, 'illegal' did not mean anything. Bullen's case highlights that adopting a belief system may not always signal change in behaviour. Rather, established behaviours may be viewed in a new light. However, this is still consistent with the use of belief systems as a lens through which to view the past. What Bullen has in common with the others is that his belief system changed the way he perceived his actions.

Bullen's (2004, 133) example is consistent with observations regarding belief systems as 'tools' for interpreting experiences (Converse, 1964, Grube *et al.*, 1994). His case also provides a counterpoint to the others, who all adopted Christian beliefs. The themes of forgiveness promulgated by such beliefs explain the admission of guilt by those who adopted them. Giordano *et al.* (2008) note that offending may continue to take place in the presence of religious beliefs and Bullen's case exemplifies a further way in which this might be done. Religious conversion may be part of the desistance of offenders, but only if the beliefs converted to support a change in behaviour.

Bullen later moderated his position on his actions, although still with reference to his Buddhist beliefs. In court, Bullen was quoted as welcoming a prison sentence because this would be good karma (The New Zealand Herald, 2006). This apparent desire to 'atone' for his offence does not alter the initial way his beliefs contributed to his offending however.

### Retelling the past

All of those considered here make reference to the 'new' life they gained as a result of the belief system they adopted, contrasting the wonder, peace and contentment of it with the prideful, decadent life they led before they accepted God. The change that Christianity brought about for him is described by Jeb Magruder:

> Gradually I was gaining some perspective. I was beginning to realize that even though a person has many different responsibilities in life… In fact, only a few really matter at all: God, my family, and whatever work Christ wanted me to do for him.
>
> (Magruder, 1978, 175)

Adopting religious beliefs helped with attempts to reconstruct the personal biography by also putting a distressing past into context (Maruna, 2001; Vaughan, 2007). Charles Colson interpreted his offence and time in prison as being part of God's design, with his work as head of the Prison Ministry a part of this:

> Could I ever understand the horrors of prison life by visiting a prison? *…of course not.* No one could understand this without being part of it, feeling the anxieties, knowing the helplessness, living in the desolation… I thought to

myself. *There is a purpose to my being [in prison], perhaps a mission the Lord has called me to.*

(Colson, 1976, 284, emphasis in original)

Also:

[God] took my greatest defeat – my fall from power and experience in prison as a broken man, the one thing in which I could not glory – and he has used it for *His* glory.

(Colson, 1976, 343, emphasis in original)

Conceptualising the past as pre-ordained helps to make sense of what has happened. Actions that were put down to pride, greed or selfishness may now be recast as being necessary if the individual was to be 'saved' by God. As McKnight makes explicit:

converts always reconstruct their personal autobiography in line with their new faith. They now have a 'new story to tell,' and we have learned that one element of this new story is the assigning of motives and causes to the world ('God did this so I would do that' or 'This happened so I would be led to this person') ...

(McKnight, 2002, 93)

In this way the belief system becomes integrated into the whole life of the believer. It has connotations for how the whole life should be led and is recognised retrospectively as the 'thing' that was missing from the life (see above). More than this though, it makes the promise that such a void will never occur again, that life now has meaning and from now on always will. There is therefore a future-oriented aspect to belief. In the aftermath of the collapse of his libel case, Jonathan Aitken did not know what the future would hold for him. However, because of his Christian faith he was untroubled:

I may have lost the whole world of my previous life, but I have found my own soul in a new life. ...Having made the commitment to God, I now look forward to following him wherever he leads with trust, hope and joyful acceptance.

(Aitken, 2000, 367)

Such feelings helped Aitken to face his future without worry, his new belief system able to convince him that he would now always be secure. Believing in God impacted upon how he felt about his life and did so in a positive manner. Conversion represented a fresh start following repentance for his sins. Colson (1976, 340) and Lawson (1992, 173) similarly recognised that life would be 'okay' because of their faith.

As much as religion provided a perspective on the past it also, necessarily, had an impact upon the future because of the shift in the values and beliefs conversion

170 *Religious conversion*

entailed. These white-collar offenders, in a similar manner to Giordano *et al.*'s (2008) participants, constructed positive meanings around religion as a way of living their life, as in Aitken's above quote, where the potential 'trials' of his future were not a worry because of his faith (2000, 367). This construction necessarily had implications for their future. What the above makes explicit when compared to Giordano *et al.*'s (2008) observations, however, is the way in which specific aspects of the past are made relevant to a particular, individual present. For example, Colson's painful experience of the 'desolation' of prison was construed by him as having a 'purpose...' within the context of his future as head of a prison ministry (1976, 284). Colson's example also outlines (more fully than Rambo elucidates) the relationship between 'crisis' (to use both Rambo's terminology and that applied here) and conversion. Colson's crisis was being 'broken' by his 'fall from power', but his conversion helped to make this meaningful (1976, 343). The utilisation of religious beliefs to satisfy individuals' crises is apparent in the above accounts. If religious conversion is attempted in answer to a crisis, then it is inevitable that the crisis will be re-evaluated in light of conversion.

### *Positive feelings*

That new beliefs can ameliorate shame and guilt underlines the importance of emotion in reinforcing change. Farrall and Calverley (2006) demonstrate that potential desisters may come to experience positive emotions[3] through engaging in new, non-deviant activities. These emotions then increase commitment to the activity, which replaces offending as a source of pleasure in the life. Giordano *et al.* (2008) report that positive emotions were a significant factor in their participants' accounts of the adoption of spiritual and religious aspects of their lives. Such is the same for these white-collar offenders. Religious belief brought them feelings of wellbeing and contentment. Charles Colson for example describes feeling 'almost serene' (Colson, 1976, 209). This serenity was echoed by David Bullen when he was interviewed by his employers, the National Australia Bank regarding his offences:

> The head of market risk was in a minor panic and I sensed fear. This was great. I was looking at doing a stint [i.e. prison sentence] and was as happy and serene as can be, while those who were after me to save their own skins were under stress.
>
> (Bullen, 2004, 137)

Stephen Lawson asked Jesus to help him with his feelings of loneliness:

> At that time, spiritual discernment was beyond me. All I knew was that within an instant the loneliness had departed. Not only had it departed, but I felt better than I had in years.
>
> (Lawson, 1992, 89)

*Religious conversion* 171

Lawson's example illustrates the way in which the positive feelings which came from belief contrasted strongly with other feelings. Engaging with a belief system is therefore an emotional endeavour as much as it is cognitive (Giordano *et al.*, 2008). This was important for confirming that adhering to a religious belief system was not only logical, but felt right. Such feelings act to enforce the efficacy of the belief system as viable. This is important for dispelling doubts over belief. Reasons for believing in the presence of God were built up in line with how believing 'felt', as Aitken makes reference to above (2000, 190).

This emotional aspect to conversion is something that Rambo (1993) and McKnight (2002) perhaps treat too lightly. Rambo's emphasis on the decision to convert, 'commitment', portrays the dynamics of conversion as rather too rational, particularly within the context of the accounts presented here. Although acknowledging that positive emotions can be elicited by conversion, Rambo's framework still implies a rational calculation, with potential converts 'deciding' (or not) to enjoy these emotions. To deny the power emotions have to drive decisions is to seemingly deny the experiences of these religious converts.

## Social aspects of belief

In addition to the inner aspects of belief, conversion to religion contained a social component as well. The social aspects of conversion can be seen through the impact of new social networks, the certification (Meisenhelder, 1982) that offenders gained through association with a belief system and the very public nature of these offenders' lives after conversion.

### *Peer groups*

Giordano *et al.* (2008) indicate that religion can provide access to pro-social others who helped converts maintain their change. The same was the case for these white-collar offenders. As is indicated above, conversion to a religion is not something that is usually undertaken alone (Rambo, 1993; McKnight, 2002). All of these men, with the exception of Bullen, drew upon new peer groups to provide support as they became believers. These groups were inevitably centred around gathering for the express purpose of worship, but such groups provided advice and examples of how to believe. Magruder writes of the importance of Christian friends for demonstrating how to act:

> *this was the kind of person I wanted to be someday* – I wanted to be able to give to other human beings the kind of love I was receiving from Jesus Christ, and I wanted to give it directly, personally.
>
> (Magruder, 1978, 143, emphasis added)

As indicated above, those adopting a belief system must learn what it means to be a believer (Rambo, 1993). This entails gaining an understanding of how an adherent to the belief system acts, how they think and what this means in the

## 172  *Religious conversion*

context of their current situation. Social networks act as a guide to living according to the belief system. For Jonathan Aitken, a prayer group he joined before going to prison helped him to understand how to pray and provided one such network:

> our Thursday morning prayer breakfasts became a vital and love-giving force in the lives of all six participants ... we not only became a mutual support group for all our respective and personal problems, we also became increasingly aware of the presence and guidance of God ...
>
> (Aitken, 2000, 267–268)

These social networks assisted neophyte believers, first, through giving counsel when problems arose and second, by providing an example of how a believer acts. For Charles Colson this example was provided by his friend Harold Hughes when he spoke at a prayer breakfast. Hughes had previously been a staunch 'enemy' of Colson's, based upon their political differences (Colson, 1976, 133):

> 'I've learned how wrong it is to hate'. Hughes went on... 'One of the men I hated most was Chuck Colson, but now that we share a commitment together in Christ, I love him as my brother. I would trust him with my life, my family, with everything I have'.
>
> (Colson, 1976, 161–162)

Social networks are a vital resource in learning what values and beliefs are commensurate with a new identity as a believer. In addition they also helped to provide these white-collar offenders with a sense of worth. Jeb Magruder noted the importance of his Christian friendship groups after he had been sentenced to prison for his role in Watergate, but before the sentence began:

> I knew that everything happening to us wasn't just happening to us. The people who loved us, our friends, our covenant brothers and sisters, even some perfect strangers, were truly sharing what we were going through and giving us their own strength when ours ran out.
>
> (Magruder, 1978, 92–93)

The importance of positive emotions is once again demonstrated by the role peer groups have in fostering these. Peer groups made offenders feel good about themselves, therefore reinforcing individuals' change.

David Bullen's conversion to Buddhism took place largely without any direct outside 'help'. However, in learning how to find enlightenment Bullen drew upon books of Buddhist teachings and also attended training courses that encouraged thinking in accordance with Buddhist perspectives. The importance of being shown how to believe is still relevant however. Bullen needed guidance as much as the others noted here, but gained that guidance from different sources.

*Religious conversion* 173

### Gaining certification

Through the process of certification individuals come to feel that others believe that their efforts to desist have been successful, and that they are therefore viewed by others as non-criminal (Meisenhelder, 1982). Part of achieving certification from others is engaging in behaviour which 'non-offenders' do such as associating with non-criminal others, based upon the assumption that who one spends time with (and where they spend that time) has implications for one's own 'character' (Lofland, 1969; Goffman, 1969).

Conversion to religion has the benefit of allowing the new believer to feel that their attempts to change have been certified. This is not least because certain religious beliefs have connotations that may lead believers to be perceived positively by the majority of witnesses. For example the archetypal Christian may be perceived as being honest and committed to helping others at all times. The new believer will benefit from such connotations, assuming others believe the conversion to the new belief system is a genuine one. Reinforcing the perception that the individual has truly changed will be their association with fellow believers (Lofland, 1969; Maruna, 2001) as the new believer takes advantage of the opportunities provided to draw upon the help and support offered. Such support allowed new believers to underpin their own change. For Charles Colson, certification of his Christian status came from Harold Hughes, a long time political opponent. Colson described to Hughes the way in which Christ came into his life:

> 'That's all I need to know. Chuck, you have accepted Jesus and He has forgiven you. I do the same' I was overwhelmed, so astonished... that I could only utter a feeble 'Thank you'. In all my life no one had ever been so warm and loving to me outside of my family. And now it was coming to me from a man who had loathed me for years...
>
> (Colson, 1976, 150)

Certification may be most pronounced, and therefore most valued however, when it comes from sources other than fellow believers, from those the individual might expect to be sceptical of their 'redeemed' character. Barry Minkow received such validation from his lawyer Dave Kenner:

> The best thing about Dave Kenner was his support for and belief in my conversion to Christianity. Even though he himself wasn't a Christian, he *never* doubted the authenticity of my faith, nor did he label me a 'born-again-until-you're-out-again' Christian.[4]
>
> (Minkow, 1995, 208, emphasis in original)

The importance for Minkow, an ex-fraudster, of having his change validated might be considered to be particularly important. As someone convicted of fraud, Minkow worried about gaining people's trust once more (Minkow, 2005, 151). His conversion helped him resolve this problem to some extent. To be recognised and responded to as a believer by one who is not is to have the conversion accepted and

174  *Religious conversion*

consequently helps a new believer to feel they can have a legitimate future. They can be regarded in new, positive terms (Goffman, 1963).

### *Authenticating conversion*

A further social aspect of conversion to religion for these men was that it was, because of the high-profile nature of their offences, conducted in a very public fashion. This prompted reflection upon and concern over how the conversion would be viewed. Four offenders – Aitken, Colson, Lawson and Minkow – worried that their conversions might be viewed as an act put on to grant them help in troubled times. Perhaps because of this worry and the high-profile nature of the conversions of these men, many made extensive changes in how they lived their lives upon completion of their prison sentences. Those who converted to Christianity – Aitken, Colson, Lawson, Minkow, Magruder – gained employment with Christian organisations. This work acted to show that their conversions were genuine, by asking the rhetorical question 'who except a genuine Christian would do this work?' This employment allowed them to draw upon their Christian identities and, in turn, being part of such organisations acted to buttress their faith, as they were surrounded by fellow believers (Giordano *et al.*, 2008). It also highlights a distinction between these offenders and Giordano *et al.*'s (2008) participants. White-collar offenders were, because of their pasts in business and administration, able to make the most of their desire to change through religious belief. They therefore had advantages that Giordano *et al.*'s offenders may not have enjoyed. In keeping with Giordano *et al.*'s (2002) framework, a desire to change is not sufficient. The opportunity must be present as well.

## Conversion narratives and change

Religious conversion and its relationship with desistance have been little studied qualitatively. Nevertheless, the processes as described by these white-collar offenders have much in common with desistance processes more generally as identified within the desistance literature. Conversion to religion apparently satisfied particular needs for white-collar offenders. It was a particular way of desisting. There are some commonalities between the findings here and those of Giordano *et al.* (2008), but equally there is much that is different. Embracing great change within the life can be welcome if it absolves the individual of blame and mitigates shame and guilt.

The relationship between religion and these offenders' desistance is complicated but, for all of these offenders, the shift in beliefs that conversion prompted led them to renounce their past lives as in some way flawed. Religion was identified as the 'something' that was missing from the lives of the majority of these offenders, with conversion bringing feelings of contentment. For most (with Bullen the exception), the change in beliefs that accompanied conversion were echoed in their ways of actions and their whole way of living – not simply their offence – was construed as wrong in some manner. Feelings of shame were elicited by their offending, but religion helped them put this 'wrong' past into a context that absolved them of responsibility.

In considering the social and inner aspects of belief, it is clear that these white-collar offenders' conversion experiences have much in common with the role of religion in the lives of Giordano *et al.*'s (2008) participants and also concordance with the way religious conversion has been considered more generally (Rambo, 1993; McKnight, 2002). What Giordano *et al.* (2008) do not make apparent however is the relationship between religion and desistance. Their account implicitly suggests that religion was responsible for the desistance of those in their sample who had stopped offending. However, in keeping with Mahoney and Pargament (2004), the accounts of white-collar offenders suggest that religion was the way in which a desire to change was realised.

Such desires came from vague feelings of unease within the life more generally that were only free to be tackled when circumstances were appropriate. Manifesting a desire for change in this way had much to do with the powerful positive emotions that religious belief prompted in offenders. Such emotions helped make religious belief attractive when compared to the existential suffering that accompanied the detection of offences. Facilitating such change was the 'training', both direct and indirect, that was provided by new peer groups, which helped offenders understand what being a believer meant for their behaviour. Further to this, religion suggested a means by which white-collar offenders could have a meaningful life. Being a believer changed the way offenders felt about their past and their future.

In identifying these benefits to adopting religious belief, this study finds much agreement with existing knowledge on religious conversion and how it relates to offending. However, it also moves beyond existing analyses in exploring in more detail the way in which religion relates to a change in offenders' perception of their life, particularly with regards to their specific past. It also provides a more nuanced consideration of the conversion experience as understood more generally, demonstrating the importance of the interaction between the crises that can leave people open to conversion and the way in which conversion is attended to, while also asserting the necessity of considering the emotional aspects of conversion.

## Notes

1 Although Rambo was writing with regard to religious conversion, it is conceivable that similar processes could apply in conversion to secular beliefs as well.
2 Isaiah 43 makes the promise of God's protection through difficult times (Aitken, 2003, 13–14).
3 For Farrall and Calverley a positive emotion is any that is pleasurable to experience (2006, 129).
4 Namely someone who is a believer while in prison, but who then stops upon release.

# 9 An existentially informed understanding of desistance

This study had several core concerns. First, it sought to identify the significant experiences white-collar offenders identify after their offending. Second, it attempted to understand the relationship between these experiences and offenders' efforts to resettle following punishment. Third, it set out to identify whether white-collar offenders' desistance was accompanied by a shift in how they felt about themselves and their behaviour and, finally, how white-collar offenders came to make sense of what had happened to them. This final concern means not simply focusing on whether or not offenders desisted, but how they experienced the process. This chapter places the observations arising from such a focus within the context of wider criminological debates on desistance from crime, identifying the contributions this study has made towards criminological knowledge more generally and outlining the implications it has for policy.

The principal contribution of this study is its bringing together of a theoretical position that has only begun to be explored within criminology to study an area that has received little attention to date and doing so with a methodology that, while not unique to this study, has not received the sustained critical reflection that it has received here. It is perhaps true that the sample drawn upon are atypical in their backgrounds relative to both other white-collar offenders and offenders more generally (although as reflected upon above, by no means are all of these men 'elite' offenders). Given this however, the similarities between these white-collar offenders and wider observations of offender resettlement are even more interesting. It would be easy to dismiss the observations presented here if they suggested a radical departure from accepted wisdom regarding desistance and resettlement. It is harder to do so when they offer support for the processes identified more broadly by criminological study.

Traditionally, research observations hold that white-collar offenders, as a group, depart quite significantly from stereotypical views of who they are (e.g. Weisburd *et al.*, 2001). This study has sought to situate an understanding of white-collar offenders' behaviour within the context of desistance and resettlement research that has focused upon 'normal' offenders. It is somewhat ironic that – despite using an offence based definition of white-collar crime – in situating white-collar offenders' desistance in this way, this study has drawn upon accounts by a group of individuals who might be thought closer to stereotyped views of white-collar

*Existentialism and desistance* 177

offenders as 'advantaged older men from stable homes living in well-kept communities' (Weisburd *et al.*, 1991, 47). In this, this study perpetuates the idea that white-collar offenders are very different from their less salubrious convicted peers, yet it also identifies many similarities. It perpetuates the stereotype of the 'typical' individual who commits a white-collar crime by drawing upon a sample of (predominantly) older men who, on the surface, have all of the 'advantages' – e.g. a stable home life, skills they can utilise after prison – that other offenders lack (Weisburd *et al.*, 1991). How, the refrain may go, can such individuals fail to desist from crime and to resettle seamlessly back in society? In response to this, the analysis has looked beyond the fact that all but one of these men appears to have desisted from crime and identified what was relevant to them as they attempted to live in the wake of conviction and punishment. The experiences white-collar offenders report echo themes of change understood by desistance research more generally. What is apparent from white-collar offenders' accounts is that while, on the surface, their experience of punishment and subsequent desistance is somewhat different from that of other offenders, the same drives and underlying motivations for behaviour are present: the desire to have their non-offender status recognised, to locate a meaningful future and to establish themselves as part of a community once more.

The concern with privileging the reality of offenders' lives is reflected in the methodology employed to examine white-collar offenders' lives. The principal advantage of drawing upon autobiographical accounts as used here is that accounts have been constructed without researcher influence. They reflect what was of significance to the author during their punishment and resettlement as identified by them. A second advantage of using these accounts is that through the writing of the autobiography the author's whole life is reflected upon and so the relevance of their offence to who they are is placed in a context alongside other significant events. More so than in an interview, the construction of an autobiography allows for considered analysis of the past and how it contributes to the present and the formation of who one is. It also focuses attention upon the future. A further advantage of using autobiographies is that they permit access to research populations that might otherwise be difficult to engage with. White-collar offenders represent one such population.

Autobiographies are particularly apposite for studying desistance because, as has been noted, moving from 'being' an offender to a non-offender is a process. The most informative studies of desistance have utilised a longitudinal methodology to track the efforts made by offenders who are attempting to reorder their lives as they make efforts to desist (Laub and Sampson, 2003; Farrall *et al.*, 2014). Autobiographies are not directly comparable to a longitudinal methodology because some autobiographies represent the recall of historical events from one point in the actor's life rather than asking them to reflect at time 1, time 2 etc. Still, the insights that autobiographies can give are strengthened by the length of time they discuss, the relationship between the past present and future of the writer's life and the fact that the observations they make are arrived at after sustained reflection. With regard to desistance-focused research then, they permit an insight into the process of

178  *Existentialism and desistance*

desistance as the writer identifies with, engages with and makes sense of it. The use of autobiographies recognises that offenders do not move from offending to non-offending in a historical vacuum. They reflect on what has gone before and interpret the future in terms of this. Autobiographies, by their very nature contain reflections on the whole life.

Autobiographical data are not without problems, however, particularly when issues of 'truth' are considered. A related issue is the use of a ghost writer to aid construction of an 'autobiography'. However, drawing upon autobiographical accounts means to privilege the author's truth, a distinct phenomenon from external, objective fact. The use of ghost writers should not complicate this distinction. An 'autobiography' may be co-authored, but this does not give the ghost writer carte blanche to invent thoughts and feelings. Ultimately, in putting their name to the book the author sanctions it as something of their own and as reflecting their own feelings.

Of course, not all white-collar offenders will have the chance to publish an account of their offending. Only the most sensational stories are worthy of publication, or so goes the refrain. Some of the offenders whose accounts are considered here were notorious; there seems little doubt of that. Nor is there doubt that it was the public interest their stories generated that made them lucrative prospects for bigger publishing houses. The sample was not homogenous in this respect though. Many published with smaller publishers. In particular, those who converted to Christianity sometimes disseminated their autobiographies through publishers sympathetic to the religious timbre of their writing. Even more noteworthy when considering that only the most high profile of offenders writes an autobiography is that two offenders (Berger and Christensen) published their own books. It is far from clear then that all the white-collar offenders who are featured here had some special quality that marked them out from other white-collar offenders. Of course, some generated interest because of who they are (or were). We can include here the politicians such as Jonathan Aitken and Jeffrey Archer who were both public figures involved in high-profile cases and who could therefore be expected to be different from white-collar offenders more generally. For every Archer and Aitken however, the sample also includes a Laite and a Lawson: offenders who apparently vanished without trace after the publication of their books. Even if there were homogeneity in these offenders' backgrounds, within the context of the existential framework utilised here it would be unwise to generalise too much. Individual lives are unique.

If there is perhaps one way in which this sample is homogenous, it is in their differences with non-white-collar offenders. They can be said to have enjoyed lives both before and after their offending that other offenders are not able to. Once again though, one of the purposes of this study has been to identify the significant experiences of this group and how these fit with observations of offenders more generally. That these white-collar offenders shared much in common with non-white-collar offenders is compelling evidence that existential angst has no regard for status or class, for financial resources or skills that might be thought to bolster employability upon release from prison.

*Existentialism and desistance* 179

This study has considered in detail how white-collar offenders experience the process of desistance from crime and of resettlement. It is – as far as can be ascertained – the first qualitative study of white-collar offenders with this focus and, as such, provides an insight into an area of criminology that until now has only been theorised. Attending to the subjective experiences of white-collar offenders has situated them closely to other observations desistance research has made. A simple focus on the presence versus absence of certain demographic characteristics such as age or social status would have been unlikely to show much similarity between white-collar and other offenders. This analysis shows that when it comes to resettlement and desistance, the many advantages white-collar offenders may have had did not ease the task of establishing who they were in the world. Resettlement was still a challenge, albeit for different reasons than for other offenders.

Two questions are relevant in considering white-collar offenders' prison and resettlement experience. The first, arising from the 'special sensitivity' debate, is whether the experience of prison is either more or less difficult for white-collar offenders (Mann *et al.*, 1980; Benson and Culen, 1988). The special sensitivity debate exemplifies the supposed divide between those who commit white-collar crime and other offenders. This is perhaps nowhere more apparent than in theorising about when the 'typical' white-collar offender, freshly plucked out of the boardroom, is placed in prison (Mann *et al.*, 1980). The environment they are subjected to upon their incarceration is suggested as being a particularly severe punishment for those more used to being 'treated as if they are special and encouraged to see themselves as such' (Shover and Hochstetler, 2006, 136). Those whose autobiographies were analysed might be thought to best epitomise the difficulty of this contrast in lives. They include former CEOs of multinational corporations (Alan Bond), politicians who were intimately involved in running their country (Charles Colson, John Dean) and others who lived lives they themselves came to define as excessive and overindulgent (Todd Volpe).

Their experience of prison did not manifest any particular difficulties that were based upon these 'high lives' however. The experience of incarceration was a shock. That much is evident. The difficulties that did manifest themselves were grounded in the initial induction to prison and the dehumanisation of the prison regime, both threatening offenders' status and attacking their sense of who they were. However, although they were initially unable to make sense of their environment the routines of prison eventually became commonplace. Offenders came to view time in prison as a boon, the alien nature of the environment was resolved by reference to familiar experiences in their pasts and loss of status was coped with through work white-collar offenders undertook with other prisoners that made them 'stand out'. Therefore, despite the difficulties inherent in prison life, it seems difficult to suggest that the white-collar offenders presented here exhibited the special sensitivity to prison that has been hypothesised (Mann *et al.*, 1980).

Prison sentences were not 'easy' for these white-collar offenders, however, contrary to assertions that they have a particular affinity for coping with imprisonment (Benson and Cullen, 1988). White-collar offenders faced the realisation

180 *Existentialism and desistance*

that they would be changed by their incarceration, by time spent away from families and also by those they shared their prison time with. The outside world had moved on without them and their place in the world had changed as a consequence of this. Their 'experience of institutional working practices' (Benson and Cullen, 1988, 210) did not make their prison time pass more quickly, nor did it help them come to terms with what form their lives would take after prison. As much as they did draw on their pasts and their knowledge of bureaucracy (for example), they did so to understand what was happening to them. In other words, they adapted in a manner similar to other prisoners by making sense of prison in terms of what they knew. Those in Farrall and Calverley's (2006) sample for example became accustomed to prison life. It was something they got used to. The same was the case for these white-collar offenders.

The second – albeit similar – question is whether the process of resettlement following a prison sentence is either easier or harder for white-collar offenders. The resettlement experiences of white-collar offenders are often theorised, but little examined. A popular suggestion is that the experience of arrest and imprisonment will mark white-collar offenders with an indelible stain that will attract stigmatisation from legitimate others when they return to society (Weisburd *et al.*, 2001; Benson and Kerley, 2001; Shover and Hochstetler, 2006). Related to the challenge presented by stigmatisation are assertions that white-collar offenders can benefit from reintegrative shaming (Braithwaite, 1985, 1989; Braithwaite and Drahos, 2002; Coricelli *et al.*, 2014). Set against this, white-collar offenders are thought to have greater resources to help them cope with resettlement, in the form of support networks that are made available as a result of their previous successful lives (Benson and Kerley, 2001; Shover and Hochstetler, 2006).

The presence or absence of stigmatisation will be subjective, but it is a clear observation of this study that several of these offenders felt stigmatised in encounters they had after their release. These encounters left them distressed but ultimately were a source of information to them about their place in the world following their release from prison. Experiencing stigmatisation may not have had any impact on their subsequent desistance, but did help them understand their position in the world and consequently what direction their lives could take after punishment. With regard to reintegrative shaming although some did feel stigatmised and thus needed to reject this deviant 'master status', in the main the stigmatisation they suffered did not originate from sources they valued closely. They did have supportive networks of family and friends.

Whether or not stigmatisation was experienced, many were eventually able to forge lives they were happy with. Some returned to the same spheres of work they had inhabited before their offending (e.g. investment banker Dennis Levine), while those who found themselves unable to do this found other fulfilling pursuits (e.g. Jonathan Aitken). Regardless, they all, as far as could be discerned here, made themselves 'successful' lives after prison (Barry Minkow's subsequent convictions do not invalidate his achievements in becoming a pastor and founding the Fraud Discovery Institute). This does not mean resettlement was straightforward. White-collar offenders faced struggles to determine their place in the world, had to cope with negative publicity regarding their offences and, for some, financial difficulties. In common with other offenders who are attempting to resettle after punishment (Uggen *et al.*, 2004) these white-collar offenders prioritised re-establishing themselves as part of a community. They had set goals they wished to achieve. In contrast to many other offenders, however, they were in possession of skills that they could make use of in achieving these goals. This is most apparent when it came to securing employment and in this their pasts served them well. Even those who wished to pursue different goals made use of their previous experience, for example by applying their business and administration skills (e.g. Magruder). These results suggest therefore, that while white-collar offenders do suffer stigmatisation, they are also in a position to make use of their successful pasts and when it comes to resettling they are able to make ostensibly 'normal' lives.

To consider the question of change for white-collar offenders is not to ask if these men were changed by their experiences. Within the context of the existential sociology framework applied here there is no question: to exist is invariably to change (Kotarba, 1984). Instead, to consider change is to study how white-collar offenders identified the shifts in the sense of self that took place and the meaning they placed upon them as part of their ongoing sense of who they were. It is also important that they adapted to change when they could not achieve their goals, focusing on other areas of their life from which they could draw fulfilment.

The experiences offenders had were sufficiently different from anything they had previously known that they could not help but impact upon them. From offenders' accounts, two means of conceiving of the past are broadly identifiable. Some offenders perceived their offence as small or having little victim impact. Placed within the context of the rest of their life it was possible for them to view their offence as an aberration by an otherwise 'good' individual as did Nick Leeson. We can also include here those who did not accept any wrong-doing on their part and those who considered themselves 'technically' guilty and/or victims of circumstance. With this conceptualisation of their offence, wholesale changes were not deemed necessary and many white-collar offenders carried on with their lives as closely as possible to the life they had prior to conviction.

The second 'group' of offenders, however, perceived their offences as more serious, this necessitating the reconstruction of the past, with the very life itself reflected upon as wrong. Identifying a particular problem with the life leads to an obligation to do something to resolve it. The way specific pasts were interpreted however is almost secondary to the fact that they needed (re)construction to make them fit with the life more generally in a meaningful way. Changes were particularly wide ranging in the impact they had upon offenders' lives through the influence they had upon what it meant to 'be' them.

As well as extent of change, offenders' engagement with it varied. Some offenders were active participants in their change. They reflected upon their deviant pasts, identified 'errors' they had made and resolved to build futures in which they would be a different person. Achieving this often included a radical reconstruction of the self e.g. as realised through religious conversion. Change was not always as sweeping in scope however. It sometimes centred around shifts in how offenders

182 *Existentialism and desistance*

spent their time or a different outlook on life, with promises made to prioritise family over work for example.

In contrast, others felt that change was put upon them by their environment and the depravations they suffered through their punishment. They were forced into having to cope with change, perhaps because conviction was identified as wrongful and accompanied by persecution. This forced offenders to endure the changes presented in their world as they suddenly became 'an offender'. Therefore, making sense of what was happening to them and their place in the world was of key importance to all of these white-collar offenders because, whether they desired change or not, it was something they had to cope with.

Offenders' perception of their own guilt is relevant in distinguishing those who changed. The analysis showed that acceptance or rejection of guilt has an impact upon the process of desistance at various stages. Those who did not admit their guilt were more anxious about stigmatisation prior to their release from prison, only changed partially and were more likely to view that change as 'inflicted' upon them. Not all of those who considered themselves guilty made new lives for themselves to the extent of those who adopted religious beliefs. Without exception, however, those who denied any wrong-doing identified little need to change who they were. These offenders only changed partially and experienced change as something that happened 'to them' rather than being agents of it. They rejected the offender label they were presented with and resented the interference of the criminal justice system in their life. Denying they were offenders meant to deny anything 'wrong' with their life that necessitated change. The changes in who they were as a result of conviction could not be ignored however and were consequently experienced as 'inflicted'. It took them time to identify any positives in their punishment and those positives were expressed along the lines of 'what does not kill me makes me stronger'.

In contrast, those who admitted their guilt and accepted the wrong of their actions were receptive to the possibility of change. They looked for solutions to correct their deficient thinking or the aspects of their lives that were at fault. They saw immediate advantage in their prison environments and took comfort by finding worthwhile pursuits. They also expressed no anxiety about the future as their release from prison drew near. Those who accepted their guilt took on the mantle of penitent offender, believing that once their prison sentence was served they could move on. By accepting society's label they could serve their punishment and earn a second chance. This feeling made them more upbeat about re-entering society.

This emphasis on how these white-collar offenders viewed their offending indicates the importance of attending to the highly personal nature of offenders' lives. A particular past is unique and therefore a unique way of living the life will come out of it. A present self is grounded in who one was, and attempts to realise a future self must be consistent with this (Sartre, 1958; Douglas, 1984). Specific examples of how the past must be constructed so as to be made meaningful in terms of the present and future come through via a focus on offenders adopting religious beliefs and taking on professional-ex roles. Being a professional-ex brings

*Existentialism and desistance* 183

with it notions of being redeemed by 'giving something back' to society and simultaneously putting a past deviant identity to use in the present. Similarly, adopting religion brings a feeling of absolution from former wrongs. What both religion and professional-ex statuses therefore do is make the past meaningful. Casting the past in this way makes apparent a set of actions that can be enacted to reinforce a particular (re)construction of the self, such as working to pay back victims or acting in accordance with a new faith. These roles enable the past, even if it is undesirable, to extend into the present and be a part of the future. The way religion and professional-ex roles were adopted emphasises the importance of offenders' willingness to view positively the opportunities they are provided with as a way of living a legitimate life. The mere fact of opportunities was not enough. There had to be a desire to engage with them (Giordano *et al.*, 2002). The fact that a considerably high proportion of white-collar offenders either converted or became a professional-ex (and in some cases both) indicates that offenders may feel these are particularly viable routes to rebuilding their lives.

Despite these similarities, however, there are also differences in the impact that professional-ex roles and religious conversion have on the life. These differences are largely constituted in the particular relationship with the past. The professional-ex draws upon a rather specific aspect of their past, i.e. a former deviant identity, and uses it to achieve quite specific goals. These goals are driven by individual-level concerns, such as Minkow's desire to 'do good'. This utilisation of the deviant past is quite particular and the professional-ex role becomes the way that goals are achieved. The white-collar offenders who formed roles as professional-exes derived some of the benefits that professional-exes more generally take from engagement with such roles (Brown, 1991; Maruna, 2001), but there were important differences in how they were realised as well. Minkow in particular was quite adversarial in his relationship with other deviants. His utilisation of his deviant past was as a set of 'skills' that he could apply to fraud prevention. Charles Colson in contrast was himself a model for change, much like Brown's professional-exes (1991).

In contrast to professional-ex roles, conversion to religion has implications for many aspects of the past. Religious beliefs provide a way of re-conceptualising not just previous deviance but the whole life, which must be re-evaluated in light of what the convert has learnt through religion. While professional-ex roles are likely focused on one particular area of the life, religious conversion is instead a way of living. Belief in God impacted upon relationships, actions undertaken and altered the salience of particular past events when viewed through the lens of belief.

Lives are lived into the future and a recurring theme throughout this analysis has been individuals' concerns for the future and the future selves offenders identified. Reactions to encounters with others, reflections on the life and threats to plans were frequently interpreted in terms of what it meant for who offenders could be. Significant for these offenders was how their past offending was related to their present life (as described in their accounts) and their future. In common with other offenders, a coherent narrative had to be drawn that put the past into a context compatible with a future that was in keeping with notions of who they wanted to

184 *Existentialism and desistance*

be (Maruna, 2001). Such constructions of the past are not merely done so as to put one's past in order, however. The way the past is constructed will have an impact upon how the life now and in the future is led. Being true to such a (re)construction of oneself is important and may necessitate change (Douglas, 1984). The broader scope of the research has situated the experiences of white-collar offenders within an understanding of the importance of self and emotions with regard to change. As the analysis makes clear, offenders are actively involved in creating the lives they wish to lead, guided in this by the way such living feels. The tenets of existential sociology – the importance of self, emotions and values – are implicitly emphasised in recent developments in desistance. Offenders who successfully desist are aided by a having a particular future self in mind (Giordano *et al.*, 2002). Identifying a particular future self implies a further important aspect of desistance, specifically that a willingness to embrace the possibility of a new way of living is an important part of attempts to desist (Giordano *et al.*, 2002; Laub and Sampson, 2003; Farrall *et al.*, 2014). Without this willingness, offenders may fail to take advantage of the opportunities the environment provides them with. Finally, offenders who desist must construct an account of their own deviant past that makes sense of it within the context of a present and future in which they are no longer an offender (Maruna and Roy, 2007). Existential sociology provides a way of uniting these elements of the desistance process and explaining desistance within one coherent framework.

Within criminology more generally, there have been calls to recognise the place that emotions have in an understanding of human behaviour (Morrison, 1995; Karstedt, 2002). Suggestions that we need to attend to the emotional aspects of offending in order to understand the lived reality of offenders' lives would seem to apply equally to considerations of their desistance. Offenders who desist may appropriate hooks for change (Giordano *et al.*, 2002), construct life narratives that put the past in positive terms (Maruna, 2001) and engage with turning points (Laub and Sampson, 2003), but they do so because of the way such endeavours feel. Emotions run thick throughout white-collar offenders' accounts as they inform us how particular encounters made them feel both in the moment and about their lives. Thus we are told of the horror of prison, the shame of stigmatisation and elation when an offender's reformed character is recognised. We learn of guilt, shame, pride and elation that offenders felt as they reflected on themselves, their lives and their place in the world. The conversion narratives of white-collar offenders perhaps best exemplify the role of emotions as a source of information about the self. Significant changes in beliefs that had ramifications for the whole life were directed by how it felt to embrace religion. Jonathan Aitken, for example, realised that conversion was as much an endeavour for the heart as the head. An existential sociology framework recognises that offenders actively choose courses of action, experience events and build up meaning in line with their sense of who they are and who they wish to be (Kotarba, 1979). Such choosing is governed in part, however, by emotions.

In locating white-collar offenders' desistance in this way, this study contributes to the embryonic field of existentially focused criminology (Lippens and Crewe, 2009). Although relatively new, this field is attracting interest for the contributions

*Existentialism and desistance* 185

it can make to existing criminological work. This study extends this corpus of work, identifying the importance of self within processes of change specifically related to punishment and resettlement for a group of offenders who have been largely neglected by the desistance literature more generally. With this emphasis, it provides a more nuanced understanding of how white-collar offenders experience prison and resettlement and also explores in more depth particular concepts such as the notion of offenders becoming a professional-ex and the role of religious conversion within the desistance process.

This study is also well situated with regard to wider desistance work. Similarities can certainly be drawn between white-collar offenders and other offenders who desist from crime. The first of these similarities is the importance of the internal, 'subjective' aspects of the desistance from crime. The desistance literature more generally has, in recent years, come to focus upon the personal experience of desistance for the individual desister (Giordano *et al.*, 2002; Farrall, 2005; Farrall *et al.*, 2014). It is not enough to cite marriage, and employment (for example) as factors associated with desistance (e.g. Laub and Sampson, 2001). An understanding of how these 'work' in terms of intrapersonal change is necessary.

Beyond the desistance literature, this study has emphasised the importance of the particular nuances of the post-punishment experience in a manner that taps into other debates. Research has identified that part of making the transition to being a non-offender is being able to communicate that change has taken place through displays of behaviour (Meisenhelder, 1982; Maruna, 2001), for example through change in locales, shifts in peer groups and other changes in behaviour, such as obtaining employment (Lofland, 1969; Meisenhalder, 1988). For the 'normal' offender such activities demonstrate a commitment to change that others can respond to (Maruna, 2001), because such changes mark their life, and therefore them, as different. These behaviours are 'appropriate' for the reformed offender and part of the process of signalling that change has taken place (Toch, 2010; Maruna, 2012).

One difficulty white-collar offenders had with the resettlement process was that returning to the world they were once a part of – the 'conventional' world – had inherent in it its own issues for their sense of self. This was particularly with regard to the way others perceived their resettlement. It would be overstating things to say that white-collar offenders were victims of their own previous success. Nevertheless, what this study asserts is that part of the resettlement process for white-collar offenders, as for other offenders, is being able to demonstrate that they are in fact ex-offenders, but that the avenues that traditionally support desistance e.g. showing reformed character through gaining employment, are not open to them. Their previous lives were too 'normal' and nothing inherent in returning to their old life indicated that they had changed and were no longer offenders (see also Hunter, 2009).

As much as with other offenders, white-collar offenders who are attempting to desist have a regard for how they themselves are seen. That such similarities can be drawn is particularly interesting when the 'elite' characteristics of the majority of the sample are considered. This suggests the importance of internal aspects of

## 186 *Existentialism and desistance*

the desistance process for all offenders. What this study adds to this work, however, is an outline of how such enactment of change operates when past lives are indicative of normalcy and replete with 'successful' overtones.

The desire to have change certified (Meisenhelder, 1982) is a recurring theme throughout this study, and this relates to the importance of self-presentation (Goffman, 1963, 1969). White-collar offenders make the aftermath of their punishment a rather public affair. The desire to be seen to have their true (that is, non-offender) character recognised may be the underlying motivation to write an autobiography (or several), and television interviews are another example of this desire. It might be said that what preoccupied all of these offenders was, if they admitted their offence, showing they had changed or, if not, indicating what had 'really happened'. Converting to religion and adopting professional-ex roles were extensions of this. The implicit goal for converts and professional-exes was to signal that change had taken place, as they took up activities that may be thought incompatible with further deviance and constructed a 'reform story' around them (Maruna, 2001). Becoming a professional-ex or converting to religion were both, therefore, particular ways to send out 'signals' as to their reformed character.

This is true of those who feel they have reformed and that their offence indicates a deep failing in their life i.e. those who admit their guilt and wish to show they have changed. It is difficult for those who reject any notion of themselves as guilty in the first place to show that they are not offenders. They lack even the basic ability to show they have changed by saying of their past 'I was wrong' (with apologies to Jim Bakker, whose autobiography has exactly that title). Their activities are focused upon publicising their desire to tell the 'truth' of events. Forewords are replete with promises to, for example, 'set the record straight' (Jett, 1999, author's note). It is, therefore, as important for white-collar offenders to have their good character recognised as it is for other offenders, but in demonstrating it they have further to go.

The conclusions of this study have several practical implications for policy, particularly when it comes to the study of non-white-collar offenders. The importance of the internal, subjective aspects of desistance indicates that criminal justice institutions concerned with the rehabilitation of offenders should attempt to identify how such changes can be facilitated within offenders by reference to this. A good example of this is with regards to the way time in prison is experienced by those incarcerated. The white-collar offenders in this study planned for the future lives they would have when they left prison. They also possessed a willingness and ability to make good use of their prison time, meaning that although it was difficult, it was not a wasted period in their life. These observations suggest that if strategies could be developed that would encourage other prisoners to look to the future instead of focusing on their pasts, as observations of prisoners have noted they are prone to do (Meisenhelder, 1985; Farrall and Calverley, 2006), then this might aid their attempts to plan legitimate futures for themselves.

Another observation of this study is that the process of resettlement took time for these offenders, who were well equipped to deal with it. Criminal justice agencies – and the public – too often expect offenders to resettle immediately and successfully after prison. This study shows that we should be prepared to give all ex-prisoners more time to reconstruct their lives (Farrall *et al.*, 2014 make this point for offenders more generally). Finally, the study shows the importance of accepting guilt for the process of internal change. This result has some concordance with recent observations within restorative justice work (e.g. Robinson and Shapland, 2008). It is important to design interventions that allow and encourage offenders to acknowledge their wrong-doing. This can also be a drawn out process, and one that is likely to be important both during and after prison.

Perhaps most importantly for implications regarding prisoner resettlement is the clear implication from this study that when it comes to considering offender resettlement we should not attribute too much primacy to 'advantages' such as particular skills or resources that offenders may have. The presence of such resources does not obviate the existential issues inherent to resettlement after punishment and it would therefore be unwise to assume desistance is inevitable or easy for any offender.

What the conclusions of this analysis also point to is that while having skills that aid in the finding of work and resources that ease the process of resettlement and desistance can be useful, there are still many issues that are equally salient to all offenders who are trying to desist from crime. These issues include coping with a change in who one is, establishing oneself in a community once again and making sense of a deviant past. This is what criminal justice agencies need to recognise and support, because this study shows that, for *all* offenders who are trying to desist, these are the key aspects of existence.

# Appendix
## Bibliography of white-collar offenders' autobiographies

Where more than one author is listed, the first named author is the offender.

Aitken, J. (2000). *Pride and Perjury*. London: Continuum.
Aitken, J. (2004). *Psalms for People under Pressure*. London: Continuum.
Aitken, J. (2004). *Prayers for People under Pressure*. London: Continuum.
Aitken, J. (2005). *Porridge and Passion*. London: Continuum.
Archer, J. (2002). *A Prison Diary Volume 1: Hell*. London: Pan Books.
Archer, J. (2003). *A Prison Diary Volume 2: Purgatory*. London: Pan Books.
Archer, J. (2004). *A Prison Diary Volume 3: Heaven*. London: Pan Books.
Bakker, J. and Abraham, K. (1996). *I Was Wrong*. Nashville, KY: Thomas Nelson.
Belfort, J. (2007). *The Wolf of Wall Street*. London: Hodder and Stoughton.
Belfort, J. (2009). *Catching the Wolf of Wall Street*. New York: Bantam.
Berger, R.L. (2003). *From the Inside: A Prison Memoir*. New York: iUniverse.
Bond, A. and Mundle, R. (2003). *Bond*. London: Harper Collins.
Bullen, D. (2004). *Fake: My Life as a Rogue Trader*. Sydney: John Wiley & Sons.
Christensen, N. (2005). *Five Years of Bad Coffee*. New York: iUniverse.
Colson, C. (1976). *Born Again*. Ada, MI: Chosen Books.
Colson, C. (1979). *Life Sentence*. London: Hodder and Stoughton.
Colson, C. (2005). *The Good Life*. Carol Stream, IL: Tyndale House.
Dean, J. (1976). *Blind Ambition*. New York: Pocket Books.
Dean, J. (1982). *Lost Honor*. Los Angeles: Stratford Press.
Guppy, D. and Davies, N. (1996). *Roll the Dice*. London: Blake Publishing.
Irving, C. (1972). *The Hoax*. London: e-reads.
Jett, J. and Chartrand, S. (1999). *Black and White on Wall Street: The Untold Story of the Man Wrongly Accused of Bringing Down Kidder Peabody*. New York: William, Morrow and Company.
Laite, W. (1972). *The United States vs. William Laite*. Washington, DC: Acropolis Books.
Lawson, S. (1992). *Daddy, Why are you Going to Jail?* Illinois: Harold Shaw.
Leeson, N. and Whitley, E. (1996). *Rogue Trader*. London: Little, Brown and Company.
Leeson, N. and Tyrrell, I. (2005). *Back from the Brink: Coping with Stress*. London: Virgin Books.
Levine, D. and Hoffer, W. (1991). *Inside Out: An Insider's Account of Wall Street*. New York: Berkeley Books.
Magruder, J. (1978). *From Power to Peace*. Texas: Word Books.
Minkow, B. (1995). *Clean Sweep: The Inside Story of the ZZZZ Best Scam...One of Wall Street's Biggest Frauds*. Nashville, KY: Thomas Nelson Inc.

*Appendix* 189

Minkow, B. (2005). *Cleaning Up: One Man's Redemptive Journey Through the Seductive World of Corporate Crime*. Nashville, KY: Nelson Current.

Pavlo, W. and Weinberg, N. (2007). *Stolen Without a Gun: Confessions from Inside History's Biggest Accounting Fraud – the Collapse of MCI WorldCom*. Tampa, FL: Etika Books.

Rose, P. and Hill, R. (2004). *My Prison Without Bars*. Emmaus, PA: Rodale.

Timilty, J. and Thomas, J. (1997). *Prison Journal*. Boston: Northeastern University Press.

Volpe, T. (2002). *Framed: Tales of the Art Underworld*. Edinburgh: Cutting Edge Press.

# References

Adams, K. (1992) Adjusting to prison life. *Crime and Justice*, 16, 275–359.
Adler, P. (1985) *Wheeling and Dealing.* New York: Columbia University Press.
Adler, P. (1992) The 'post' phase of deviant careers. *Deviant Behaviour*, 13, 2, 103–126.
Aitken, J. (2014) *Jonathan Aitken.* Available online at www.jonathanaitken.org [accessed 12th August 2014].
Altheide, D.L. (1977) The sociology of Alfred Schutz. In Douglas, J.D. and Johnson, J.M. (eds) *Existential Sociology.* London: Cambridge University Press, pp. 133–152.
Archer, J. (2014) *Jeffery Archer.* Available online at www.jeffreyarcher.co.uk/site [accessed 12th August 2014].
Attig, T. (2002) Questionable assumptions about assumptive worlds. In Kauffman, J. (ed.) *Loss of the Assumptive World.* London: Routledge, pp. 55–68.
Baier, C.J. and Wright, B.R.E. (2001) If you love me, keep my commandments. *Journal of Research in Crime and Delinquency*, 38, 1, 3–21.
Barnett, A., Blumstein, A. and Farrington, D. (1989) A prospective test of a criminal career model. *Criminology*, 27, 2, 373–388.
BBC Sunday AM (2006) *Life After Prison.* 26th February. Available online at http://news.bbc.co.uk/1/hi/programmes/sunday_am/4752414.stm [accessed 5th August 2014].
Belfort, J. (2014) *Jordan Belfort: Corporate Training, Investments and Wealth Building Strategies.* Available online at http://jordanbelfort.com/ [accessed 12th August 2014].
Benson, M.L. (1985) Denying the guilty mind. *Criminology*, 23, 4, 583–607.
Benson, M.L. (2013) Editors' introduction. *Journal of Contemporary Criminal Justice*, 29, 3, 324–330.
Benson, M.L. and Cullen, F.T. (1988) The special sensitivity of white-collar offenders to prison. *Journal of Criminal Justice*, 16, 207–215.
Benson, M.L. and Moore, E. (1992) Are white-collar and common offenders the same? *Journal of Research in Crime and Delinquency*, 29, 3, 251–272.
Benson, M.L. and Kerley, K.R. (2001) Life course theory and white-collar crime. In Pontell, H.N. and Shichor, D. (eds) *Contemporary Issues in Crime and Criminal Justice.* Upper Saddle River, NJ: Prentice-Hall, pp.121–136.
Blumstein, A., Cohen, J. and Farrington, D. (1988a) Criminal career research. *Criminology*, 26, 1, 1–35.
Blumstein, A., Cohen, J. and Farrington, D. (1988b) Longitudinal and criminal career research. *Criminology*, 26, 1, 57–74.
Blumstein, A., Cohen, J., Das, S. and Moitra, S.D. (1988) Specialization and seriousness during adult criminal careers. *Journal of Quantitative Criminology*, 4, 4, 303–345.

## References 191

Bottoms, A., Shapland, J., Costello, A., Holmes, D. and Muir, G. (2004) Towards desistance. *Howard Journal of Criminal Justice*, 43, 4, 368–389.

Bovens, L. (1999) The value of hope. *Philosophy and Phenomenological Research*, 59, 3, 667–681.

Braithwaite, J. (1985) White-collar crime. *Annual Review of Sociology*, 11, 1–25.

Braithwaite, J. (1989) *Crime Shame and Reintegration*. Cambridge: Cambridge University Press.

Braithwaite, J. and Drahos, P. (2002) Zero tolerance, naming and shaming? *The Australian and New Zealand Journal of Criminology*, 35, 3, 269–288.

Brewer, B.W., Selby, C.L., Linder, D.E. and Petitpas, A.J. (1999) Distancing oneself from a poor season. *Journal of Personal and Interpersonal Loss*, 4, 2, 149–163.

Brown, J.D. (1991) The professional ex. *Sociological Quarterly*, 32, 2, 219–230.

Brune, M., Haasen, C., Krausz, M., Yagdiran, O., Bustos, E. and Eisenman, D. (2002) Belief systems as coping factors for traumatized refugees. *European Journal of Psychiatry*, 17, 8, 451–458.

Bulmer, M. (1984) *The Chicago School of Sociology*. London: University of Chicago Press.

Burnett, R. and Maruna, S. (2004) So prison works does it? The criminal careers of 130 men released from prison under Michael Howard. *Howard Journal of Criminal Justice*, 43, 4, 390–404.

Bushway, S.D., Piquero, A.R., Broidy, L.M., Cauffman, E. and Mazerolle, P. (2001) An empirical framework for studying desistance as a process. *Criminology*, 39, 2, 491–516.

Buttimer, A. (1976) Grasping the dynamism of lifeworld. *Annals of the Association of American Geographers*, 66, 2, 277–292.

Calverley, A. (2013) *Cultures of Desistance*. London: Routledge.

Charles Colson Legacy Fund (2014) *Remembering Chuck Colson*. Available online at http://chuckcolson.org/ [accessed 12th August 2014].

Chu, D.C. (2007) Religiosity and desistance from drug use. *Criminal Justice and Behavior*, 34, 5, 661–679.

Clark, C. (2002) Taming the 'brute being'. In Kotarba, J.A. and Johnson, J.M. (eds) *Postmodern Existential Sociology*. Lanham, MD: Rowman and Littlefield, pp.155–182.

Clarke, R.V. and Cornish, D.B. (1985) Modelling offenders' decisions. *Crime and Justice*, 6, 147–185.

Cleaver, K. and Katsiaficas, G. (eds) (2001) *Liberation, Imagination and the Black Panther Party*. New York: Routledge.

CNN (2004) *Stewart Convicted on All Charges*. 10th March. Available online at http://money.cnn.com/2004/03/05/news/companies/martha_verdict/ [accessed 7th August 2014].

CNN (2005) *CNN Live Saturday: Interview with Barry Minkow*. 5th March. Available online at http://transcripts.cnn.com/TRANSCRIPTS/0503/05/cst.02.html [accessed 12th August 2014].

Cohen, S. and Taylor, L. (1972) *Psychological Survival*. Harmondsworth: Penguin.

Converse, P.E. (1964) The nature of belief systems in mass publics. In Apter, D.E. (ed.) *Ideology and Discontent*. New York: Free Press, pp.206–261.

Copes, H., Vieraitis, L.M., Cardwell, S.M. and Vasquez, A. (2013) Accounting for identity theft. *Journal of Contemporary Criminal Justice*, 29, 3, 351–368.

Coricelli, G., Rusconi, E., and Villeval, M. (2014) Tax evasion and emotions. *Journal of Economic Psychology*, 40, 49–61.

Corr, C.A. (2002) Coping with challenges to assumptive worlds. In Kauffman, J. (ed.) *Loss of the Assumptive World*. London: Routledge, pp.127–138.

## 192   References

Cotterhill, P. and Letherby, G. (1993) Weaving stories. *Sociology*, 27, 1, 67–79.

Craib, I. (1976) *Existentialism and Sociology*. London: Cambridge University Press.

Cressey, D.R. (1971) *Other People's Money*. Belmont, CA: Wadsworth.

Crewe, B. (2011) Depth, weight, tightness. *Punishment & Society*, 13, 5, 509–529.

Croall, H. (2001) *Understanding White-Collar Crime*. Buckingham: Open University Press.

Cullen, F.T., Jonson, C.L. and Nagin, D.S. (2011) Prisons do not reduce recidivism. *The Prison Journal*, 91, 3, 48S–65S.

Cusson, M. and Pinnsoneault, P. (2014) The decision to give up crime. In Cornish, D.B. and Clarke, R.V. (eds) *The Reasoning Criminal*. Piscataway, NJ: Transaction, pp.72–82.

Davidson, L. (2002) The spirit of the hills: mountaineering in northwest Otago, New Zealand, 1882–1940. *Tourism Geographies*, 4, 1, 44–61.

de Man, P. (1979) *The Rhetoric of Romanticism*. New York: Columbia University Press.

Denzin, N.K. (1987) *The Recovering Alcoholic*. London: Sage.

Douglas, J.D. (1977) Aspects of existential sociology. In Douglas, J.D. and Johnson, J.M. (eds) *Existential Sociology*. London: Cambridge University Press, pp.3–74.

Douglas, J.D. (1984) The emergence, security and growth of the sense of self. In Kotarba, J.A. and Fontana, A. (eds) *The Existential Self in Society*. Chicago, IL: University of Chicago Press, pp.69–99.

Douglas, J.D. and Johnson, J.M. (eds) (1977) *Existential Sociology*. London: Cambridge University Press.

Drahota, J.A.T. and Eitzen, E.S. (1998) The role exit of professional athletes. *Sociology of Sport Journal*, 15, 3, 263–278.

Ebaugh, H.R.F. (1984) Leaving the convent. In Kotarba, J.A. and Fontana, A. (eds) *The Existential Self in Society*. Chicago, IL: University of Chicago Press, pp.156–176.

Ebaugh, H.R.F. (1988) *Becoming an Ex*. Chicago, IL: University of Chicago Press.

Edelhertz, H. (1970) *The Nature, Impact and Prosecution of White-Collar Crime*. Washington, DC: USGPO.

Elliot, D.S. (1994) Serious violent offenders. *Criminology*, 32,1 , 1–21.

Erben, M. (1993) The problem of other lives. *Sociology*, 27, 1, 5–13.

Erikson, K. (1965) *Childhood and Society*. London: Hogarth.

Espeland, W. (1984) Blood and money. In Kotarba, J.A. and Fontana, A. (eds) *The Existential Self in Society*. Chicago, IL: University of Chicago Press, pp.131–155.

Etika (2014) *About Etika LLC*. Available online at http://etikallc.com/about-white-collar-crime/ [accessed 12th August 2014].

Evans, M. (1993) Reading lives. *Sociology*, 27, 1, 5–13.

Farrall, S. (ed.) (2000) *The Termination of Criminal Careers*. Aldershot: Dartmouth Publishing.

Farrall, S. (2002) *Rethinking What Works with Offenders*. Cullompton: Willan.

Farrall, S. (2005) On the existential aspects of desistance from crime. *Symbolic Interaction*, 28, 3, 367–386.

Farrall, S. and Bowling, B. (1999) Structuration, human development and desistance from crime. *British Journal of Criminology*, 39, 2, 253–268.

Farrall, S. and Maruna, S. (2004) Desistance-focused criminal justice policy research. *The Howard Journal of Criminal Justice*, 43, 4, 358–367.

Farrall, S. and Calverley, A. (2006) *Understanding Desistance from Crime*. London: Open University Press.

Farrall, S., Hunter, B., Sharpe, G. and Calverley, A. (2014) *Criminal Careers in Transition*. Oxford: Oxford University Press.

*References* 193

Farrington, D. (1986) Age and crime. *Crime and Justice*, 7, 189–250.

Farrington, D. (1992) Criminal career research in the United Kingdom. *British Journal of Criminology*, 32, 4, 521–534.

Farrington, D. (1997) Human development and criminal careers. In Maguire, M., Morgan, R. and Reiner, R. (eds) *The Oxford Handbook of Criminology*, 2nd edition. Oxford: University Press, pp.361–408.

Farrington, D. and Hawkins, J.D. (1991) Predicting participation, early onset and later persistence in officially recorded offending. *Criminal Behaviour and Mental Health*, 1, 1, 1–33.

Financial Times (2014) *Nick Leeson Warns that Banks are Still Under Threat from Rogue Trading*. 15th January. Available online at www.ft.com/cms/s/0/fb63ab62-76e6-11e3-a253-00144feabdc0.html#axzz3AADGywi4 [accessed 12th August 2014].

Flynn, N. (2010) *Criminal Behaviour in Context*. London: Willan.

Fontana, A. (1984) Introduction. In Kotarba, J.A. and Fontana, A. (eds) *The Existential Self in Society*. Chicago, IL: University of Chicago Press, pp.3–17.

Fontana, A. (2002) Short stories from the salt. In Kotarba, J.A. and Johnson, J.M. (eds) *Postmodern Existential Sociology*. Lanham, MD: Rowman and Littlefield, pp.201–218.

Fontana, A. and Van de Water, R. (1977) The existential thought of Jean Paul Sartre and Maurice Merleau-Ponty. In Douglas, J.D. and Johnson, J.M. (eds), *Existential Sociology*. London: Cambridge University Press, pp.101–129.

Ford, G.G. (1996) An existential model for promoting life change. *Journal of Substance Abuse Treatment*, 13, 2, 151–158.

Fortune (1990) *The Inside Story of an Inside Trader*. 21st May. Available online at http://money.cnn.com/magazines/fortune/fortune_archive/1990/05/21/73553/index.htm [accessed 4th August 2014].

Fortune (2005a) *Remodelling Martha*. 14th November. Available online at http://money.cnn.com/magazines/fortune/fortune_archive/2005/11/14/8360708/index.htm [accessed 5th August 2014].

Fortune (2005b) *Where Are They Now*. 18th April. Available online at http://money.cnn.com/magazines/fortune/fortune_archive/2005/04/18/8257002/index.htm [accessed 12th August 2014].

Fortune (2014) *Barry Minkow, Fraudster, Nonpareil, Gets Five More Years*. 15th May. Available online at http://fortune.com/2014/05/06/barry-minkow-con-man-nonpareil-gets-five-more-years/ [accessed 12th August 2014].

Frank, J.D. (1977) Nature and functions of belief systems. *American Psychologist*, 32, 7, 555–559.

Frankl, V.E. (1978) *The Unheard Cry for Meaning*. London: Hodder and Stoughton.

Friedrichs, D.O. (2009) *Trusted Criminals*. Belmont, CA: Wadsworth.

Garfinkel, H. (1956) Conditions of successful degradation ceremonies. *American Journal of Sociology*, 61, 5, 420–424.

Geis, G. (1968) The heavy electrical equipment antitrust cases of 1961. In Geis, G. (ed.) *White-Collar Criminal*. Piscataway, NJ: Transaction, pp.103–118.

Giddens, A. (1984) *The Constitution of Society*. Cambridge: Polity Press.

Giordano, P.C., Cernkovich, S.A. and Rudolph, J.L. (2002) Gender, crime and desistance. *American Journal of Sociology*, 107, 4, 990–1064.

Giordano, P.C., Cernkovich, S.A. and Holland, D.D. (2003) Changes in friendship relations over the life course. *Criminology* 41, 2, 293–327.

Giordano, P., Schroeder, R.D. and Cernkovich, S.A. (2007) Emotions and crime over the life course. *American Journal of Sociology*, 112, 6, 1603–1661.

194    *References*

Giordano, P.C, Longmore, M.A., Schroeder, R.D. and Seffrin, P.M. (2008) A life-course perspective on spirituality and desistance from crime. *Criminology*, 46, 1, 99–132.

Goffman, E. (1961) *Asylums*. New York: Anchor Books.

Goffman, E. (1963) *Stigma*. Harmondsworth: Penguin Books.

Goffman, E. (1969) *The Presentation of Self in Everyday Life*. Harmondsworth: Penguin Books.

Gottfredson, M. and Hirschi, T. (1986) The true value of lambda would appear to be zero. *Criminology*, 24, 2, 213–234.

Gottfredson, M. and Hirschi, T. (1987) The methodological adequacy of longitudinal research on crime. *Criminology,* 25, 3, 581–614.

Gottfredson, M. and Hirschi, T. (1988) Science, public policy, and the career paradigm. *Criminology*, 26, 1, 37–56.

Gottfredson, M. and Hirschi, T. (1990) *A General Theory of Crime*. Stanford, CA: Stanford University Press.

Greenberg, D.F. (ed.) (1996a) *Criminal Careers Volume 1*. Aldershot: Dartmouth.

Greenberg, D.F. (ed.) (1996b) *Criminal Careers Volume 2*. Aldershot: Dartmouth.

Grossman, R. (1984) *Phenomenology and Existentialism*. London: Routledge & Kegan Paul.

Grube, J.W., Mayton II, D.M. and Ball-Rockeach, S.J. (1994) Inducing change in values, attitudes, and behaviours. *Journal of Social Issues*, 50, 4, 153–173.

Gusdorf, G. (1980) Conditions and limits of autobiography. In Olney, J. (ed.) *Autobiography: Essays Theoretical and Critical*. Princeton, NJ: Princeton University Press, pp.28–48.

Harding, D.J. (2003) Jean Valjean's dilemma. *Deviant Behaviour*, 24, 6, 571–595.

Hayim, G.J. (1996) *Existentialism and Sociology*. Piscataway, NJ: Transaction.

Heidegger, M. (1926) *Being and Time*. Translated by Macquarrie, J. and Robinson, E. [1962]. New York: Harper.

Henking, S. (1992) Protestant religious experience and the rise of American sociology. *Journal of the History of the Behavioural Sciences*, 28, 4, 325–339.

Hersh, T. (1980) The phenomenology of belief systems. *Journal of Humanistic Psychology*, 20, 2, 58–69.

Hirschi, T. (1969) *Causes of Delinquency*. Berkeley, CA: University of California Press.

Horney, J.D., Osgood, W., and Marshall, I.H. (1995) Criminal careers in the short-term. *American Sociological Review*, 60, 5, 655–673.

Howard, J. (2008) Negotiating an exit. *Social Psychology Quarterly*, 71, 2, 177–192.

Hughes, M. (1998) Turning points in the lives of young inner-city men forging destructive criminal careers. *Social Work Research*, 22, 3, 143–151.

Hunter, B. (2009) White-collar offenders after the fall from grace. In Lippens, R. and Crewe, D. (eds) *Criminology and Existentialism*. London: Routledge, pp.145–168.

Hunter, B. (2011) 'I can't make my own future'. In Farrall, S., Hough, M., Maruna, S., and Sparks, R. (eds) *Escape Routes*. Abingdon: Routledge, pp.221–239.

Irving, C. (2014) *The Official Website of Clifford Irving*. Available online at http://clifford irving.com/ [accessed 12th August 2014].

Irwin, J. (1980) *Prisons in Turmoil*. Boston, MA: Little & Brown.

Irwin, J. and Owen, B. (2005) Harm and the contemporary prison. In Liebling, A. and Maruna, S. (eds) *The Effects of Imprisonment*. Padstow: Willan, pp.94–117.

Jamieson, R. and Grounds, A. (2005) Release and adjustment. In Liebling, A. and Maruna, S. (eds) *The Effects of Imprisonment*. Padstow: Willan, pp.33–65.

Jett, J. (2014) *Stripped*. Available online at www.joseph-jett.com/ [accessed 12th August 2014].

## References    195

Jolliffe, D. and Hedderman, C. (2012) Investigating the impact of custody on reoffending using propensity score matching. *Crime & Delinquency*, [online] 1–27.

Justia (2014) *Analysis and Commentary by John Dean*. Available online at http://verdict.justia.com/author/dean [accessed 12th August 2014].

Jesilow, P., Pontell, H.M. and Geis, G. (1993) *How Doctors Defraud Medicaid*. Berkeley, CA: University of California Press.

Johnson, J.M. (2002) The stalking process. In Kotarba, J.A. and Johnson, J.M. (eds) *Postmodern Existential Sociology*. Lanham, MD: Rowman and Littlefield, pp.183–197.

Johnson, J.M. and Kotarba, J.A. (2002) Postmodern existentialism. In Kotarba, J.A. and Johnson, J.M. (eds) *Postmodern Existential Sociology*. Lanham, MD: Rowman and Littlefield, pp.3–14.

Jose-Kampfer, C. (1990) Coming to terms with existential death. *Social Justice*, 17, 2, 110–125.

Josselson, R. and Lieblich, A. (eds) (1993) *The Narrative Study of Lives vol. 1*. London: Sage.

Karstedt, S. (2002) Emotions and criminal justice. *Theoretical Criminology*, 6, 3, 299–317.

Karstedt, S., Levi, M. and Godfrey, B. (2006) Introduction. *British Journal of Criminology*, 46, 6, 971–975.

Katz J. (1988) *Seductions of Crime*. New York: Basic Books.

Kauffman, J. (2002) Safety and the assumptive world. In Kauffman, J. (ed.) *Loss of the Assumptive World*. London: Routledge, pp.205–212.

Kenyon, G.M. (2000) Philosophical foundations of existential meaning. In Reker, G.T. and Chamberlain, K. (eds) *Exploring Existential Meaning*. London: Sage, pp.7–22.

Kierkegaard, S.A. (1844) *The Concept of Dread*. Translated by Lowrie, W. [1946]. Princeton, NJ: Princeton University Press.

Klingemann, H.K.H. (1999) Addiction careers and careers in addiction. *Substance Use and Misuse*, 34, 11, 1505–1526.

Kotarba, J.A. (1979) Existential sociology. In McNall, S. (ed.) *Theoretical Perspectives in Sociology*. New York: St. Martin's Press, pp.348–368.

Kotarba, J.A. (1984) A synthesis. In Kotarba, J.A. and Fontana, A. (eds) *The Existential Self in Society*. London: University of Chicago Press, pp.222–234.

Kotarba, J.A. and Fontana, A. (eds) (1984) *The Existential Self in Society*. Chicago, IL: Chicago University Press.

Kotarba, J.A. and Bentley, P. (1988) Workplace wellness participation and the becoming of self. *Social Science and Medicine*, 26, 5, 551–558.

Kotarba, J.A. and Johnson, J.M. (eds) (2002) *Postmodern Existential Sociology*. Lanham, MD: Rowman and Littlefield.

Laub, J.H. and Sampson, R.J. (1993) Turning points in the life course. *Criminology*, 31, 3, 301–325.

Laub, J.H. and Sampson, R.J. (2001) Understanding desistance from crime. *Crime and Justice*, 28, 1–69.

Laub, J.H. and Sampson, R.J. (2003) *Shared Beginnings, Divergent Lives*. London: Harvard University Press.

Laub, J.H., Nagin, D.S. and Sampson, R.J. (1998) Trajectories of change in criminal offending. *American Sociological Review*, 63, 2, 225–238.

Lazarus, R.S. (1999) Hope. *Social Research*, 66, 2, 653–678.

LeBel, T.P. (2007) An examination of the impact of formerly incarcerated persons helping others. *Journal of Offender Rehabilitation*, 46, 1, 1–24.

## 196    References

Leeson, N. (2014) *Nick Leeson*. Available online at www.nickleeson.com/ [accessed 7th August 2014].

Leibrich, J. (1996) The role of shame in going straight. In Galaway, B. and Hudson, J. (eds) *Restorative Justice*. New York: Criminal Justice Press, pp.283–302.

Lejeune, P. (1982) The autobiographical contract. In Todorov, T. (ed.) *French Literary Theory Today*. Translated by Carter, R. Cambridge: Cambridge University Press, pp.192–222.

Lester, M. (1984) Self. In Kotarba, J.A. and Fontana, A. (eds) *The Existential Self in Society*. Chicago, IL: University of Chicago Press, pp.18–68.

Leverentz, A. (2010) People, places, and things. *Journal of Contemporary Ethnography*, 39, 6, 646–681.

Levi, M. (1981) *The Phantom Capitalists*. London: Cambridge University Press.

Levi, M. (1988) *The Prevention of Fraud*. Crime Prevention Unit, Paper 17. London: HMSO.

Levi, M. (1994) Masculinities and white-collar crime. In Newburn, T. and Stanko, E. (eds) *Just Boys Doing Business?* Abingdon: Routledge, pp.234–252.

Lewis, H.B. (1971) *Guilt and Shame in Neurosis*. New York: International Universities Press.

Lexington Herald (2014) *Watergate Figure Jeb Stuart Magruder, Who Later Became a Minister in Lexington, Dies at 79*. 15th May. Available online at www.kentucky.com/2014/05/15/3244758/watergate-figure-jeb-stuart-magruder.html [accessed 12th August 2014].

Lippens, R. and Crewe, D. (eds) *Criminology and Existentialism*. London: Routledge.

Loader, I. and deHaan, W. (2004) On the emotions of crime, punishment and social control. *Theoretical Criminology*, 6, 3, 243–253.

Lofland, J. (1969) *Deviance and Identity*. Englewood Cliffs, NJ: Prentice-Hall.

Lynd, H.M. (1958) *On Shame and the Search for Identity*. New York: Science Editions.

Macquarrie, J. (1972) *Existentialism*. London: Penguin Books.

Maguire, M. and Raynor, P. (2006) How the resettlement of prisoners promotes desistance from crime. *Criminology and Criminal Justice*, 6, 1, 19–38.

Mahoney, A. and Pargament, K.I. (2004) Sacred changes. *Journal of Clinical Psychology*, 60, 5, 481–492.

Manion, J. (2002) The moral relevance of shame. *American Philosophical Quarterly*, 39, 1, 73–90.

Mann, K., Wheeler, S. and Sarat, A. (1980) Sentencing the white-collar offender. *American Criminal Law Review*, 14, 479–500.

Manning, P. (1973) Existential sociology. *Sociological Quarterly*, 14, 2, 200–225.

Maruna, S. (1997) Going straight. In Lieblich, A. and Josselson, R. (eds) *The Narrative Study of Lives Vol. 5*. London: Sage, pp.59–93.

Maruna, S. (2001) *Making Good*. Washington, DC: American Psychological Association Books.

Maruna, S. (2012) Elements of successful desistance signalling. *Criminology and Public Policy*, 11, 1, 73–86.

Maruna, S. and Farrall, S. (2004) Desistance from crime. *Kölner Zeitschrift für Soziologie & Sozialpsychologie*, 43, 171–194.

Maruna, S. and Roy, K. (2007) Amputation or reconstruction? *Journal of Contemporary Criminal Justice*, 23, 1, 104–124.

McAdams, D.P. (1993) *The Stories We Live By*. New York: Guilford.

McKnight, S. (2002) *Turning to Jesus*. Louisville, KY: Westminster John Knox Press.

## References    197

Meisenhelder, T. (1977) An exploratory study of exiting from criminal careers. *Criminology*, 15, 3, 319–334.

Meisenhelder, T. (1982) Becoming normal. *Deviant Behaviour*, 3, 2, 137–153.

Meisenhelder, T. (1985) An essay on time and the phenomenology of imprisonment. *Deviant Behaviour*, 6, 1, 39–56.

Messinger, S.L. and Warren, C.A.B. (1984) The homosexual self and the organisation of experience. In Kotarba, J.A. and Fontana, A. (eds) (1984) *The Existential Self in Society*. Chicago, IL: University of Chicago Press, pp.196–206.

Moffitt, T.E. (1993) Life-course persistent and adolescent-limited anti-social behaviour. *Psychological Review*, 100, 4, 674–701.

Morgan, S. (1999) Prison lives. *The Howard Journal of Criminal Justice*, 38, 3, 328–340.

Morrison, W. (1995) *Theoretical Criminology*. London: Cavendish Publishing.

MSLO (1999) *Annual Report 1999*.

MSLO (2008) *News Release*. 19th February.

Nietzsche, F. (1886) *Beyond Good and Evil*. Translated by Faber, M. [1998]. Oxford: Oxford: University Press.

Nietzsche, F. (1887) *The Gay Science*. Translated by Kauffman, W. [1974]. New York: Vintage Books.

Nelken, D. (2012) White-collar and corporate crime. In Maguire, M., Morgan, R., and Reiner, R. (eds) *The Oxford Handbook of Criminology*, 5th edition. Oxford: Oxford University Press, pp.623–659.

Oleson, J.C. (2003) The celebrity of infamy. *Crime, Law & Social Change*, 40, 4, 391–408.

Paloutzian, R.F. (1981) Purpose in life and value changes following conversion. *Journal of Personality and Social Psychology*, 41, 6, 1153–1160.

Paloutzian, R.F., Richardson, J.T. and Rambo, L.R. (1999) Religious conversion and personality change. *Journal of Personality*, 67, 6, 1047–1079.

Patrick, D.R. and Bignall, J.E. (1984) Creating the competent self. In Kotarba, J.A. and Fontana, A. (eds) *The Existential Self in Society*. London: University of Chicago Press, pp.207–221.

Petersilia, J. (2003) *When Prisoners Come Home: Parole and Prisoner Re-entry*. Oxford: Oxford University Press.

Pezzin, L.E. (1995) Earning prospects, matching effects, and the decision to terminate a criminal career. *Journal of Quantitative Criminology*, 11, 1, 29–50.

Piquero, N.L. (2012) The only thing we have to fear is fear itself. *Crime & Delinquency*, 58, 3, 362–379.

Piquero, N.L. and Benson, M.L. (2004) White-collar crime and criminal careers. *Journal of Contemporary Criminal Justice*, 20, 2, 148–165.

Pitulac, T. and Nastuta, S. (2007) Choosing to be stigmatized. *Journal of Religions and Ideologies*, 16, 1, 80–97.

Plummer, K. (1983) *Documents of Life*. London: George Allen & Unwin.

Plummer, K. (2001) *Documents of Life 2*. London: Sage.

Rambo, L.R. (1993) *Understanding Religious Conversion*. New Haven, CT: Yale University Press.

Retzinger, S.M. (1991) *Violent Emotions: Shame and Rage in Marital Quarrels*. London: Sage.

Richards, S.C. and Jones, R.S. (2004) Beating the perpetual incarceration machine: overcoming structural impediments to re-entry. In Maruna, S. and Immarigeon, R. (eds) *After Crime and Punishment*. Portland, OR: Willan, pp.201–232.

Robinson, G. and Shapland, J. (2008) Reducing recidivism. *The British Journal of Criminology*, 48, 3, 337–358.

198    *References*

Rose, P. (2014) *Pete Rose*. Available online at www.peterose.com/ [accessed 12th August 2014].

Rowbotham, J. (2007) Editorial. *Liverpool Law Review*, 28, 319–326.

Sampson, R.J. and Laub, J.H. (1993) *Crime in the Making*. Cambridge, MA: Harvard University Press.

Sampson, R.J. and Laub, J.H. (2005a) A life course view of the development of crime. *Annals of the American Academy of Political and Social Sciences*, 602, 12–45.

Sampson, R.J. and Laub, J.H. (2005b) A general age graded theory of crime. In Farrington, D. (ed.) *Integrated Developmental and Life Course Theories of Offending*. Piscataway, NJ: Transaction Press, pp.165–181.

Sapsford, R.J. (1978) Life-sentence prisoners. *British Journal of Criminology*, 18, 2, 128–145.

Sartre, J.-P. (1958) *Being and Nothingness*. Translated by Barnes, H.E [1980]. New York: Philosophical Library.

Sartre, J.-P. (1963) *Saint Genet*. Translated by Fretchman, B. [1984]. New York: Pantheon.

Scheff, T.J. (2000) Shame and the social bond. *Sociological Theory*, 18, 1, 84–99.

Scheff, T.J. and Retzinger, S.M. (1991) *Emotions and Violence*. Lexington, MA: Lexington.

Schneider, C.D. (1992) *Shame, Exposure and Privacy*. London: W.W. Norton & Company.

Schrock, D. (2002) Emotional stories. In Kotarba, J.A. and Johnson, J.M. (eds) *Postmodern Existential Sociology*. Lanham, MD: Rowman and Littlefield, pp.219–234.

Schutz, A. (1967) *Collected Papers*, Vol. 1. Edited and introduced by Natanson, M. The Hague: Nijhoff.

Scott, G. (2004) It's a sucker's outfit. *Ethnography*, 5, 1, 107–140.

Securities and Exchange Commission (2006) *Litigation Release No. 19794*. 7th August.

Shaffir, W. and Kleinknecht, S. (2005) Death at the polls. *Journal of Contemporary Ethnography*, 34, 6, 707–738.

Shapiro, S.P. (1990) Collaring the crime not the criminal. *American Sociological Review*, 55, 3, 346–365.

Sharp, S.F. and Hope, T.L. (2001) The professional-ex revisited. *Journal of Contemporary Ethnography*, 30, 6, 678–703.

Sheridan, D. (1993) Writing to the archive. *Sociology*, 27, 1, 27–40.

Shover, N. (1983) The later stages of ordinary property offender careers. *Social Problems*, 31, 2, 208–218.

Shover, N. (1985) *Aging Criminals*. Thousand Oaks, CA: Sage.

Shover, N. (1996) *Great Pretenders*. Boulder, CO: Westview.

Shover, N. and Thompson, C.Y. (1992) Age, differential expectations, and crime desistance. *Criminology*, 30, 1, 89–104.

Shover, N. and Wright, J.P. (eds) (2001) *Crimes of Privilege*. New York: Oxford University Press.

Shover, N. and Hochstetler, A. (2006) *Choosing White-Collar Crime*. London: Cambridge University Press.

Shover, N. and Hunter, B. (2010) Blue-collar, white-collar. In Bernasco, W. (ed.) *Criminals on Crime*. Cullompton: Willan, pp.205–227.

Simpson, C. (2004) When hope makes us vulnerable. *Bioethics*, 18, 5, 428–447.

Simpson, S. (2013) White-collar crime. *Annual Review of Sociology*, 39, 309–331.

Simpson, S. and Weisburd, D. (eds) (2009) *The Criminology of White-Collar Crime*. New York: Springer.

Slapper, G. and Tombs, S. (1999) *Corporate Crime*. London: Longman.

## References    199

Smith, B. and Sparkes, A.C. (2005) Men, sport, spinal cord injury, and narratives of hope. *Social Science & Medicine*, 61, 5, 1095–1105.

Smith, S. and Watson, J. (2002) *Reading Autobiography*. Minneapolis, MN: University of Minnesota Press.

Stewart, M. (2005) *The Martha Rules*. New York: Rodale Books.

Strauss, A.L. and Corbin, J.M. (1998) *Basics of Qualitative Research*. Thousand Oaks, CA: Sage.

Sutherland, E. (1932) Review of 'The natural history of a delinquent career. *American Journal of Sociology*, 38, 1, 135–136.

Sutherland, E. (1940) White-collar criminality. *American Sociological Review*, 5, 1, 1–11.

Sutherland, E. (1945) Is white-collar crime crime? *American Sociological Review*, 10, 2, 132–139.

Sutherland, E. (1983) *White-Collar Crime*. New Haven, CT: Yale University Press.

Sykes, G. (1958) *The Society of Captives*. Princeton, NJ: Princeton University Press.

Sykes, G.M. and Messinger, S.L. (1960) The inmate social system. In Cloward, R., Cressey, D.A., Grosser, G.H., McCleery, R., Ohlin, L.E., Sykes, G.M. and Messinger, S.L. (eds) *Theoretical Studies in Social Organization of the Prison*. New York: Social Science Research Council, pp.5–19.

Taylor, G. (1985) *Pride, Shame and Guilt*. Oxford: Clarendon Press.

The Australian (2014) *Alan Bond's Getting the Band Back Together*. 11th June. Available online at www.theaustralian.com.au/business/alan-bonds-getting-the-band-back-together/story-e6frg8zx-1226949909163?nk=01aad087654abec3b957bcff41ee1909 [accessed 12th August 2014].

The New Zealand Herald (2006) *Convicted Trader Looking After Next Life*. 3rd June. Available online at http://subs.nzherald.co.nz/organisation/story.cfm?o_id=127& ObjectID=10384806 [accessed 5th August 2014].

The Jim Bakker Show (2008) *The Jim Bakker show*. Available online at www.jim bakkershow.com/ [accessed 12th August 2014].

Time Magazine (2001) *Wall Street's New Honor Code*. 25th June. Available online at http://content.time.com/time/magazine/article/0,9171,1000181,00.html [accessed 6th August 2014].

Toch, H. (1992) *Living in Prison*. New York: American Psychological Association.

Toch, H. (2010) 'I am not now who I used to be then'. *The Prison Journal*, 90, 1, 4–11.

Uggen, C. (2000) Work as a turning point in the life course of criminals. *American Sociological Review*, 65, 4, 529–546.

Uggen, C. and Kruttschnitt, C. (1998) Crime in the breaking. *Law and Society Review*, 32, 2, 339–366.

Uggen, C., Manza, J. and Behrens, A. (2004) Less than the average citizen. In Maruna, S. and Immarigeon, R. (eds) *After Crime and Punishment*. Portland, OR: Willan, pp.261–293.

Vaughan, B. (2007) The internal narrative of desistance. *British Journal of Criminology*, 47, 3, 390–404.

Vaughan, D. (2001) Sensational cases, flawed theories. In Pontell, H.N. and Shichor, D. (eds) (2001) *Contemporary Issues in Crime and Criminal Justice*. Upper Saddle River, NJ: Prentice-Hall, pp. 45–66.

Visher, C.A. and Travis, J.T. (2003) Transitions from prison to community. *Annual Review of Sociology*, 29: 89–113.

Visher, C.A. and Travis, J.T. (2011) Life on the outside. *The Prison Journal*. 91, 3, 102s–119s.

## 200  References

Volpe, T. (2012) *Todd Michael Volpe*. Available online at www.todvolpe.com/ [accessed 12th August 2014].

Warr, M. (1988) Life course transitions and desistance from crime. *Criminology*, 36, 1, 183–216.

Weisburd, D., Waring, E.J. and Chayet, E.F. (2001) *White-Collar Crime and Criminal Careers*. Cambridge: Cambridge University Press.

Weisburd, D., Wheeler, S., Waring, E.J. and Bode, N. (1991) *Crimes of the Middle Classes*. London: Yale University Press.

Wheeler, S. (1992) The problem of white-collar crime motivation. In Weisburd, D. and Schlegel, K. (eds) *White-Collar Crime Reconsidered*. Boston, MA: Northeastern University Press, pp.108–123.

Wheeler, S., Weisburd, D. and Bode, N. (1982) Sentencing the white-collar offender: rhetoric and reality. *American Sociological Review*, 47, 641–659.

Wheeler, S., Mann, K. and Sarat, A. (1988) *Sitting in Judgement: The Sentencing of White-Collar Offenders*. New Haven, CT: Yale University Press.

White, W.L. (2000) The history of recovered people as wounded healers II. *Alcoholism Treatment Quarterly*, 18, 2, 1–25.

Wired for Books (1984) *Audio Interviews with Clifford Irving*. Available online at http://wiredforbooks.org/cliffordirving/ [accessed 5th August 2014].

Wolfgang, M.E., Figlio, R.M., and Sellin, J.T. (1972) *Delinquency in a Birth Cohort*. Chicago, IL: University of Chicago Press.

Wright, R.A., Bryant, K.M. and Miller, J.M. (2001) Top criminals/top criminologists: *Journal of Contemporary Criminal Justice*, 17, 4, 383–399.

Yalom, I. (1980) *Existential Psychotherapy*. New York: Basic Books.

# Index

action 31
age: and crime 14, 24, 25
ageing: and desistance 16
agency 22–3; and change 121–7; human 19, 19–20
Aitken, Jonathan: active change 121; admission of guilt 93; anxiety at application to Oxford University 115; asking forgiveness 165; autobiography 53, 54; belief system 156; blocked paths 101; Christian faith 118; confidence as prisoner 87; debarred from re-entering politics 103; on difficulties after leaving prison 99; on facing the future with new belief system 169; failing to return to politics 111; intellectual challenge of God's existence 162; on libel case with *The Guardian* 158, 163; on *metanoia* 160; on penitence 167; philosophising on failing to re-enter politics 113; on prayer groups 172; prison sentence and time served 66, 87; on privacy in prison 72; professional-ex activity 133; professions 109; reconciling new beliefs with past wrongdoings 163; studying theology 114; substantial change 117, 118; success 114; threat of violence in prison 68; uncertainty about the future 96; utilising skills for fellow prisoners 78; on visa refusal 102
Altheide, D. L.: on phenomenological sociology 41
anxiety 29–30; anxious prisoners 87–90; coping with 90–1; guilt acceptance 93; role exit 130

Archer, Jeffrey: anxiety about the future 87; autobiography 53, 54; blocked paths 101; contact with prison personnel 78; on facing the future 89–90; on fearing negative change in prison 77; fears negative change in prison 125; negative passive change 124; partial change 117; passive change 121; prison diaries 125; prison sentence and time served 66–7, 87; professions 109; rejection of guilt 93; reports positive change after prison 125; on structuring time in prison 73
The Australian 109
authentic existence 29
autobiographical writing 5–6
autobiographies: analysing 55–6; characteristics 48; comparing accounts 56–8; comparison with other life telling methods 48; confirming existence to oneself 48; in criminology 50; definition 46; factual accuracy 51; methodological issues in studying 50–1; posthumous propaganda 48; in sociology 49, 50; subjectivity 47; telling of the self 46–9; truth 47, 48, 49, 51; white-collar offenders 52–4
awareness 158

bad faith 29
bad self 40
Bakker, Jim: autobiography 53, 54; blocked paths 101; confidence as prisoner 87; on leaving prison 94; partial change 117; passive change 121; positive passive change 124; prison

## 202  Index

sentence and time served 66, 87; professions 109; on structuring time in prison 73; on tasting freedom 95

barcodes 68

Barings Bank 99

becoming: self 28

behavioural change 20

Belfort, Jordan: autobiography 53, 54; prison sentence and time served 66; professional-ex activity 133; professions 109

beliefs 34–5

belief systems 92, 118–19; accepting 158–61; adoption of new 156–66; authenticating conversion 174; becoming aware 158; confirming the efficacy of beliefs 164–6; context of conversion 157–8; definition 151–2; doubts 161–2; emotional aspects 171; gaining certification 173–4; inner aspects 166–71; learning to believe 163–4; peer groups 171–2; positive feelings 170–1; religion and white-collar offenders 156; religious 152; retelling the past 168–70; secular 152; shame, guilt and relinquishing of control 166–8; social aspects 171–4; surrender 167; value of 152; *see also* religion; religious conversion

Benson, M. L.: adult life experiences 26; on white-collar offenders in prison 65

Berger, Robert L.: on anxiety about the future 87, 88; autobiography 53, 54; blocked paths 101; car service business 91; on health benefits of imprisonment 71; justification of actions 120; on life before and after prison 124; negative passive change 124; partial change 117; passive change 121; on potential for failure 91; on prison life 68; prison sentence and time served 66, 87; professional-ex activity 133; on rebuilding from scratch 91; on reflections of prison time 74–5; rejection of guilt 93; returning to old life 90; on stigma 101; technical guilt 93

blocked paths 101, 102–4; definition 100

Bond, Alan: anxiety about the future 87;

autobiography 53, 54; blocked paths 101; partial change 117; passive change 121; positive passive change 124; prison sentence and time served 66, 87; professions 109; rejection of guilt 93; on using prison experience in business life 123; utilising skills for fellow prisoners 78

Bottoms, A.: interactive framework 22–3

Bowling, B.: environment and desistance 21–2

Braithwaite, J.: theory of shaming 44

Buddhism 156, 172

Bullen, David: autobiography 53, 54; belief system 156; conversion to Buddhism 156, 159; on despondency with life 157; on feeling serene 170; guidance from Buddhist sources 172; neutralising feelings of shame and guilt 159; on the new way of viewing illegal trades 167–8; single moment of religious connection 162

Calverley, A.: on prison life 62

Cernkovich, S. A.: cognitive transformation 19–20

certification 145, 173–4

change: and agency 121–7; 'appropriating hooks for change' 20; dimensions of 116–17; healing wounds and the passage of time 125–7; new lives 116, 117–19; partial 119–21; passive 122–4; receiving 122–5; redemption 122; seeking to 121–2; in self 116–21; substantial 117–19

Charles Colson Legacy Fund 109

Chayet, E. F. 11, 13; age and crime 24; stability in adulthood 26

Chicago School of Sociology 49

choice: freedom of 29, 29–30; new starts for ex-prisoners 98; reduction of 31

Christensen, Nelson: admission of guilt 93; autobiography 53, 54; blocked paths 101; confidence as prisoner 87; on leaving prison 94; on prison identification 67–8; prison sentence and time served 66, 87; on receiving a clean slate 92–3; resettlement 86; on structuring time in prison 73; utilising

skills for fellow prisoners 78
Christianity: conversion to 114; drawing strength from faith in 92; faith in 118; recognising sins 167; relinquishing control 166
Christian Solidarity Worldwide 118
civic functions 83, 84
civic reintegration 112
civil rights 103
cognitive transformation 19–20, 43–4
Cohen, S.: prison life 63; shattering experience of prison life 64
Colson, Charles: active change 121; admission of guilt 93; arrest of son 121; autobiography 53, 54; belief system 156; blocked paths 101; certification 173; Christian faith 118, 134; confidence as prisoner 87; employing ex-identity 132; fame 59; on fatherhood 121–2; on Harold Hughes 172, 173; intellectual challenge of God's existence 162; on leaving prison 97; on new life path 99; on prison as part of God's design 168–9; prison sentence and time served 66, 87; professional-ex activity 133; professional-ex role *see* Colson, Charles (professional-ex role); professions 109; reconciling new beliefs with past wrongdoings 163; redemption 122; resettlement 86; speaking to President Richard Nixon 117–18; substantial change 117, 118; success 114
Colson, Charles (professional-ex role): achieving something significant 135; advantages of role 149; becoming a professional-ex 134–5; case summary 134; conversion to Christianity 138–9; epiphany moment 137; forced choice 139; on fulfilling future dreams 135; fulfilment and therapy 145–6; generative pursuits 143; hesitation 138; making meaning of past experiences 143; necessity of deviant past 141; on realising prison care project 137; setting up prison ministry 138–9, 140; training disciples for prison ministry 142; on the uncertainties of being a Christian 136; uncertainty 142;

uncertainty of achieving goals 136; use of deviant past 147; on vision of future prison ministry 137
commitment: religious conversion 153–4, 167
community work 112
confident offenders 21
confident prisoners 87, 92–4
consequences: religious conversion 154
context 153
conversion, religious 57–8
Costello, A.: interactive framework 22–3
credibility 140–1
crime: and age 14, 24, 25; emotional need 42
criminal career, concept of 13–14
criminal law: utilising skills for fellow prisoners 78
criminology: and autobiographies 50; and emotion 184; and existential sociology 42–4
crisis: religious conversion 153
Cullen, S. T.: on white-collar offenders in prison 65
culture and habitus 22
Cusson, M. 16

Dean, John: active change 121; admission of guilt 93; autobiography 53, 54; blocked paths 101; confidence as prisoner 87; denied participation in civic activities 103; on experience of writing 119; financial considerations for writing autobiography 99; on judging others 102; negative encounters 101; on new starts 98; partial change 117; perspective gained from imprisonment 119; on planning the rest of his life 98; on pondering the future 96; prison sentence and time served 87; professions 109; on receiving job offers 101; on reduced civil rights 103; resettlement into previous profession 110
dehumanisation 67–8, 80
deprivations: prisoners 64
desistance: autobiographies, value of 177–8; correlates 16–17; defining and conceptualising 15; existential

sociology 184; experiences of desisters 21; future self 184; guilt 182; legitimate employment 43; length of prison sentences 62; literature 185; primary 15; promotion of 148; reduced opportunities for agency in prison 62; and religion 154–6; research 14, 24–5; resettlement *see* resettlement; secondary 15; and shame 37–40; stability in adulthood 26; stigmatisation 180; support groups and family members 84; *see also* ex-prisoners; professional-exes; professional-ex roles; pro-social identities
despair 30
despondency 103
detection, crime 16
deviant pasts 18, 130, 131, 140–1, 147, 148
difference: characteristic of existentialism 41
doubts: belief systems 161–2
Douglas, J. D.: self without values 34; sense of self 33

Ebaugh, H. R. F. 89
Edelhertz, H. 11
education programmes: utilising skills for fellow prisoners 78
emotions: desistance process 43, 184; interacting with the world 29–31, 35; role in crime 42
employment: and crime 25; and desistance 16–17, 43; of ex-prisoners 85; and prison 61; problems facing ex-prisoners 102
encounter: religious conversion 153
environment: and desistance 21–2
Etika 109
existentialism: action 31; belief systems 152; characteristics of existence 28–9; difference 41; emotions and the world 29–31; nature of existence 28–9; past, present and future 31–2
existential sociology 4–5; and criminology 42–4; feelings and emotions 35; meaningful self-identity 33–4; and phenomenological sociology 40–1; shame 35–40; values and beliefs 34–5
exoneration: generative pursuit 131, 144–5

ex-prisoners: achievable goals 84; awareness of others' perceptions 102; concealing criminal past 130; immediate action required on release 96; importance of normalcy 100; inadequate support structures 84–5; new starts and choices 98; old identities 95; peer groups and family members 84; post-release world 100–4; pro-social identities 83–4; *see also* leaving prison

failing (resettlement) 111–13; alternative projects 113; events 116
Farrall, S. 15, 23; employment and desistance 17; environment and desistance 21–2; experiences of desisters 21; offenders' groupings 21; on prison life 62
feelings: interacting with the world 29–31, 35
finance sector 119
Fontana, A. 80
Ford, G. G.: power of shame 36
Fortune 109
Fraud Discovery Institute (FDI) 133, 149
freedom: of choice 29, 29–30; choices for ex-prisoners 98; leaving prison 94–100; reduction of choices 31
fulfilment: generative pursuit 131, 145–6
future self 43–4, 80, 91, 184

gang membership 42
generative pursuits 131, 143–6
ghost writers 178
Giordano, P. C. 23; cognitive transformation 19–20
goals: achievable 84; personal 115, 116; uncertainty of achieving 136
God: existence 164–5; faith in 92; fearing rejection of 161; forgiveness 92, 166; intellectual challenge of existence 162
good self 40
Gottfredson, M. 14
*The Guardian* 158, 163
guilt 30, 36, 166–8, 182; acceptance 93; admission 93; neutralising feelings of 159; rejection 93; sharing guilty feelings 160; technical 93

*Index* 205

Guppy, Darius: admission of guilt 93; autobiography 53, 54; blocked paths 101; confidence as prisoner 87; justification of actions 120; on leaving prison 96–7; partial change 117; passive change 121; on positive experience of prison life 123–4; positive passive change 124; prison sentence and time served 66, 87
Gusdorf, G.: on autobiographies 48

habitus, culture and 22
healing wounds 125–7
Heidegger, Martin 32
Hirschi, T. 14
Hochstetler, A.: recidivism and white-collar offenders 25
Holmes, D.: interactive framework 22–3
honour groups 36
hooks, for change 20
hope 30, 31, 45n1
Howard, Michael 103
Hughes, Harold 172
Hughes, Howard 120
human agency 19, 19–20
Hunter, B. 12

identification, prison 67–8
identity: deviant 84; ex-prisoner 95; fit with self 84; manipulation 84; new 83; people and places 84; post-prison 83; pro-social 83, 84; socially constructed 85; *see also* pro-social identities; role exit; self
ImClone Systems Inc. 1
immediate aftermath 94
imprisonment: existential death for women 42
inauthentic existence 29
individual being *see* existentialism
induction, prison 67–70
inside knowledge 141
interaction: religious conversion 153
Irving, Clifford: autobiography 53, 54; desire to return to former life 120; partial change 117, 120, 121; passive change 121; positive passive change 124; professions 109
Irwin, J. 63–4

Jett, Joseph: autobiography 53, 54; on drawing strength from conviction 126–7; partial change 117; passive change 121; positive passive change 124; professions 109
The Jim Bakker Show 109
Jose-Kampfer, C.: existential death 63; female imprisonment 42
Justia 109

Katz, J.: emotional pleasure of crime 42
Kenner, David 173
Kerley, K. R.: adult life experiences 26

Laite, William: anxiety about the future 87; autobiography 53, 54; on being unable to find employment 102; blocked paths 101; failing to return to politics 111, 127; on fears of leaving prison 88–9; on first impressions of prison life 67; negative passive change 124; partial change 117; passive change 121; prison sentence and time served 66, 87; on protection in prison from the outside world 88; on rebuilding life 89; rejection of guilt 93; on returning as Mayor 112
Laub, J. H. 23; life courses 18–19; marriage and desistance 17
Lawson, Stephen: active change 121; admission of guilt 93; angst 157; on asking forgiveness 165; autobiography 53, 54; belief system 156; blocked paths 101; Christian faith 118; confidence as prisoner 87; disappointment at friends' refusal of financial help 164; distraught 159; on faith in God 92; on fearing God's rejection 161; on God's forgiveness 166; on loneliness 170; on loss of identity 159; prison sentence and time served 66, 87; professional-ex activity 133; on proof of God's existence 164–5; reconciling new beliefs with past wrongdoings 163; substantial change 117, 118
leaving prison: blocked paths 102–4; ex-prisoner identity 95; first impressions 94–7; immediate action

## 206   Index

required on release 96; immediate aftermath 94; importance of normalcy 100; new lives and familiar activities 99–100; new starts 98–9; quiet life 96–7; removal of prison uniform 95; stigma 100–2; uncertainty about the future 96; *see also* ex-prisoners; prisoners

Leeson, Nick: anxiety about the future 87; autobiography 53, 54; awareness of impact on family 119–20; blocked paths 101; career after leaving prison 120; coping strategies in prison 70; exceptional offences 58–9; justification of actions 120–1; partial change 117, 120; passive change 121; perspective gained from imprisonment 119–20; positive passive change 124; prison sentence and time served 66, 87; professional-ex activity 133; professions 109; on reconnecting with roots 99; rejection of guilt 93; technical guilt 93; on using prison time 71

legal restrictions 85

legitimacy: generative pursuit 131, 144–5

Lejeune, P.: on autobiographies 46

Lennar Corporation 133

Levi, M. 12

Levine, Dennis: active change 121; admission of guilt 93; arrest 59; autobiography 53, 54; blocked paths 101; confidence as prisoner 87; financial consultancy 114, 127; forgiveness post-prison sentence 121; on impact on family 99; partial change 117; on pondering the future 96; prison sentence and time served 66, 87; professions 109; redemption 122; on second chances 92; on seeking change 122; on using prison time for reflection 70, 71; on withdrawing from the finance industry 119

Lewis, James 141

Lexington Herald 109

life courses 18–19

life narratives *see* autobiographies

Lloyds Bank 120

low-security prisons 80

Lynd, H. M. 36

Macquarrie, J.: authentic and inauthentic existence 29; characteristics of existence 28–9

Magruder, Jeb: active change 121; admission of guilt 93; autobiography 53, 54; belief system 156; blocked paths 101; Christian faith 118; on Christian friendship groups 172; confidence as prisoner 87; conversion to Christianity 115; on coping with prison life 69; on the importance of Christian friends 171; on the importance of Christianity 168; intellectual challenge of God's existence 162; prison sentence and time served 66, 87; professions 109; on restlessness with life 157; substantial change 117, 118; success 114

Manion, J. 36

marriage: and crime 25; and desistance 17; white-collar offenders 85

Marsh, Ben 123

Martha Stewart Living Omnimedia (MSLO) 1

Maruna, S. 15, 23; autobiographies 50, 51; environment and desistance 21–2; redemption script 17–18

McKnight, S.: on converts conceptualising the past 169

Meisenhelder, T.: futility of prison life 43

*metanoia* 160

Michael (juvenile criminal) 1–2

military service 19

Minkow, Barry: active change 121; admission of guilt 93; autobiography 53, 54; belief system 156; blocked paths 101; certification 173; Christian faith 118; confidence as prisoner 87; on David Kenner 173; failing of new business 112; on inconsistencies between new beliefs and lying 164; prison sentence and time served 66, 87; professional-ex activity 133; professional-ex role *see* Minkow, Barry (professional-ex role); professions 109; reconviction 128, 133; on setting up a new business 112; on sharing guilty feelings 160; single moment of religious connection 162; on

*Index* 207

structuring time in prison 74; substantial change 117, 118; success 114; on taking stock of life 113
Minkow, Barry (professional-ex role): advantages of role 149; advice for potential business investors 138; becoming a professional-ex 134–5; case summary 133; certification 145; contribution to fraud prevention 137, 139, 140; on credibility 140–1; epiphany moment 137; exoneration and legitimacy 144–5; fears of failing as a fraud investigator 142; generative pursuits 143; hesitation 139; importance of job as pastor 149; on making amends 135; making meaning of past experiences 143; necessity of deviant past 141; role as pastor 144; self-presentation 136; on the uncertainties of making restitution 136; uncertainty 142; use of deviant past 147, 148
Morgan, S.: autobiographies 50
Morrison, W.: emotional component of offending 42
Muir, G.: interactive framework 22–3
MX Factors 139

Nagin, D. S.: marriage and desistance 17
napping 76
Nelken, D. 12–13
new starts 98–9
Nietzsche, Friedrich 29
Nixon, Richard 117, 118

ontology: anxiety 90, 152; crippling failure 113; insecurity 33, 68, 152, 159, 161; threat to sense of wellbeing 64
optimists: offenders 21
Oxford University 114, 115

partial change 117, 119–21; avoiding same mistakes 119–20; justification of actions 120–1; no desire of offenders to change character 119–20
passive change 122–4
Pavlo, Walter Junior: autobiography 53, 54; professional-ex activity 133; professions 109; resettlement into previous profession 110

peace: desired after leaving prison 96–7
peer groups 171–2
peer pressure 36
penitence 167
pessimists: offenders 21
phenomenological sociology: and existential sociology 40–1
Pinsonneault, P. 16
Plummer, K.: on life history research 47–8; systematic thematic analysis 55
*The Polish Peasant in Europe and America* 49
posthumous propaganda 48
prayer groups 172
primary desistance 15
prison: ageing offenders' attitude to 16; concept of time in 43, 63–4; and employment 61; experiences of prisoners 43; induction 67–70; life in 62, 63; living 94–100; lobbying for reform 90; low-security 80; sentences 62
*Prison Diary* (Archer) 86
prisoners: acceptance of wrongdoing 93; adjusting to prison 69–70; anticipating release 86–94; anxious 87–90; assault on the self 75–8; autobiographies 50; code for behaviour 64–5; confident 87, 92–4; coping with anxiety 90–1; deprivations 64; dislocation 63; first impressions of prison life 67–70; futureless 43; future planning 62; leaving prison *see* leaving prison; loss of previous life 68; ontological decline 64; prison accounts 66–7; prison time 70–4; prison uniform 64; quiet life on leaving prison 96–7; reflection 63, 80, 81; sensitivities of white-collar offenders 65–6; shock at prison induction 67–8; shock of incarceration 65; strategies to pass time quickly 63–4; structuring time 73–4; threat of violence 68; using time in prison 70–2, 79; veering between optimism and pessimism 91; *see also* ex-prisoners
Prison Fellowship 132, 134, 146
professional-exes: advantages of deviant past 131; credibility 140–1; embarkation 140; finding the role

208 *Index*

136–7; generative pursuits 131; hesitation 138–9; identities and credibility 140–1; initial idea 135; stages in becoming 134–40; statuses 132; taking up the ex-role 137–8
professional-ex roles: assistance with desistance 131; definition 130; fragility of 141–2; generative pursuits 131; making a virtue out of a stigma 132; parallel to other life changes 148; promotion of desistance 148; restructuring of the past 142–3; therapeutic settings 130–1; *see also* Colson, Charles (professional-ex role); Minkow, Barry (professional-ex role)
programmed potential 22
pro-social identities: civic roles 83, 84; family and work roles 84; pro-social roles 83–4

quest: religious conversion 153, 160

Rambo, L. R.: stages of religious conversion 153–4
recidivism 25, 86
redemption 122
redemption script 17–18
reflection 70, 71, 72, 74–5, 80, 81
relationships: importance to ex-prisoners 84
religion: belief and white-collar offenders 156; and desistance from crime 154–6; sense of security 92; *see also* belief systems; Christianity
religious conversion 57–8; absolution of shame and guilt 153; to Christianity 114; commitment 153–4, 167; commitment to change 152–3; consequences 154; context 153, 157–8; conversion of Charles Colson to Christianity 138–9; conversion of David Bullen to Buddhism 156, 159; conversion of Jeb Magruder to Christianity 115, 156, 159; crisis 153; definition 152; dimensions 154; encounter 153; interaction 153; quest 153; stages of 153; surrendering control of life 153; transformation of the self 152; *see also* belief systems; Christianity

relinquishment of control 166
remorse 93
reparations 112
replacement self 20
resettlement 85–6; agency and change 121–7; alternative projects 113; civic reintegration 112; failing 111–13, 116; life after punishment 127–8; new lives 117–19; radical changes in self-identity 115; reparations 112; returning to the familiar 108–10; succeeding 114–16
role exit: anxiety 130; deviant past 130; identity vacuum 130; leaving a role 130; reactions of others 130; unique perspective 129; *see also* professional-exes; professional-ex roles
romantic partnerships: and desistance 17
Rose, Pete: admission of guilt 93; autobiography 53, 54; blocked paths 101; confidence as prisoner 87; on coping with prison life 69; prison sentence and time served 66, 87; professions 109
routines 90
Royce Aerospace Materials 90
Rudolph, J. L.: cognitive transformation 19–20

Sampson, R. J. 23; life courses 18–19; marriage and desistance 17
Sartre, Jean-Paul 29, 57; past, present and future 32
Scheff, T. J. 36
Schneider, C. D.: on shame 36
Schutz, Alfred 40
Scott, G. 42
secondary desistance 15
Securities and Exchange Commission 1, 92, 126, 145
self: action 31; assault on 75–8; autobiographies 46–9; 'becoming' 28; constant growth 116; despair 30; deterioration of 124–5; fit with identity 84; future 43–4, 80, 91, 184; guilt 30; hope 30, 31; new lives 117–19; past, present and future 31–2; re-establishment of the coherent 126; reflecting on 74–5; relatedness 29; responding to changes 116–21;

restructuring of the past 126; sense of 33; stripping of 67; uniqueness 28–9; *see also* existentialism; existential sociology; identity; role exit
self-identity 33–4, 130
self-relatedness 29
self-respect 36
sentences, prison 62
shame 34, 35–7, 122, 166–8; and desistance 37–40; theory of 44
Shapland, J.: interactive framework 22–3
Sheridan, D. 48
Shover, N. 12; advantages of autobiographies 51; recidivism and white-collar offenders 25
situational contexts 22
slave morality 29
Smith, S.: on autobiographies 47
social control: romantic partnerships 17
social interaction 85
social networks 171–2
sociology: and autobiographies 49; autobiographies 50
spirituality 155
status: loss of 85–6
Stewart, Martha 1–2
stigma 85–6, 89, 100–2, 103–4, 132, 180
stories *see* autobiographies
strip searches 79
structures 22
substantial change 117–19
succeeding (resettlement) 114–16; process of 116; radical changes in self-identity 115
support networks 81; white-collar offenders 85–6
surrender 167
survival strategies 80
Sutherland, E. 10
Sykes, G.: ontological decline of prisoners 64; pains of imprisonment 64
systematic thematic analysis 55

Tao Te Ching 162
Taylor, G. 36
Taylor, L.: prison life 63; shattering experience of prison life 64
technical guilt 93
termination: and desistance 15

therapy: generative pursuit 131, 145–6
time: experienced in prison 43, 63–4; passage of 125–7; structuring time in prison 73–4; using time in prison 70–2, 79
Timilty, Joseph: anxiety about the future 87, 88; autobiography 53, 54; blocked paths 101; on coping with prison life 69; on freedom of leaving prison 95; justification of actions 121; lobbying for prison reform 90; on napping during the day 76; on negative experience of prison 124; negative passive change 124–5; on new starts 98; partial change 117; passive change 121; prison sentence and time served 66–7, 87; rejection of guilt 93; returning to politics 91; technical guilt 93
tragedy 31
Travis, J. T.: post-release circumstances 83
true self 40
truth: in autobiographies 47, 48, 49
turning points 18–19

uniform, prison 64, 95
uniqueness, self 28–9; loss of 64
Unlock 131

values 34–5
violence: threat in prison 68
Visher, C. A.: post-release circumstances 83
Volpe, Tod: active change 121; admission of guilt 93; autobiography 53, 54; blocked paths 101; on changing self 75; confidence as prisoner 87; partial change 117; on prison as protection from outside world 71; prison sentence and time served 66, 87; professions 109

Wall Street 119
Waring, E. J. 11, 13; age and crime 24, 25; stability in adulthood 26
Watergate 69, 96, 99, 101, 103, 134
Watson, J.: on autobiographies 47
Weisburd, D. 11; age and crime 24, 25; stability in adulthood 26

210 *Index*

white-collar crime: criminal careers 13–14; definitions 10–11; research 11–13

white-collar offenders: adjusting to prison 69–70; and age 24, 25; anticipating release 86–94; assault on the self 75–8; autobiographies 52–4, 55–6; celebrity 59; changes to self 116–21; changing self during prison term 74–5; comparing autobiographical accounts 56–8; concealment of offences 70–1; differences with criminal peers 76; drawing on past experiences 81; first impressions of prison life 67–70; future self 43, 80; identifying 13; leaving prison 94–100; prison accounts 66–7; prison life as contrast with old lives 79; prison time 70–4; questions about life after a prison sentence 83–5; and religious belief 156; removal of individuality in prison 68; research 12; resettlement 85–6; seeking like-minded prisoners as companions 77–8; shock at prison induction 67–8; shock of incarceration 65; structuring time 73–4; threat of violence in prison 68; using prison time for reflection 71, 72, 79, 81; using time 70–2; utilising skills for fellow prisoners 78

*Wired for Books* 120

Young Life 115

ZZZZ Best 133, 138, 159

CPSIA information can be obtained
at www.ICGtesting.com
Printed in the USA
LVHW080812230420
653743LV00006B/58